# 4th Workshop on Arabic Corpus Linguistics (WACL-4)



Abu Dhabi, United Arab Emirates
20 January 2025

ISBN: 979-8-3313-1375-3

**Printed from e-media with permission by:**

Curran Associates, Inc.
57 Morehouse Lane
Red Hook, NY 12571

**Some format issues inherent in the e-media version may also appear in this print version.**



Printed with permission by Curran Associates, Inc. (2026)

For permission requests, please contact the Association for Computational Linguistics at the address below.

Association for Computational Linguistics
209 N. Eighth Street
Stroudsburg, Pennsylvania 18360

Phone: 1-570-476-8006
Fax: 1-570-476-0860

acl@aclweb.org

**Additional copies of this publication are available from:**

Curran Associates, Inc.
57 Morehouse Lane
Red Hook, NY 12571 USA
Phone: 845-758-0400
Fax: 845-758-2633
Email: curran@proceedings.com
Web: www.proceedings.com

The 31st International Conference on Computational Linguistics

# WACL-4

## The 4th Workshop on Arabic Corpus Linguistics

**Proceedings of the Workshop**

January 20, 2025

https://wp.lancs.ac.uk/wacl4

Order copies of this and other ACL proceedings from:

Association for Computational Linguistics (ACL)
209 N. Eighth Street
Stroudsburg, PA 18360
USA
Tel: +1-570-476-8006
Fax: +1-570-476-0860
acl@aclweb.org

# Preface

Welcome to the Fourth Workshop on Arabic Corpus Linguistics (WACL-4), held online on January 20, 2025, in conjunction with the 31st International Conference on Computational Linguistics (COLING 2025) in Abu Dhabi, UAE.

The field of Arabic language research using corpora and corpus-based methods has undergone remarkable growth over the past decade. What began as a series of isolated initiatives has evolved into a dynamic and rapidly expanding domain of inquiry, encompassing a wide range of topics in both corpus and computational linguistics. Building on the success of the previous workshops—WACL-1 (2011), WACL-2 (2013, hosted at the Corpus Linguistics Conference at Lancaster University), and WACL-3 (2019, hosted at the Corpus Linguistics Conference at Cardiff University)—WACL-4 (2025, hosted at COLING) continues to provide a dedicated venue for advancing research and promoting collaboration in this vibrant field.

The primary objectives of WACL-4 are to showcase the latest developments in the creation, annotation, and application of Arabic corpora and to foster interdisciplinary collaboration. This year, we place a special emphasis on Arabic dialects, including non-standard and regional varieties, aiming to deepen our understanding of Arabic in its many forms and to support research on under-resourced linguistic varieties. The workshop also seeks to encourage advancements in Natural Language Processing (NLP) tailored for Arabic, focusing on integrating corpora into NLP workflows, developing new computational tools, and evaluating existing systems to enhance their performance in processing Arabic text.

We received 22 submissions most of which 13 were accepted. Each submission underwent rigorous review by at least three reviewers, ensuring the quality and relevance of the accepted contributions, resulting in an acceptance rate of 59

We thank the authors, reviewers, and organizing committee for their efforts and support. We hope these proceedings inspire new research and collaborations to advance the field.

Saad Ezzini, General Chair, on behalf of the organizing committee of the WACL-4 workshop.

## Organizing Committee

Saad Ezzini, King Fahd University of Petroleum and Minerals, Saudi Arabia (General Chair)
Hamza Alami, Sidi Mohamed Ben Abdellah University, Morocco (Programme Co-Chair)
Ismail Berrada, Mohammed VI Polytechnic University, Morocco (Programme Co-Chair)
Abdessamad Benlahbib, Sidi Mohamed Ben Abdellah University, Morocco (Programme Co-Chair)
Abdelkader El Mahdaouy, Mohammed VI Polytechnic University, Morocco (Review Chair)
Salima Lamsiyah, University of Luxembourg, Luxembourg (Publication Chair)
Hatim Derrouz, Ibn Tofail University, Morocco (Publicity Co-Chair)
Amal Haddad, University of Granada, Spain (Publicity Co-Chair)
Mustafa Jarrar, Birzeit University, Palestine (Advisory Committee)
Mo El-Haj, Lancaster University, UK (Advisory Committee)
Ruslan Mitkov, Lancaster University, UK (Advisory Committee)
Paul Rayson, Lancaster University, UK (Advisory Committee)

## Programme Committee

Almoataz B. Al-Said, Cairo University, Egypt
Abdessamad Benlahbib, Sidi Mohamed Ben Abdellah University, Morocco
Ashraf Boumhidi, Sidi Mohamed Ben Abdellah University, University, Morocco
Abdelkader El Mahdaoui, Mohammed VI Polytechnic University, Morocco
Hamza Alami, Sidi Mohamed Ben Abdellah University, Morocco
Hatim Derrouz, Ibn Tofail University, Morocco
Hicham Hammouchi, University of Luxembourg, Luxembourg
Ismail Berrada, Mohammed VI Polytechnic University, Morocco
Maram Alharbi, Lancaster University, UK
Nagham F. Hamad, Birzeit University, Palestine
Nizar Habash, New York University Abu Dhabi, UAE
Nora Al-Twairesh, King Saud University, Saudi Arabia
Noorhan Abbas, Leeds University, UK
Saad Ezzini, King Fahd University of Petroleum and Minerals, Saudi Arabia
Salima Lamsiyah, University of Luxembourg, Luxembourg
Salmane Chafik, Mohammed VI Polytechnic University, Morocco
Samir El Amrani, University of Luxembourg, Luxembourg
Wajdi Zaghouani, Hamad Bin Khalifa University, Qatar

# Table of Contents

*ArabicSense: A Benchmark for Evaluating Commonsense Reasoning in Arabic with Large Language Models*
Salima Lamsiyah, Kamyar Zeinalipour, Samir El Amrany, Matthias Brust, Marco Maggini, Pascal Bouvry and Christoph Schommer . . . . . 1

*Lahjawi: Arabic Cross-Dialect Translator*
Mohamed Motasim Hamed, Muhammad Hreden, Khalil Hennara, Zeina Aldallal, Sara Chrouf and Safwan AlModhayan . . . . . 12

*Lost in Variation: An Unsupervised Methodology for Mining Lexico-syntactic Patterns in Middle Arabic Texts*
Julien JB Bezançon, Rimane Karam and Gaël Lejeune . . . . . 25

*SADSLyC: A Corpus for Saudi Arabian Multi-dialect Identification through Song Lyrics*
Salwa Saad Alahmari . . . . . 38

*Enhancing Dialectal Arabic Intent Detection through Cross-Dialect Multilingual Input Augmentation*
Shehenaz Hossain, Fouad Shammary, Bahaulddin Shammary and Haithem Afli . . . . . 44

*Dial2MSA-Verified: A Multi-Dialect Arabic Social Media Dataset for Neural Machine Translation to Modern Standard Arabic*
Abdullah Salem Khered, Youcef Benkhedda and Riza Batista-Navarro . . . . . 50

*Web-Based Corpus Compilation of the Emirati Arabic Dialect*
Yousra A. El-Ghawi . . . . . 63

*Evaluating Calibration of Arabic Pre-trained Language Models on Dialectal Text*
Ali Al-Laith and Rachida Kebdani . . . . . 68

*Empirical Evaluation of Pre-trained Language Models for Summarizing Moroccan Darija News Articles*
Azzedine Aftiss, Salima Lamsiyah, Christoph Schommer and Said Ouatik El Alaoui . . . . . 77

*Dialect2SQL: A Novel Text-to-SQL Dataset for Arabic Dialects with a Focus on Moroccan Darija*
Salmane Chafik, Saad Ezzini and Ismail Berrada . . . . . 86

*AraSim: Optimizing Arabic Dialect Translation in Children's Literature with LLMs and Similarity Scores*
Alaa Hassan Bouomar and Noorhan Abbas . . . . . 93

*Navigating Dialectal Bias and Ethical Complexities in Levantine Arabic Hate Speech Detection*
Ahmed Haj Ahmed, Rui-Jie Yew, Xerxes Minocher and Suresh Venkatasubramanian . . . . . 103

# Conference Program

**Monday, January 20, 2025**

**9:00–9:10** ***Welcome and Opening Remarks***

9:10–9:50 *Invited Talk by Imed Zitouni: Bridging the Gap: Arabic Search in the Age of LLMs*

**Session 1**

9:50–10:10 *ArabicSense: A Benchmark for Evaluating Commonsense Reasoning in Arabic with Large Language Models*
Salima Lamsiyah, Kamyar Zeinalipour, Samir El Amrany, Matthias Brust, Marco Maggini, Pascal Bouvry and Christoph Schommer

10:10–10:30 *Lahjawi: Arabic Cross-Dialect Translator*
Mohamed Motasim Hamed, Muhammad Hreden, Khalil Hennara, Zeina Aldallal, Sara Chrouf and Safwan AlModhayan

**10:30–11:00** ***Coffee Break***

**Session 2**

11:00–11:20 *Lost in Variation: An Unsupervised Methodology for Mining Lexico-syntactic Patterns in Middle Arabic Texts*
Julien JB Bezançon, Rimane Karam and Gaël Lejeune

11:20–11:40 *SADSLyC: A Corpus for Saudi Arabian Multi-dialect Identification through Song Lyrics*
Salwa Saad Alahmari

11:40–12:00 *Enhancing Dialectal Arabic Intent Detection through Cross-Dialect Multilingual Input Augmentation*
Shehenaz Hossain, Fouad Shammary, Bahaulddin Shammary and Haithem Afli

12:00–12:20 *Dial2MSA-Verified: A Multi-Dialect Arabic Social Media Dataset for Neural Machine Translation to Modern Standard Arabic*
Abdullah Salem Khered, Youcef Benkhedda and Riza Batista-Navarro

**12:20–13:20** ***Lunch Break***

**Session 3**

13:20–13:40 *Web-Based Corpus Compilation of the Emirati Arabic Dialect*
Yousra A. El-Ghawi

13:40–14:00 *Evaluating Calibration of Arabic Pre-trained Language Models on Dialectal Text*
Ali Al-Laith and Rachida Kebdani

14:00–14:20 *Empirical Evaluation of Pre-trained Language Models for Summarizing Moroccan Darija News Articles*
Azzedine Aftiss, Salima Lamsiyah, Christoph Schommer and Said Ouatik El Alaoui

14:20–14:40 *Dialect2SQL: A Novel Text-to-SQL Dataset for Arabic Dialects with a Focus on Moroccan Darija*
Salmane Chafik, Saad Ezzini and Ismail Berrada

14:40–15:00 *AraSim: Optimizing Arabic Dialect Translation in Children's Literature with LLMs and Similarity Scores*
Alaa Hassan Bouomar and Noorhan Abbas

15:00–15:20 *Navigating Dialectal Bias and Ethical Complexities in Levantine Arabic Hate Speech Detection*
Ahmed Haj Ahmed, Rui-Jie Yew, Xerxes Minocher and Suresh Venkatasubramanian

**15:20–16:00** ***Coffee Break***

**16:00–16:30** ***Best Paper Award, Closing Remarks, and Wrap-Up by Dr Saad Ezzini***

# ArabicSense: A Benchmark for Evaluating Commonsense Reasoning in Arabic with Large Language Models

**Salima Lamsiyah[1*], Kamyar Zeinalipour[2*], Samir El Amrany[1*], Matthias Brust[1], Marco Maggini[2], Pascal Bouvry[1], Christoph Schommer[1],**

[1]Faculty of Science, Technology and Medicine (FSTM), University of Luxembourg
[2]University of Siena, DIISM, Via Roma 56, 53100 Siena, Italy
**Correspondence:** kamyar.zeinalipour2@unisi.it

## Abstract

Recent efforts in natural language processing (NLP) commonsense reasoning research have led to the development of numerous new datasets and benchmarks. However, these resources have predominantly been limited to English, leaving a gap in evaluating commonsense reasoning in other languages. In this paper, we introduce the ArabicSense Benchmark, which is designed to thoroughly evaluate the world-knowledge commonsense reasoning abilities of large language models (LLMs) in Arabic. This benchmark includes three main tasks: first, it tests whether a system can distinguish between natural language statements that make sense and those that do not; second, it requires a system to identify the most crucial reason why a nonsensical statement fails to make sense; and third, it involves generating explanations for why statements do not make sense. We evaluate several Arabic BERT-based models and causal LLMs on these tasks. Experimental results demonstrate improvements after fine-tuning on our dataset. For instance, AraBERT v2 achieved an 87% F1 score on the second task, while Gemma and Mistral-7b achieved F1 scores of 95.5% and 94.8%, respectively. For the generation task, LLaMA-3 achieved the best performance with a BERTScore F1 of 77.3%, closely followed by Mistral-7b at 77.1%. All codes and the benchmark is publicly available. [1] [2] [3][4] [5]

## 1 Introduction

Commonsense reasoning (CSR) plays a critical role in understanding natural language. It involves making inferences based on commonsense knowledge, which encompasses general facts about the physical world and human behavior that people intuitively understand during communication. This implicit knowledge forms the backdrop for everyday conversations. Both humans and natural language processing (NLP) systems require CSR to comprehend the flow of daily events. Therefore, Commonsense reasoning remains a persistent challenge in artificial intelligence (AI) and natural language processing, in particular, evaluating and enhancing the commonsense reasoning capabilities of large language models (LLMs) is essential for advancing general natural language understanding (NLU) systems (Davis and Marcus, 2015).

Despite recent progress in creating commonsense reasoning benchmarks, most of them are available only in English (Davis, 2023), leaving a significant gap in resources for evaluating Arabic pre-trained language models. For example, the Arabic benchmark proposed by Al-Tawalbeh and Al-Smadi (2020) for commonsense validation and explanation is merely a translation of the English dataset from SemEval-2020's Commonsense Validation and Explanation (ComVE) task (Wang et al., 2019). Similarly, recent efforts by Beheitt and Ben HajHmida (2023) have focused on translating the Explanations for CommonsenseQA (Arabic-ECQA) and Open Mind Common Sense (Arabic-OMCS) datasets from English versions provided by IBM Research (Aggarwal et al., 2021). Thus, there is currently no dataset specifically developed from scratch for commonsense reasoning in Arabic. Indeed, translating English commonsense datasets into Arabic causes many challenges because direct translations often fail to capture cultural nuances and linguistic subtleties, resulting in inaccuracies

* Equal contribution
[1]https://github.com/EL-Amrany/Arabic-Commonsense-Reasoning
[2]https://huggingface.co/datasets/Kamyar-zeinalipour/ArabicSense
[3]https://huggingface.co/Kamyar-zeinalipour/Mistral-7b-CS-AR
[4]https://huggingface.co/Kamyar-zeinalipour/gemma2-9b-CS-AR
[5]https://huggingface.co/Kamyar-zeinalipour/P-Llama3-8B



*Proceedings of The 4th Workshop on Arabic Corpus Linguistics (WACL-4)*, pages 1–11
January 20th, 2025. 

and a loss of contextual relevance. Additionally, the structural differences between the two languages further complicate accurate translation, undermining the effectiveness of the datasets for evaluating commonsense reasoning in Arabic.

Developing high-performance text classification models critically depends on the availability of high-quality training data. However, collecting and curating such data is often costly and time-consuming, particularly for specialized tasks that require domain-specific knowledge. To address this challenge, researchers have begun exploring the use of large language models (LLMs) to generate synthetic datasets as an alternative approach. In this paper, we leverage the capabilities of GPT-4 (Achiam et al., 2023) to create ArabicSense, a dataset specifically designed for Arabic commonsense reasoning. We focus on two natural language understanding tasks and one natural language generation task, which are detailed below. Illustrative examples of these tasks are provided in Figure 1.

- **Task A: Commonsense Validation** — The model is presented with two sentences ($S_1$ and $S_2$) that are similar in structure. The task is to identify which one of the two sentences does not make sense.
- **Task B: Commonsense Explanation (Multiple Choice)** — After identifying a nonsensical statement, the model is given three potential reasons ($r_1$, $r_2$, and $r_3$) explaining why the statement contradicts commonsense. The task is to select the correct reason. This assesses the model's understanding of the specific logical inconsistencies within the statement.
- **Task C: Commonsense Explanation (Generation)** — The model is required to generate a coherent explanation in natural language for why a given statement is against commonsense. The quality of the generated explanations is evaluated using BERTscore measure.

In our empirical study, we evaluate six BERT-based models — AraBERT (Antoun et al., 2020), ARBERT (Abdul-Mageed et al., 2021), MARBERT (Abdul-Mageed et al., 2021), CamelBERT[6], ArabicBERT (Safaya et al., 2020), and mBERT (Pires et al., 2019) — on the classification tasks described in Task A and Task B. Additionally, we

**Task A: Commonsense Validation**

*Which statement among the two is against commonsense?*

**$S_1$:** الفهد يعد أسرع حيوان على وجه الأرض، إذ تصل سرعته إلى 120 كيلومترًا في الساعة في المسافات القصيرة

(**$S_1$**: The cheetah is considered the fastest animal on Earth, as its speed can reach up to 120 kilometers per hour over short distances.)

**$S_2$:** الفهود تستطيع الطيران لمسافات قصيرة باستخدام أجنحة صغيرة مخبأة تحت جلدها، مما يجعلها قادرة على الهروب من الضواري الأكبر حجمًا بسهولة

(**$S_2$**: Cheetahs can fly short distances using small wings hidden under their skin, allowing them to easily escape from larger predators.)

**Task B: Commonsense Explanation (Multiple Choice)**

*Select the most corresponding reason why this statement is against common sense.*

**$r_1$:** الفهود تفضل السباحة للهروب من الضواري لأنها تعتمد على براعتها في الماء

(**$r_1$**: Cheetahs prefer swimming to escape from predators, as they rely on their agility in the water.)

**$r_2$:** الفهود تستطيع الاختباء تحت الأرض بفضل جلودها المتغيرة اللون التي تجعلها غير مرئية

(**$r_2$**: Cheetahs can hide underground thanks to their color-changing skin, which makes them invisible.)

**$r_3$:** الفهود ليس لديها أجنحة ولا يمكنها الطيران؛ فهي تعتمد على سرعتها في الجري للهرب من الضواري

(**$r_3$**: Cheetahs do not have wings and cannot fly; they rely on their running speed to escape predators.)

**Task B: Commonsense Explanation (Generation)**

*Generate the reason why this statement is against common sense.*

**r:** الفهود لا تملك القدرة على الطيران حيث تفتقر إلى الأجنحة، بل تعتمد على سرعتها العالية في الفرار من الكائنات المفترسة

**r:** (Cheetahs do not have the ability to fly as they lack wings; instead, they rely on their high speed to escape predators.)

Figure 1: Samples of our dataset

[6]https://github.com/CAMeL-Lab/CAMeLBERT

assess three state-of-the-art causal language models — Mistral-7b (Jiang et al., 2023), LLaMA-3 (Dubey et al., 2024), and Gemma[7] — using both zero-shot and fine-tuning approaches. The results demonstrate the effectiveness and quality of ArabicSense as a challenging commonsense reasoning benchmark for the Arabic language. Consequently, we present **ArabicSense** to the community as the first commonsense benchmark specifically designed to test commonsense world-knowledge and reasoning abilities of Arabic pre-trained language models.

The main contributions of this paper are summarized as follows:

- We present **ArabicSense**, the first commonsense reasoning benchmark developed specifically for the Arabic language.

- We develop three interrelated tasks to assess both natural language understanding and generation capabilities of pre-trained language models in Arabic commonsense reasoning.

- We leverage GPT-4 and prompting, to automatically generate high-quality synthetic data for commonsense reasoning in Arabic.

- We conduct a comprehensive evaluation of six BERT-based models and three state-of-the-art causal language models using zero-shot and fine-tuning approaches.

## 2 Related Work

**Commonsense Reasoning Benchmarks.** The NLP community has made significant progress in constructing commonsense datasets like ConceptNet (Speer et al., 2017) and ATOMIC (Hwang et al., 2021), as well as more specialized resources focused on physical (Bisk et al., 2020) and social commonsense (Sap et al., 2019). These resources have been widely incorporated into various downstream tasks (Lin et al., 2019; Guan et al., 2020; Liu et al., 2021) to assess AI's reasoning in commonsense scenarios. However, most of these benchmarks are English-centric, limiting their applicability for evaluating other languages (Davis, 2023).

Some Arabic benchmarks have been directly translated from English datasets (Al-Tawalbeh and Al-Smadi, 2020; Beheitt and Ben HajHmida, 2023). However, this approach often fails to capture the unique linguistic features and cultural nuances of the Arabic language, which are essential for accurate commonsense reasoning. Some studies have leveraged these translated datasets to evaluate the performance of pre-trained Arabic language models. For instance, Alshanik et al. (2023) explored commonsense validation and explanation through their participation in the SemEval 2020 Task 4, where their model achieved 84.7% accuracy in validation and a BLEU score of 24 for explanation generation. Finally, Khaled et al. (2023) conducted a comparative study on several Arabic BERT models for commonsense tasks, identifying ARBERTv2 as the top performer with 84.4% and 74.9% accuracy in validation and explanation tasks, respectively.

Despite initial efforts in Arabic commonsense reasoning, the field remains significantly underexplored compared to English-centric research. More work is needed to create dedicated datasets that capture the linguistic and cultural nuances of Arabic, making it essential to develop benchmarks specifically for evaluating Arabic commonsense reasoning.

**LLMs for Synthetic Data Generation.** Large language models (LLMs) are widely recognized for their strong generalization ability across a broad range of tasks (Achiam et al., 2023; Jiang et al., 2023; Dubey et al., 2024). However, optimizing these models for specific tasks remains a significant challenge. While zero-shot and few-shot prompting provide some level of flexibility (Dong et al., 2022), fine-tuning on task-specific data generally yields better results, particularly for specialized or out-of-domain tasks (Liu et al., 2022). Nonetheless, creating high-quality datasets is a time-consuming and resource-intensive process requiring specialized domain expertise. Synthetic data generation, which refers to artificially created data that replicates the characteristics of real-world data (Little, 1993), has emerged as a crucial solution for accelerating model training, particularly for small language models. It plays a significant role in all stages of training, including pre-training, instruction-tuning, and reinforcement learning from human feedback (Mitra et al., 2024).

A dataset is considered fully synthetic when the questions or instructions, the potential context, and the answers are all generated artificially. Examples of such methods include Self-Instruct (Wang et al., 2023), Unnatural Instructions (Honovich

[7] https://ai.google.dev/gemma/docs

et al., 2023), and Alpaca[8]. These models generate general-purpose synthetic data, while other approaches focus on task-specific fine-tuning by rephrasing existing datasets (Yin et al., 2023). A key limitation of fully synthetic data generation is the repetition and low quality of the generated samples. For example, Unnatural Instructions and Self-Instruct both reported significant redundancy in their data, with correctness rates around 54%-56.5%, while Alpaca's correctness rate was as low as 17%, making much of the data unsuitable for fine-tuning models. Indeed, partially synthetic data generation, which incorporates human-curated input, context, or output, helps improve data quality and diversity (Maini et al., 2024). However, these methods often depend on resource-intensive processes and limit task flexibility because of their reliance on human-generated components. In addition, inspired by self-instruct methods, several works have explored various languages, including Turkish, Arabic, English, and Italian. (Zeinalipour et al., 2024a; Zugarini et al., 2024; Zeinalipour et al., 2024c,b), Recently, Mitra et al. (2024) introduced AgentInstruct, a model that autonomously generates diverse, high-quality synthetic data from raw documents. It leverages powerful models like GPT-4 and tools such as search and code interpreters to create large-scale datasets tailored to both general and domain-specific skills, significantly improving the fine-tuning process. Inspired by AgentInstruct, we developed the first Arabic benchmark designed to evaluate commonsense reasoning in pre-trained Arabic language models.

## 3 ArabicSense: A New Benchmark Dataset

The aim of this work is twofold: to create a dataset for evaluating Arabic commonsense reasoning in LLMs and to improve their performance in this area. To achieve this, we generate diverse, high-quality data specifically designed for training LLMs in Arabic commonsense reasoning. This section outlines the methodology used to create the ArabicSense dataset, followed by the human validation process and an analysis of the dataset.

### 3.1 Methodology

The development of the ArabicSense dataset involves transforming unstructured seed data into three distinct tasks designed to assess various aspects of commonsense reasoning in Arabic: Commonsense Validation, Multiple-Choice Commonsense Explanation, and Generative Commonsense Explanation. We use the GPT-4 model to convert the seed data into diverse examples for each task. The following outlines the main steps used for building the dataset.

**Seed Data Collection.** We curated a collection of raw seed data exclusively from Arabic-language sources on Wikipedia [9]. The seed data covers a wide range of domains, including culture, geography, art, history, philosophy, and other relevant topics. Wikipedia is chosen for its diverse and extensive coverage of these subjects in Arabic, ensuring the dataset reflects varied contexts and knowledge areas essential for world-knowledge commonsense reasoning. More specifically, our data collection process began by extracting the opening sections of Arabic Wikipedia articles, with a specific emphasis on the bolded keywords found in the introduction. Alongside this keyword extraction, we also gathered vital metadata for each article, including details such as view counts, relevance scores, brief summaries, key headings, related terms, categorization information, and URLs.

**Transformation of Seed Data Using GPT-4**: To create the three tasks, we formulated specific prompts for each task and used GPT-4 (Achiam et al., 2023) to transform the seed data accordingly. Each task was generated with carefully crafted prompts that tailored the raw data into the required format, ensuring variety and depth in the examples.

- **Task A: Commonsense Validation** — The GPT-4 model was prompted to generate pairs of sentences ($S_1$ and $S_2$) that are similar in wording and structure. One of the sentences in each pair was logical, while the other was nonsensical, designed to challenge the model's commonsense reasoning ability.

- **Task B: Commonsense Explanation (Multiple Choice)** — After identifying the nonsensical sentence, GPT-4 was used to generate three possible reasons ($r_1$, $r_2$, and $r_3$), one of which was correct, explaining why the sentence contradicts commonsense. This task assesses the model's understanding of the specific logical inconsistencies in the sentence.

[8]https://github.com/tatsu-lab/stanford_alpaca

[9]https://en.wikipedia.org/wiki/Wikipedia:Lists_of_popular_pages_by_WikiProject

- **Task C: Commonsense Explanation (Generation)** — For this task, we prompt GPT-4 to generate a coherent explanation in natural language for why a given statement contradicts commonsense.

### 3.2 Refinement and Human Validation

The dataset was iteratively refined through human evaluations to ensure clarity, diversity, and quality across all three commonsense reasoning tasks. We assessed human performance on each task using three expert annotators who evaluated 200 random samples from each task. Our experts, who are native Arabic speakers and experienced NLP researchers, were not involved in the original data collection. Their expertise allows them to clarify misunderstandings in the annotation guidelines and produce more accurate and thoughtful annotations compared to crowd workers. The annotators were asked to rate each response using the following criteria:

- **RATING-A (Excellent):** The response is highly accurate, insightful, and completely relevant to the task. It shows a deep understanding of commonsense reasoning, providing a flawless and satisfying answer with no errors.

- **RATING-B (Good):** The response is generally correct and acceptable, but may contain minor errors, ambiguities, or imperfections. These issues do not significantly detract from the quality or overall validity of the response.

- **RATING-C (Adequate):** The response is relevant to the task but contains errors or oversights. While parts of the answer are valid, significant issues reduce its reliability, and it may veer off-topic in certain areas.

- **RATING-D (Poor):** The response is minimally relevant or partially incorrect. It may include some valid information but is weak in terms of commonsense reasoning. The answer may not fully address the task or be partially invalid.

- **RATING-E (Unacceptable):** The response is irrelevant, completely incorrect, or nonsensical. It fails to demonstrate an understanding of the task and does not provide a valid answer, possibly even contradicting commonsense knowledge.

The results revealed that 98% of the data across all tasks was rated as "A," demonstrating the exceptional quality of the proposed dataset. Furthermore, we measure the consistency of the review process with Fleiss's kappa[10], a statistical measure that evaluates inter-annotator agreement. Our expert annotators achieved a near-perfect Fleiss's kappa score, as shown in Table 1, demonstrating high reliability in the validation of the synthetic data. This high level of agreement highlights the robustness and effectiveness of our data generation method.

| Tasks | Fleiss's Kappa |
|---|---|
| Task A | 0.97% |
| Task B | 0.96% |
| Task C | 0.97% |

Table 1: Annotators agreement for the three tasks.

### 3.3 Dataset Analysis

The dataset used in this study is derived from Wikipedia articles, with commonsense statements extracted from sections of these articles. All views, word counts, and daily averages correspond to the statistics of these Wikipedia pages. The dataset for Task A includes 3954 training samples, 848 validation samples, and 848 test samples, with an average of 123,164 views per article and 217.40 words per sample, showing similar statistics across validation and test sets. Task B, which involves predicting the reason a statement is non-commonsensical, uses the same dataset sizes and maintains consistent statistics for views, word count, and daily averages. Task C, focused on generating explanations for nonsensical statements, follows the same size and structure as Task B, resulting in a balanced dataset across all tasks. Detailed statistical information for each task and split is presented in Table 2.

### 3.4 Experimental Setup

This study evaluates the performance of large language models for Arabic commonsense reasoning using the ArabicSense benchmark. The experimental setup involves two sets of models: BERT-based encoders (AraBERTv2 (Antoun et al., 2020), ARBERT (Abdul-Mageed et al., 2021), MARBERTv2, CamelBERT [11], ArabicBERT (base and large) (Safaya et al., 2020), and mBERT (Pires et al., 2019)) and three causal LLMs (Mistral-7b

[10]https://fr.wikipedia.org/wiki/Kappa_de_Fleiss

[11]https://github.com/CAMeL-Lab/CAMeLBERT

| Task | Split | Count | Mean Views | Mean Word Count |
|---|---|---|---|---|
| **Task A** | Train | 3954 | 123,164 | 217.40 |
| | Validation | 848 | 126,339 | 220.22 |
| | Test | 848 | 133,027 | 224.21 |
| **Task B** | Train | 3954 | 123,164 | 217.40 |
| | Validation | 848 | 126,339 | 220.22 |
| | Test | 848 | 133,027 | 224.21 |
| **Task C** | Train | 3954 | 123,164 | 217.40 |
| | Validation | 848 | 126,339 | 220.22 |
| | Test | 848 | 133,027 | 224.21 |

Table 2: Dataset Statistics for the Three Tasks. The statistics correspond to the original Wikipedia articles from which the commonsense statements were generated.

(Jiang et al., 2023), LLaMA-3 (Dubey et al., 2024), and Gemma[12]). The BERT-based encoders are evaluated on the first two tasks, while the causal LLMs are assessed across all three tasks. The detailed experimental setups for each task are described below.

For **Task A**, which involves binary classification to distinguish between commonsensical and nonsensical statements, all BERT-based models were fine-tuned using a batch size of 8, employing the AdamW optimizer (Loshchilov, 2017) with a learning rate of $2e^{-5}$. To prevent overfitting, dropout regularization (Srivastava et al., 2014) was applied with a rate of 0.1. Additionally, to ensure reproducibility, a fixed random seed of 42 was used across all models and random number generators (NumPy, PyTorch).

For **Task B**, models were tasked with multiclass classification, where they were required to identify the correct reason why a nonsensical statement deviates from commonsense. Similar to Task A, all BERT-based models were fine-tuned using a batch size of 8 and the AdamW optimizer with a learning rate of $2e^{-5}$. Input sequences consisted of three sentences, concatenated using the [SEP] token (Devlin, 2018) and tokenized using the AutoTokenizer from HuggingFace, with a maximum sequence length of 128 tokens. Regularization techniques, including dropout with a rate of 0.1, is applied to prevent overfitting.

In **Task C**, we evaluated the performance of LLMs to generate explanations for why nonsensical statements deviate from commonsense. The causal LLMs tested for this task included Mistral-7b, LLaMA-3, and Gemma. Fine-tuning was performed using two NVIDIA A6000 GPUs, each equipped with 48 GB of GPU memory, which was necessary to handle the large sequence lengths and computation requirements for this generation task. The models were fine-tuned for 4 epochs with a maximum sequence length of 1024 tokens. We applied a learning rate of $1e^{-4}$, combined with a cosine scheduler and a weight decay of $1e^{-4}$. To optimize memory usage, we utilized gradient accumulation over 4 steps, and employed techniques such as gradient checkpointing and flash attention. Additionally, we applied LoRA (Low-Rank Adaptation) (Hu et al., 2021) with a rank of 16 and an alpha of 32 to further enhance memory efficiency during training. The batch size for both training and evaluation was set to 8, and model checkpoints were saved at the end of each epoch for reproducibility and future evaluations.

For all tasks, early stopping (Prechelt, 2002) was used to monitor validation loss and prevent overfitting.

### 3.5 Evaluation Measures

For the classification tasks (**Task A** and **Task B**), we used accuracy, precision, recall, and F1-score to thoroughly assess the effectiveness of the models. For the text generation task (**Task C**), we evaluated both the fluency and semantic quality of the generated content using BERTScore (Zhang et al., 2019). It utilizes pre-trained transformer models to compare embeddings of the generated and reference texts, providing a more robust measure of semantic similarity.

### 3.6 Results

#### 3.6.1 Task A and Task B Evaluation Results

To verify the quality of the generated ArabicSense dataset, we designed a comprehensive eval-

[12] `https://ai.google.dev/gemma/docs`

uation strategy for the text classification tasks, Task A (Commonsense Validation) and Task B (Commonsense Explanation). The evaluation was performed in two phases, starting with BERT-based encoders and then extending to causal LLMs. In the first phase, we evaluated six pre-trained BERT-based language models—AraBERT v2, MarBERT, CamelBERT, ArabicBERT base, ArabicBERT large, and mBERT—on the dataset without fine-tuning. This initial phase assessed the baseline performance of these models, leveraging only their pre-trained knowledge. As shown in Table 3, the models struggled to perform well on both tasks, with accuracy scores for Task A ranging from 0.33 to 0.34 and Task B accuracy ranging from 0.32 to 0.36. Similarly, precision, recall, and F1 scores were generally low, indicating the difficulty these models faced in distinguishing between sensible and nonsensical sentences, as well as identifying logical inconsistencies in Task B.

In the second phase, we fine-tuned the same BERT-based models on the ArabicSense dataset to evaluate the impact of task-specific training. The results, as presented in Table 4, show improvements across all metrics for both tasks. For Task A, AraBERT v2 achieved the highest performance, with an accuracy, precision, recall, and F1 score of 0.87. Similarly, for Task B, AraBERT v2 also obtained an accuracy and F1 score of 0.83, closely followed by other models like ArabicBERT (base) and MarBERT, which achieved strong results across metrics. These findings demonstrate that fine-tuning improves the models' ability to perform commonsense reasoning in Arabic, validating the quality and effectiveness of the ArabicSense dataset.

Next, we extended our evaluation to causal large language models (LLMs), including Gemma, LLaMA-3, and Mistral-7b, testing their performance in both zero-shot and fine-tuned settings. In the zero-shot setting (Table 5), Gemma performed the best, achieving an F1 score of 0.867 for Task A and 0.921 for Task B. LLaMA-3 and Mistral-7b showed weaker performance on Task A, with F1 scores of 0.659 and 0.601, respectively, although they achieved moderate results on Task B, with F1 scores of 0.863 and 0.805. These results indicate that without fine-tuning, causal LLMs face challenges in handling Arabic commonsense reasoning tasks. After fine-tuning the causal LLMs on our dataset (Table 6), all models showed performance improvements. For instance, Gemma's F1 score increased to 0.947 for Task A and 0.944 for Task B, demonstrating its ability to handle complex reasoning after fine-tuning. Similarly, Mistral-7b, which initially performed poorly, achieved an F1 score of 0.948 for Task A and 0.934 for Task B. LLaMA-3 also showed marked improvement, reaching F1 scores of 0.945 for Task A and 0.930 for Task B. These results highlight the critical role of fine-tuning in enhancing the performance of LLMs for nuanced commonsense reasoning tasks in Arabic.

#### 3.6.2 Task C Evaluation Results

Table 7 presents BERTscore results for Task C (Commonsense Explanation Generation) using both zero-shot learning and fine-tuning for three different causal models: Gemma, LLaMa-3, and Mistral-7b. The BERTscore results show that fine-tuning on the ArabicSense dataset improves the performance of all models—Gemma, LLaMa-3, and Mistral-7b—compared to zero-shot learning. Gemma, which had the lowest zero-shot F1 score (0.656), saw the most improvement after fine-tuning, with an F1 score increase to 0.759. Similarly, LLaMa-3 and Mistral-7b improved from 0.747 and 0.728 F1 scores to 0.773 and 0.771, respectively. This highlights that the ArabicSense dataset enhances the models' ability to generate coherent explanations for why statements are against commonsense, validating its effectiveness for Task C. Furthermore, these results confirm the importance of fine-tuning on task-specific datasets to achieve optimal performance, particularly for tasks that require a deeper understanding of logical relationships.

Overall, by comparing the performance of BERT-based models and causal LLMs before and after fine-tuning, we demonstrate the effectiveness of the ArabicSense dataset in enhancing model performance. The consistent improvement across both encoder-based and causal models highlights the robustness of our dataset for training models to handle commonsense reasoning challenges in Arabic.

## 4 Conclusion

In this paper, we introduced **ArabicSense**, the first comprehensive benchmark designed to evaluate the commonsense reasoning abilities of large language models (LLMs) in Arabic. Through the creation of three distinct tasks: commonsense validation (task A), commonsense explanation (task B), and commonsense explanation generation (task C), we

| Model without Fine-Tuning | Task A | | | | Task B | | | |
|---|---|---|---|---|---|---|---|---|
| | **Accuracy** | **Precision** | **Recall** | **F1** | **Accuracy** | **Precision** | **Recall** | **F1** |
| AraBERT v2 | 0.33 | 0.21 | 0.32 | 0.22 | 0.33 | 0.18 | 0.32 | 0.18 |
| MarBERT | 0.34 | 0.34 | 0.34 | 0.34 | 0.36 | 0.35 | 0.35 | 0.35 |
| CamelBERT | 0.33 | 0.33 | 0.33 | 0.33 | 0.34 | 0.22 | 0.34 | 0.21 |
| ArabicBERT (base) | 0.34 | 0.22 | 0.33 | 0.19 | 0.34 | 0.34 | 0.34 | 0.34 |
| ArabicBERT (large) | 0.34 | 0.11 | 0.33 | 0.17 | 0.33 | 0.14 | 0.32 | 0.16 |
| mBERT | 0.33 | 0.11 | 0.33 | 0.16 | 0.32 | 0.10 | 0.33 | 0.16 |

Table 3: Evaluation of the pretrained language models **without fine-tuning** on Tasks A and B.

| Model with Fine-Tuning | Task A | | | | Task B | | | |
|---|---|---|---|---|---|---|---|---|
| | **Accuracy** | **Precision** | **Recall** | **F1** | **Accuracy** | **Precision** | **Recall** | **F1** |
| AraBERT v2 | 0.87 | 0.86 | 0.87 | 0.87 | 0.83 | 0.83 | 0.83 | 0.83 |
| MarBERT | 0.81 | 0.78 | 0.85 | 0.82 | 0.83 | 0.83 | 0.83 | 0.83 |
| CamelBERT | 0.82 | 0.81 | 0.84 | 0.82 | 0.80 | 0.80 | 0.79 | 0.80 |
| ArabicBERT base | 0.84 | 0.82 | 0.87 | 0.85 | 0.81 | 0.82 | 0.81 | 0.81 |
| ArabicBERT large | 0.75 | 0.80 | 0.67 | 0.73 | 0.84 | 0.84 | 0.84 | 0.84 |
| mBERT | 0.75 | 0.72 | 0.84 | 0.77 | 0.76 | 0.76 | 0.75 | 0.76 |

Table 4: Evaluation of the pretrained language models **with fine-tuning** on Tasks A and B.

| Model with Zero-shot | Task A | | | | Task B | | | |
|---|---|---|---|---|---|---|---|---|
| | **Accuracy** | **Precision** | **Recall** | **F1** | **Accuracy** | **Precision** | **Recall** | **F1** |
| Gemma | 0.869 | 0.880 | 0.854 | 0.867 | 0.921 | 0.922 | 0.920 | 0.921 |
| LLama-3 | 0.690 | 0.733 | 0.598 | 0.659 | 0.863 | 0.865 | 0.860 | 0.863 |
| Mistral-7b | 0.523 | 0.517 | 0.718 | 0.601 | 0.805 | 0.804 | 0.806 | 0.805 |

Table 5: Comparison results of the Causal LLMs using **zero-shot** on Task A and Task B.

| Model with Fine-tuning | Task A | | | | Task B | | | |
|---|---|---|---|---|---|---|---|---|
| | **Accuracy** | **Precision** | **Recall** | **F1** | **Accuracy** | **Precision** | **Recall** | **F1** |
| Gemma | 0.947 | 0.948 | 0.946 | 0.947 | 0.944 | 0.944 | 0.944 | 0.944 |
| LLama-3 | 0.945 | 0.948 | 0.942 | 0.945 | 0.930 | 0.930 | 0.930 | 0.930 |
| Mistral-7b | 0.948 | 0.946 | 0.950 | 0.948 | 0.934 | 0.934 | 0.934 | 0.934 |

Table 6: Comparison results of the Causal LLMs after **fine-tuning** on Task A and Task B.

| Model | Zero-shot | | | Fine-tuning | | |
|---|---|---|---|---|---|---|
| | **Precision** | **Recall** | **F1** | **Precision** | **Recall** | **F1** |
| Gemma | 0.641 | 0.672 | 0.656 | 0.765 | 0.754 | 0.759 |
| LLama-3 | 0.733 | 0.763 | 0.747 | 0.774 | 0.773 | 0.773 |
| Mistral-7b | 0.735 | 0.722 | 0.728 | 0.768 | 0.774 | 0.771 |

Table 7: BERTscore results using **zero-shot learning** and **Fine Tuning** on Task C.

addressed the gap in commonsense reasoning resources available for Arabic. The dataset was generated using GPT-4 and refined through human validation, ensuring its quality and relevance to the Arabic language context.

Our empirical evaluations, conducted across six pre-trained Arabic BERT-based models and three state-of-the-art causal LLMs, clearly demonstrate that the models' performance improves after fine-tuning on our dataset. The results show that fine-tuning these models on ArabicSense enables them to handle the nuances of Arabic commonsense reasoning with good accuracy, precision, recall, and F1 scores. These findings confirm the utility and quality of ArabicSense as a benchmark for advancing research and model development in this domain. The codes and resources will be made publicly available to support further exploration and enhancement of Arabic common-sense reasoning tasks.

## 5 Limitations

Despite promising results, our study has several limitations. ArabicSense focuses on three specific tasks of commonsense reasoning, which may not cover the entire spectrum of commonsense knowledge. Commonsense reasoning encompasses a wide range of domains, and further expansions to include additional reasoning dimensions (e.g., causal or temporal reasoning) could enhance the benchmark's coverage. Additionally, while the dataset was generated using advanced models such as GPT-4 and validated by humans to ensure quality, it remains synthetic in nature. Synthetic data generation may introduce biases or fail to capture certain real-world nuances that naturally occurring datasets might better reflect. Future work could explore hybrid approaches that combine synthetic and real-world data to enhance the quality of the dataset.

## References


Muhammad Abdul-Mageed, AbdelRahim Elmadany, and El Moatez Billah Nagoudi. 2021. ARBERT & MARBERT: Deep bidirectional transformers for Arabic. In *Proceedings of the 59th Annual Meeting of the Association for Computational Linguistics and the 11th International Joint Conference on Natural Language Processing (Volume 1: Long Papers)*, pages 7088–7105, Online. Association for Computational Linguistics.

Josh Achiam, Steven Adler, Sandhini Agarwal, Lama Ahmad, Ilge Akkaya, Florencia Leoni Aleman, Diogo Almeida, Janko Altenschmidt, Sam Altman, Shyamal Anadkat, et al. 2023. Gpt-4 technical report. *arXiv preprint arXiv:2303.08774*.

Shourya Aggarwal, Divyanshu Mandowara, Vishwajeet Agrawal, Dinesh Khandelwal, Parag Singla, and Dinesh Garg. 2021. Explanations for CommonsenseQA: New Dataset and Models. In *Proceedings of the 59th Annual Meeting of the Association for Computational Linguistics and the 11th International Joint Conference on Natural Language Processing (Volume 1: Long Papers)*, pages 3050–3065, Online. Association for Computational Linguistics.

Saja Al-Tawalbeh and Mohammad Al-Smadi. 2020. A benchmark arabic dataset for commonsense explanation. *arXiv preprint arXiv:2012.10251*.

Farah Alshanik, Ibrahim Al-Sharif, and Mohammad W Abdullah. 2023. Commonsense validation and explanation for arabic sentences. In *International Conference on Emerging Trends and Applications in Artificial Intelligence*, pages 101–112. Springer.

Wissam Antoun, Fady Baly, and Hazem Hajj. 2020. AraBERT: Transformer-based model for Arabic language understanding. In *Proceedings of the 4th Workshop on Open-Source Arabic Corpora and Processing Tools, with a Shared Task on Offensive Language Detection*, pages 9–15, Marseille, France. European Language Resource Association.

Mohamed El Ghaly Beheitt and Moez Ben HajHmida. 2023. Generation of arabic commonsense explanations. In *Asian Conference on Intelligent Information and Database Systems*, pages 527–537. Springer.

Yonatan Bisk, Rowan Zellers, Jianfeng Gao, Yejin Choi, et al. 2020. Piqa: Reasoning about physical commonsense in natural language. In *Proceedings of the AAAI conference on artificial intelligence*, volume 34, pages 7432–7439.

Ernest Davis. 2023. Benchmarks for automated commonsense reasoning: A survey. *ACM Computing Surveys*, 56(4):1–41.

Ernest Davis and Gary Marcus. 2015. Commonsense reasoning and commonsense knowledge in artificial intelligence. *Communications of the ACM*, 58(9):92–103.

Jacob Devlin. 2018. Bert: Pre-training of deep bidirectional transformers for language understanding. *arXiv preprint arXiv:1810.04805*.

Qingxiu Dong, Lei Li, Damai Dai, Ce Zheng, Zhiyong Wu, Baobao Chang, Xu Sun, Jingjing Xu, and Zhifang Sui. 2022. A survey on in-context learning. *arXiv preprint arXiv:2301.00234*.

Abhimanyu Dubey, Abhinav Jauhri, Abhinav Pandey, Abhishek Kadian, Ahmad Al-Dahle, Aiesha Letman, Akhil Mathur, Alan Schelten, Amy Yang, Angela Fan, et al. 2024. The llama 3 herd of models. *arXiv preprint arXiv:2407.21783*.

Jian Guan, Fei Huang, Zhihao Zhao, Xiaoyan Zhu, and Minlie Huang. 2020. A knowledge-enhanced pretraining model for commonsense story generation. *Transactions of the Association for Computational Linguistics*, 8:93–108.

Or Honovich, Thomas Scialom, Omer Levy, and Timo Schick. 2023. Unnatural instructions: Tuning language models with (almost) no human labor. In *Proceedings of the 61st Annual Meeting of the Association for Computational Linguistics (Volume 1: Long Papers)*, pages 14409–14428, Toronto, Canada. Association for Computational Linguistics.

Edward J Hu, Yelong Shen, Phillip Wallis, Zeyuan Allen-Zhu, Yuanzhi Li, Shean Wang, Lu Wang, and Weizhu Chen. 2021. Lora: Low-rank adaptation of large language models. *arXiv preprint arXiv:2106.09685*.

Jena D Hwang, Chandra Bhagavatula, Ronan Le Bras, Jeff Da, Keisuke Sakaguchi, Antoine Bosselut, and

Yejin Choi. 2021. (comet-) atomic 2020: On symbolic and neural commonsense knowledge graphs. In *Proceedings of the AAAI conference on artificial intelligence*, volume 35, pages 6384–6392.

Albert Q Jiang, Alexandre Sablayrolles, Arthur Mensch, Chris Bamford, Devendra Singh Chaplot, Diego de las Casas, Florian Bressand, Gianna Lengyel, Guillaume Lample, Lucile Saulnier, et al. 2023. Mistral 7b. *arXiv preprint arXiv:2310.06825*.

M Moneb Khaled, Aghyad Al Sayadi, and Ashraf Elnagar. 2023. Commonsense validation and explanation in arabic text: A comparative study using arabic bert models. In *2023 24th International Arab Conference on Information Technology (ACIT)*, pages 1–6. IEEE.

Bill Yuchen Lin, Xinyue Chen, Jamin Chen, and Xiang Ren. 2019. KagNet: Knowledge-aware graph networks for commonsense reasoning. In *Proceedings of the 2019 Conference on Empirical Methods in Natural Language Processing and the 9th International Joint Conference on Natural Language Processing (EMNLP-IJCNLP)*, pages 2829–2839, Hong Kong, China. Association for Computational Linguistics.

Roderick JA Little. 1993. Statistical analysis of masked data. *Journal of Official statistics*, 9(2):407.

Haokun Liu, Derek Tam, Mohammed Muqeeth, Jay Mohta, Tenghao Huang, Mohit Bansal, and Colin A Raffel. 2022. Few-shot parameter-efficient fine-tuning is better and cheaper than in-context learning. *Advances in Neural Information Processing Systems*, 35:1950–1965.

Ye Liu, Yao Wan, Lifang He, Hao Peng, and S Yu Philip. 2021. Kg-bart: Knowledge graph-augmented bart for generative commonsense reasoning. In *Proceedings of the AAAI conference on artificial intelligence*, volume 35, pages 6418–6425.

I Loshchilov. 2017. Decoupled weight decay regularization. *arXiv preprint arXiv:1711.05101*.

Pratyush Maini, Skyler Seto, Richard Bai, David Grangier, Yizhe Zhang, and Navdeep Jaitly. 2024. Rephrasing the web: A recipe for compute and data-efficient language modeling. In *Proceedings of the 62nd Annual Meeting of the Association for Computational Linguistics (Volume 1: Long Papers)*, pages 14044–14072, Bangkok, Thailand. Association for Computational Linguistics.

Arindam Mitra, Luciano Del Corro, Guoqing Zheng, Shweti Mahajan, Dany Rouhana, Andres Codas, Yadong Lu, Wei-ge Chen, Olga Vrousgos, Corby Rosset, et al. 2024. Agentinstruct: Toward generative teaching with agentic flows. *arXiv preprint arXiv:2407.03502*.

Telmo Pires, Eva Schlinger, and Dan Garrette. 2019. How multilingual is multilingual BERT? In *Proceedings of the 57th Annual Meeting of the Association for Computational Linguistics*, pages 4996–5001, Florence, Italy. Association for Computational Linguistics.

Lutz Prechelt. 2002. Early stopping-but when? In *Neural Networks: Tricks of the trade*, pages 55–69. Springer.

Ali Safaya, Moutasem Abdullatif, and Deniz Yuret. 2020. KUISAIL at SemEval-2020 task 12: BERT-CNN for offensive speech identification in social media. In *Proceedings of the Fourteenth Workshop on Semantic Evaluation*, pages 2054–2059, Barcelona (online). International Committee for Computational Linguistics.

Maarten Sap, Hannah Rashkin, Derek Chen, Ronan Le Bras, and Yejin Choi. 2019. Social IQa: Commonsense reasoning about social interactions. In *Proceedings of the 2019 Conference on Empirical Methods in Natural Language Processing and the 9th International Joint Conference on Natural Language Processing (EMNLP-IJCNLP)*, pages 4463–4473, Hong Kong, China. Association for Computational Linguistics.

Robyn Speer, Joshua Chin, and Catherine Havasi. 2017. Conceptnet 5.5: An open multilingual graph of general knowledge. In *Proceedings of the AAAI conference on artificial intelligence*, volume 31.

Nitish Srivastava, Geoffrey Hinton, Alex Krizhevsky, Ilya Sutskever, and Ruslan Salakhutdinov. 2014. Dropout: a simple way to prevent neural networks from overfitting. *The journal of machine learning research*, 15(1):1929–1958.

Cunxiang Wang, Shuailong Liang, Yue Zhang, Xiaonan Li, and Tian Gao. 2019. Does it make sense? and why? a pilot study for sense making and explanation. In *Proceedings of the 57th Annual Meeting of the Association for Computational Linguistics*, pages 4020–4026, Florence, Italy. Association for Computational Linguistics.

Yizhong Wang, Yeganeh Kordi, Swaroop Mishra, Alisa Liu, Noah A. Smith, Daniel Khashabi, and Hannaneh Hajishirzi. 2023. Self-instruct: Aligning language models with self-generated instructions. In *Proceedings of the 61st Annual Meeting of the Association for Computational Linguistics (Volume 1: Long Papers)*, pages 13484–13508, Toronto, Canada. Association for Computational Linguistics.

Da Yin, Xiao Liu, Fan Yin, Ming Zhong, Hritik Bansal, Jiawei Han, and Kai-Wei Chang. 2023. Dynosaur: A dynamic growth paradigm for instruction-tuning data curation. In *Proceedings of the 2023 Conference on Empirical Methods in Natural Language Processing*, pages 4031–4047, Singapore. Association for Computational Linguistics.

Kamyar Zeinalipour, Achille Fusco, Asya Zanollo, Marco Maggini, and Marco Gori. 2024a. Harnessing llms for educational content-driven italian crossword generation. *arXiv preprint arXiv:2411.16936*.

Kamyar Zeinalipour, Yusuf Gökberk Keptiğ, Marco Maggini, and Marco Gori. 2024b. Automating turkish educational quiz generation using large language models. *arXiv preprint arXiv:2406.03397*.

Kamyar Zeinalipour, Yusuf Gökberk Keptiğ, Marco Maggini, Leonardo Rigutini, and Marco Gori. 2024c. A turkish educational crossword puzzle generator. In *International Conference on Artificial Intelligence in Education*, pages 226–233. Springer.

Tianyi Zhang, Varsha Kishore, Felix Wu, Kilian Q Weinberger, and Yoav Artzi. 2019. Bertscore: Evaluating text generation with bert. *arXiv preprint arXiv:1904.09675*.

Andrea Zugarini, Kamyar Zeinalipour, Surya Sai Kadali, Marco Maggini, Marco Gori, and Leonardo Rigutini. 2024. Clue-instruct: Text-based clue generation for educational crossword puzzles. *arXiv preprint arXiv:2404.06186*.

# Lahjawi: Arabic Cross-Dialect Translator

**Mohamed Motasim Hamed, Muhammad Hreden, Khalil Hennara**
**Zeina Aldallal, Sara Chrouf, Safwan AlModhayan**
Misraj AI
Khobar, Saudi Arabia
{hamed,hreden,hennara,aldallal,sara.chrouf,safwan}@misraj.ai

## Abstract

In this paper, we explore the rich diversity of Arabic dialects by introducing a suite of pioneering models called Lahjawi. The primary model, Lahjawi-D2D, is the first designed for cross-dialect translation among 15 Arabic dialects. Furthermore, we introduce Lahjawi-D2MSA, a model designed to convert any Arabic dialect into Modern Standard Arabic (MSA). Both models are fine-tuned versions of ***Kuwain-1.5B***[1] an in-house built small language model, tailored for Arabic linguistic characteristics. We provide a detailed overview of Lahjawi's architecture and training methods, along with a comprehensive evaluation of its performance. The results demonstrate Lahjawi's success in preserving meaning and style, with BLEU scores of 9.62 for dialect-to-MSA and 9.88 for dialect-to-dialect tasks. Additionally, human evaluation reveals an accuracy score of 58% and a fluency score of 78%, underscoring Lahjawi's robust handling of diverse dialectal nuances. This research sets a foundation for future advancements in Arabic NLP and cross-dialect communication technologies.

## 1 Introduction

Arabic is the official language of 22 countries, with an estimated 400 million speakers globally (Mohammed Ameen and Abdulrahman Kadhim, 2023), It stands out as one of the world's most linguistically rich. With more than 120 morphological patterns (Shaalan et al., 2019), Arabic offers a multitude of word formations that significantly amplify its expressive capacity. In everyday communication, Arabs primarily use dialects, which vary significantly across countries and regions, posing challenges for cross-dialect communication, particularly in informal contexts.

The importance of Arabic dialect translation has grown significantly over the last decade, driven by increasing demand for digital communication and cultural exchanges. While early research focused on Modern Standard Arabic (MSA) translation, the need for comprehensive cross-dialectal translation has recently gained attention due to the language's rich diversity. This diversity presents substantial challenges, including significant vocabulary disparities (see Table 1), varying sentence structures, and region-specific idiomatic expressions like folk proverbs. Additionally, grammatical differences in verb conjugations and plural forms further increase complexity. Despite advancements in Arabic Natural Language Processing (NLP), several challenges persist:

- *Lack of Cross-Dialect Translation Models*: lack of models addressing the dialect-to-dialect translation.
- *Absence of Comprehensive Solutions*: Current models fail to provide a holistic approach that addresses the full spectrum of Arabic dialectal diversity and translation needs.

To address these challenges, we present Lahjawi, a set of dialect translation models designed to address the challenges of cross-dialect communication in Arabic. Our key contribution, Lahjawi-D2D, is the first model developed for cross-dialect translation, covering 15 distinct Arabic dialects. Additionally, we introduce Lahjawi-D2MSA, which translates any Arabic dialect into Modern Standard Arabic (MSA). This work advances Arabic dialect translation and contributes to the broader goal of enhancing inclusivity and linguistic diversity in NLP.

The remainder of this paper is organized as follows: Section 2 reviews related works, Section 3 details our dataset creation steps, Section 4 presents our model and the proposed method, Sec-

[1]***Kuwain-1.5B* (كُوَيِّن)**: *an in-house built small language model designed to address the unique linguistic characteristics of Arabic.*



*Proceedings of The 4th Workshop on Arabic Corpus Linguistics (WACL-4)*, pages 12–24
January 20th, 2025. 

| MSA | Levantine Arabic | Egyptian Arabic | Translation |
|---|---|---|---|
| كيف حالك؟ | كيفك؟ | إزيك؟ | How are you? |
| أريد الذهاب للمنزل | بدي أروح عالبيت | عايز أروح البيت | I want to go home |
| ماذا يحدث؟ | شو عم بصير؟ | إيه اللي بيحصل؟ | What's happening? |

Table 1: Examples of dialectal variations in Arabic

tion 5 outlines our experimental setup. Section 6 discusses the findings, interprets them to existing research, and explores their broader implications. Section 7 acknowledges the approach limitations and suggests directions for future research. Through this structured approach, we deliver an in-depth analysis of Lahjawi's capabilities, highlighting its potential impact on Arabic NLP and cross-dialectal communication.

## 2 Related Work

Recent advancements in dialect translation research have been explored in various dimensions, with notable efforts focusing on translation from individual dialects to Modern Standard Arabic (MSA) and translation involving multiple dialects into MSA (AlMusallam and Ahmad, 2024). The former involves converting a specific dialect into MSA, aiming for precise linguistic alignment between regional speech and formal Arabic. The latter examines the translation of multiple dialects into MSA, offering broader applicability across diverse dialectal variations and enhancing mutual intelligibility. Beyond these, cross-dialect translation involves translating texts from one specific Arabic dialect directly into another, bypassing the need for Modern Standard Arabic (MSA) as an intermediary. This approach is particularly relevant for improving communication between speakers of different dialects. However, despite its practical importance, research in this area remains limited. This may be because most other languages do not exhibit the same level of dialectal variation as Arabic. As a result, cross-dialect translation is a challenge unique to Arabic and a few other languages, which might explain the relatively limited attention it has received from researchers. Consequently, only one foundational work (Meftouh et al., 2015) has addressed this underexplored domain.

### 2.1 Single Dialect Translation To MSA

Recent research in Arabic dialect translation has primarily focused on converting specific dialects to Modern Standard Arabic (MSA). Studies on Jordanian (Al-Ibrahim and Duwairi, 2020), Tunisian (Sghaier and Zrigui, 2020; Kchaou et al., 2020), and Egyptian (Faheem et al., 2024) dialects have highlighted various challenges and approaches. For instance, Jordanian-to-MSA translation has achieved high accuracy at both word and sentence levels (Al-Ibrahim and Duwairi, 2020), while Tunisian dialect translation has faced difficulties with longer, idiomatic phrases (Sghaier and Zrigui, 2020; Kchaou et al., 2020). Egyptian dialect research has emphasized the importance of both monolingual and parallel data in low-resource settings (Faheem et al., 2024). Multi-dialectal approaches, such as (Khered et al., 2023), have shown success in translating Egyptian, Emirati, Jordanian, and Palestinian dialects to MSA using separate models for each dialect.

Methodologies in this field have evolved from traditional rule-based systems to advanced Deep Learning techniques. Early rule-based machine translation (RBMT) systems (Sghaier and Zrigui, 2020) struggled with complex phrases, while statistical machine translation (SMT) (Kchaou et al., 2020) offered moderate improvements through data augmentation. Deep learning methods, particularly recurrent neural networks (RNNs) and transformer models, have shown superior accuracy. For example, RNN-based approaches (Al-Ibrahim and Duwairi, 2020) demonstrated high accuracy for Jordanian dialect translation, while transformer models (Torjmen and Haddar, 2024; Khered et al., 2023) significantly outperformed rule-based approaches. Semi-supervised approaches (Faheem et al., 2024) have effectively combined parallel and monolingual data, outperforming both supervised and unsupervised models in low-resource contexts.

### 2.2 Multiple Dialects Translation To MSA

Recent advancements in multi-dialect translation to MSA have centered on model fine-tuning, data augmentation, and applying large language models (LLMs). Fine-tuning pre-trained transformer models, particularly AraT5, has shown significant improvements in translation quality for various dialects including Palestinian, Jordanian, and Egyptian (AlMusallam and Ahmad, 2024; Alahmari, 2024; Derouich et al., 2023). Joint models trained on multiple dialects (Khered et al., 2023) have leveraged cross-dialectal information to achieve high performance.

Data augmentation and dataset expansion have been crucial strategies. Studies like (Nacar et al., 2024) and (Fares, 2024) have employed back-translation and incorporated multiple corpora to expand training data, leading to substantial improvements in translation performance. The introduction of novel datasets, such as SADA (Abdelaziz et al., 2024), created using automated translation methods with ChatGPT 3.5, has further enhanced model training.

The application of LLMs has shown great potential, especially in low-resource settings. Research utilizing models like GPT-3.5, AraT5, and No Language Left Behind (NLLB) (Atwany et al., 2024) has achieved high BLEU scores across multiple dialects. Notably, the Arabic Train Team demonstrated the superior performance of the Jais (Sengupta et al., 2023), an Arabic-focused model, which outperformed GPT-3.5, GPT-4, and NLLB in translating dialects into MSA (Demidova et al., 2024). Additionally, the fine-tuning of models like LLaMA-3 using Parameter-Efficient Fine-Tuning (PEFT) methods (Ibrahim, 2024) has demonstrated the effectiveness of resource-efficient approaches for complex dialect translations. These advancements underscore the growing impact of LLMs and the importance of dialect-specific datasets and efficient fine-tuning techniques in improving translation quality across Arabic dialects.

### 2.3 Cross-Dialect Translation

While most research in Arabic dialect translation has focused on converting dialects into Modern Standard Arabic (MSA), cross-dialect translation has received comparatively less attention. A notable exception is the work by (Meftouh et al., 2015), who introduced PADIC, a parallel corpus of five Arabic dialects from the Maghreb and the Middle East (Algerian, Tunisian, Syrian, and Palestinian). PADIC represents an early attempt at facilitating machine translation between dialects themselves. The study found that dialects from the same region, such as Algerian and Tunisian, achieved better translation accuracy due to their linguistic similarities. In contrast, dialects from different areas, like Syrian and Algerian, posed greater challenges due to their divergence. This groundbreaking work underscores both the potential and the current limitations of machine translation systems when applied to under-resourced Arabic dialects.

## 3 Dataset Preparation and Preprocessing

Our multi-dialect Arabic translation model was developed using a combination of open-source datasets: MADAR (Bouamor et al., 2018), PADIC (Meftouh et al., 2015), NADI (2023) (Abdul-Mageed et al., 2023), Dial2MSA (Mubarak, 2018), Arabic STS (Al Sulaiman et al., 2022), UFAL Parallel Corpus of North Levantine 1.0 (Sellat et al., 2023) and Multidialectal Parallel Corpus of Arabic(MDPCA) (Bouamor et al., 2014). These datasets were processed uniformly using two distinctive templates, with system prompts employed throughout, one for translating any dialect-to-MSA, and another for translating between specific dialects (see Figure 1).

Applying these templates results in two types of datasets: Dialect-to-MSA, and Dialect-to-Dialect datasets. The *Dialect-to-MSA (D2MSA)* dataset consists of 197,042 samples, which are used to train the Lahjawi-D2MSA models. Figure 2 shows the distribution of dialects within this dataset. As shown in the figure, the dataset exhibits significant dialect imbalance, with Syrian Arabic dominating at 66%, while other dialects have minimal representation ranging from 0.8% to 5.7%.

The *Dialect-to-Dialect (D2D)* dataset contains 266,871 samples and is used to train the Lahjawi-D2D model. This dataset was created by generating every possible combination of dialect pairs from all previously mentioned datasets, encompassing a wide range of dialect variations. The dataset includes 210 possible dialect translation pairs (see Figure 3). The dataset shows significant skewness in the number of samples for each pair across the 15 dialects, with an over-representation of Levantine dialects, specifically Syrian, Palestinian, and Jordanian, and Maghrebi dialects, particularly Tunisian, Moroccan, and Algerian.

We implemented a straightforward preprocessing pipeline to standardize the training data. This process includes the normalization of Arabic characters and numerals, as well as the standardization of punctuation and spacing. These preprocessing

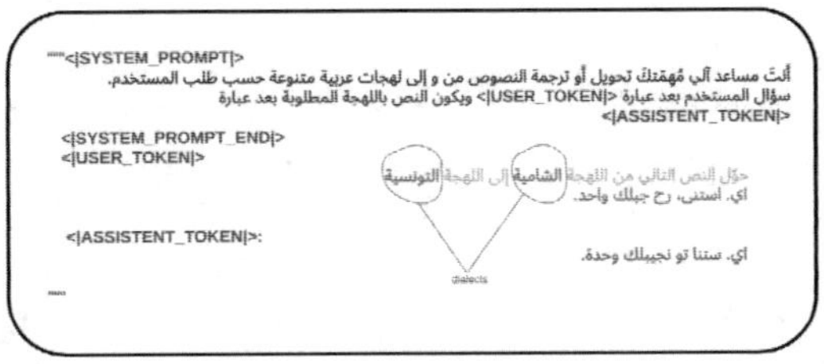


Figure 1: Illustration of the two system prompt templates used in Lahjawi. (Left) Template for translating any dialect-to-MSA, with **system prompt** in dark red, **input** in light blue, and **output** in green. (Right) Template for translating between specific dialects, with **system prompt** in dark red, **template question** in orange, **dialect** name in red, **input** in light blue, and **output** in green.

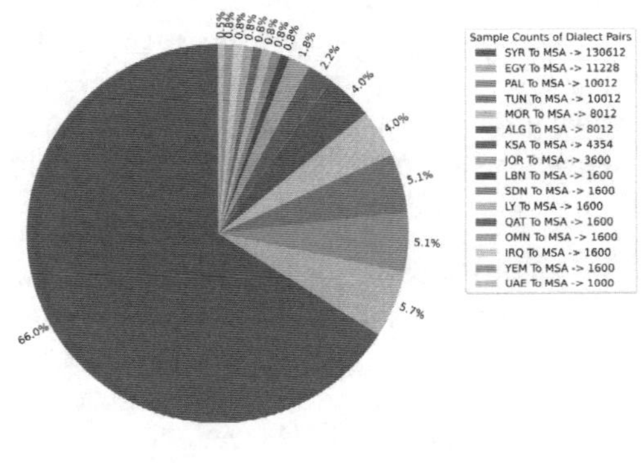


Figure 2: The distribution of dialect-to-MSA samples in D2MSA dataset

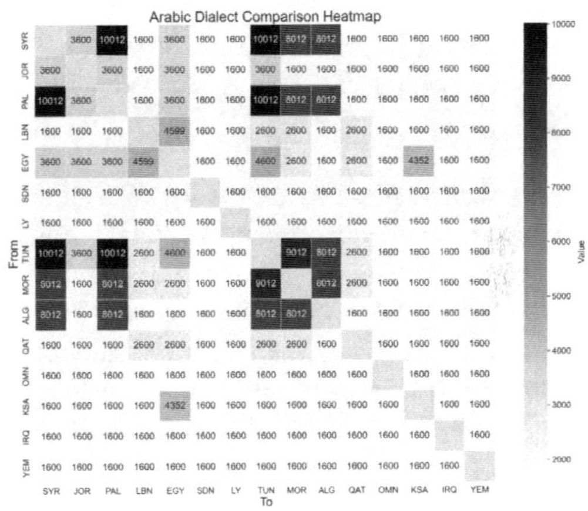


Figure 3: Heatmap of Arabic Dialect Comparison

steps ensure consistency across the datasets, enabling more accurate and reliable model training. To evaluate the performance of our models, we utilized two datasets.

The first dataset is the NADI-2024 DA-MSA test and development data (Abdul-Mageed et al., 2024), which is available in four dialects: Egyptian, Emirati, Jordanian, and Palestinian. This benchmark facilitates the comparison of our results with others. Additionally, we selected the MADAR parallel corpus test set (Bouamor et al., 2018) to assess our model's performance on additional dialects, considering the absence of a standardized benchmark for testing the translation of other dialects into MSA. We applied the same benchmark to evaluate Lahjawi-D2D for cross-dialectical translation, leveraging the fact that MADAR offers parallel translations between our targeted dialects.

## 4 Model

**Lahjawi** models are a fine-tuned adaptation of an in-house small language model *Kuwain 1.5B*, specifically optimized for the challenging task of Arabic dialect translation. In our approach, we reformulated the translation problem into a Question-Answering (QA) framework, which enabled more precise and focused training. This reframing allowed us to capture the nuances of dialect-specific translations better.

As outlined in the previous section, we implemented a consistent template transformation across the entire training dataset, tailoring the input-output structures to align with dialect-specific translation tasks, as illustrated in Figure 1. This step was crucial in adapting the general-purpose *Kuwain* model to specialize in translating input text from one dialect to another, based on the prompt provided.

The fine-tuning process followed the next-token prediction paradigm, with system prompts and embedding tokens carefully masked to ensure the model focused on relevant dialectal context. The training was conducted over three epochs using a *cosine learning rate schedule*, with meticulously adjusted hyperparameters to maximize performance. These optimizations ensured the model's ability to capture both subtle and overt linguistic distinctions across the dialects, delivering robust translation quality across diverse sentence structures. See Appendix A for configuration details.

By combining the strengths of the *Kuwain* model with our specialized fine-tuning approach, Lahjawi models are uniquely positioned to address the complexities of Arabic dialect translation. This tailored methodology enables Lahjawi to serve as a powerful tool for facilitating cross-dialectal communication, offering more accurate and context-aware translations between the various Arabic dialects.

## 5 Experiments and Results

This section presents the results from four experiments conducted on Arabic dialect translation. Each experiment was designed to evaluate different aspects of the translation process. The *first experiment*, Lahjawi-QuadD, follows the methodology of several papers participating in NADI 2024 competition (Abdul-Mageed et al., 2024), to translate from specific Arabic dialects to MSA, serving as a benchmark to compare results. The *second experiment*, Lahjawi-4Isolate, was inspired by (Khered et al., 2023), which suggested that training a model separately for each dialect improves performance. However, our results contradicted this hypothesis, leading us to the *third experiment*, Lahjawi-D2MSA, which investigated the impact of increasing the number of dialects on overall performance. The *fourth and final experiment*, Lahjawi-D2D, represents our primary contribution to developing the first-ever model for direct translation between Arabic dialects.

### 5.1 Lahjawi-QuadD: A Comprehensive Model on 4 Dialects

The experiment focused on fine-tuning a model to translate four Arabic dialectsJordanian, Palestinian, Emirati, and Egyptianinto Modern Standard Arabic (MSA), as part of the NADI-2024 (Abdul-Mageed et al., 2024) subtask DA-MSA machine translation. The model was trained on sample sizes of 3,600 for Jordanian, 10,012 for Palestinian, 14,227 for Egyptian, and 1,000 for Emirati. The data is a subset of D2MSA data for translating input text to MSA. Table 2 presents the model's evaluation measured by the BLEU metric, for the NADI-2024 DA-MSA test data across various Arabic translation systems.

### 5.2 Lahjawi-4Isolate: The Effect of Separates Models Training

In this experiment, four distinct models were trained, each specifically dedicated to translating one of the four target dialects in the NADI-2024 into Modern Standard Arabic (MSA). The main objective of this experiment was to explore the impact of training separate models for each dialect versus using a unified model, as done in the first experiment. The results in Table 2 illustrate the inefficiency of training separate models for each dialect, demonstrating that the previous experiment significantly enhances translation quality compared to this one. Results and findings will be discussed in the section 6

### 5.3 Lahjawi-D2MSA: A Unified Model for Translating All Arabic Dialects to MSA

This experiment focused on developing a robust model for translating various Arabic dialects into Modern Standard Arabic (MSA). The training utilized (D2MSA) dataset, enabling the model to handle the linguistic variations effectively across these diverse dialects. The dataset includes 197,042 samples, with detailed information on the dialects and their corresponding sample sizes provided in Figure 2. Tables 2 and 3 present the BLEU metrics of the unified model derived from the NADI-2024 DA-MSA and MADAR test data, respectively.

Table 4 in Appendix B demonstrates Lahjawi-D2MSA translation examples from different Arabic dialects to Modern Standard Arabic (MSA). The table specifically presents the original dialect sentences alongside their corresponding Lahjawi-D2MSA outputs, illustrating how the translations capture the essence of the original expressions while adapting them to the standardized form of Arabic.

### 5.4 Lahjawi-D2D: A Model for Cross-Dialect Translation

Lahjawi-D2D is an Arabic model for Arabic cross-dialect translation, capable of translating between 15 dialect pairs shown in Figure 3. The model was developed using a standardized format for conversion between any two dialects. The model's performance was evaluated using the BLEU metric on the MADAR test data, with results detailed

| System | Overall | Egy. | Emi. | Jor. | Pal. |
|---|---|---|---|---|---|
| Arabic Train | 20.44 | 16.57 | 23.38 | 21.37 | 20.62 |
| Alson | 17.46 | 16.76 | 17.53 | 20.94 | 18.43 |
| ASOS | 17.13 | 14.82 | 19.39 | 15.80 | 18.38 |
| CUFE | 16.09 | 14.86 | 17.35 | 15.98 | 16.82 |
| Lahjawi-QuadD | 13.55 | 12.64 | 12.51 | 14.96 | 14.20 |
| Lahjawi-D2MSA | 13.30 | 11.39 | 11.37 | 17.40 | 13.67 |
| Lahjawi-4Isolate | 12.13 | 10.54 | 15.27 | 7.87 | 14.41 |
| MBZUAI BLEU | 10.54 | 8.53 | 11.51 | 11.79 | 10.44 |
| VBNN | 9.24 | 8.62 | 6.30 | 11.79 | 10.54 |
| AraT5v2 | 6.87 | 9.38 | 4.61 | 4.90 | 8.13 |
| mT5 | 2.81 | 3.08 | 2.33 | 3.11 | 2.95 |
| MBZUAI BADG | 2.78 | 3.03 | 2.53 | 1.98 | 2.58 |
| AraBART | 0.87 | 0.77 | 0.81 | 1.11 | 0.88 |

Table 2: Performance Metrics: BLEU Scores Across Various Arabic Translation Systems Evaluated on NADI-2024 DA-MSA Test Data.

| **Dialect** | **Test BLEU** | **Dialect** | **Test BLEU** |
|---|---|---|---|
| KSA | 10.81 | ALG | 9.40 |
| OMN | 11.31 | LY | 7.89 |
| QAT | 8.77 | MOR | 8.58 |
| IQR | 8.37 | TUN | 6.47 |
| JOR | 11.52 | EGY | 10.55 |
| LBN | 11.29 | SDN | 8.97 |
| PAL | 11.24 | YEM | 7.80 |
| SYR | 11.39 | | |
| **Overall: 9.62** | | | |

Table 3: *Lahjawi-D2MSA* BLEU Scores on MADAR Test Datasets for Arabic Dialects

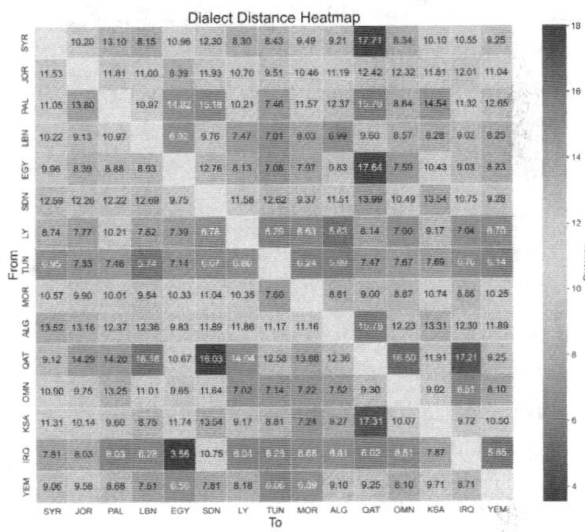


Figure 4: Lahjawi-D2D's BLEU scores on MADAR test set.

in Figure 4. Additionally, human assessments were conducted on 50 sentences for the most commonly spoken dialects, including Syrian, Jordanian, Palestinian, Tunisian, Egyptian, Saudi, and Moroccan. These evaluations, which assess accuracy and fluency, were assigned scores ranging from 1 to 5. The combined outcomes of the human evaluations and the BLEU scores provide valuable insights into the model's effectiveness in cross-dialect translation. Table 5 and 6 in Appendix C demonstrate Lahjawi-D2D translations examples from the Egyptian, and Syrian dialects to various Arabic dialects respectively. It highlights how dialectal variations affect phrasing and vocabulary, showcasing similarities and unique features across all dialects.

## 6 Discussion

First, we will examine the impact of the first experiment involved training a comprehensive model on four dialects collectively (*Lahjawi-QuadD*), compared to the second experiment focused on training separate individual models for each of these dialects (*Lahjawi-4Isolate*). As shown in Table 2, training a comprehensive model demonstrated a relatively consistent performance across all dialects, showing slightly better results in Jordanian and Palestinian dialects. Despite the limited number of samples for the Jordanian dialect in the training data, this did not significantly impact the model's performance. This could potentially be attributed to the benefits of shared knowledge across dialects, leading to improved overall model performance.

Observing the results of training individual models for each dialect reveals that separate

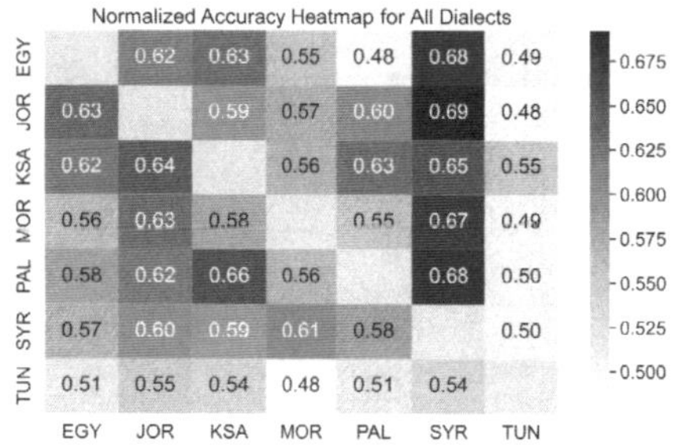


(a)

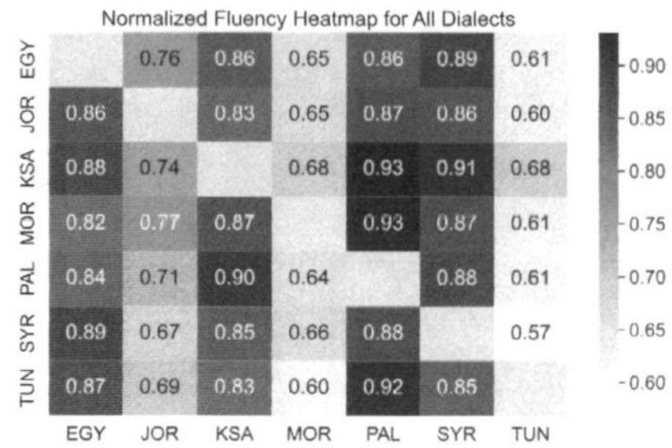


(b)

Figure 5: Dialect-to-Dialect Human evaluation: (a) accuracy scores, (b) fluency score.

training does not consistently lead to better performance, particularly for the Jordanian model, which showed a notable drop in accuracy. This aligns with findings from (AlMusallam and Ahmad, 2024), who observed that the Jordanian and Palestinian dialects tend to achieve high accuracy with minimal differences between them when used together for training, likely due to their close similarity to each other and Modern Standard Arabic (MSA).To confirm this, we compared the Jordanian and Palestinian models on the NADI development set. The results were as follows: Jordanian achieved a BLEU score of 5.67, while Palestinian achieved 14.12, Interestingly, when we tested the Palestinian model on Jordanian data, it scored 19.34, while the Jordanian model scored 6.84 on Palestinian data. These results suggest that the Jordanian dataset is relatively small, and given the similarity between the two dialects, combining them leads to improved BLEU scores. Despite the limited number of training samples for the Emirati dialect, the model performed well. This success could be attributed to the fact that *Kuwain* was exposed to more Gulf dialects during the pre-training phase, leading to a better understanding and representation of the Emirati dialect within the model.

As for the third experiment, training*Lahjawi-D2MSA* as a unified model on 15 dialects yields slightly different scores, with similar overall averages. These small differences indicate that increasing the number of dialects adds translation challenges in some dialects due to the increase in complexity, while others may benefit from the existence of other dialects since similar words and contexts may be the same in different dialects. Nevertheless, the model demonstrated strong adaptability across the diverse linguistic variations.

Compared to other models, our model Lahjawi-D2MSA produced mediocre results. In contrast, teams like Arabic Train (Demidova et al., 2024) and CUFE(Ibrahim, 2024), with superior models such as the Jais-13B and LLaMA-8B multilingual model, leveraged much larger architectures. Additionally, teams like Alson (AlMusallam and Ahmad, 2024) and ASOS (Nacar et al., 2024) enhanced their performance by augmenting their datasets with higher quality and more extensive data. This suggests that using a larger model along with higher-quality data could significantly improve performance.

In Table 3, Lahjawi-D2MSA demonstrates higher performance with Levantine dialects, which aligns with the significant representation of the Syrian Levantine dialect in the training dataset. Additionally, Gulf and Egyptian dialects exhibit decent translation performance, although not as robust as the Levantine dialects. However, the model encounters difficulties with Maghribi dialects, especially Tunisian. These challenges may stem from linguistic differences and the complexity inherent in those dialects, diverging from Modern Standard Arabic (MSA). This underscores the importance of additional training or refining the model to handle underrepresented dialects.

Analyzing the results presented in Figure 4 the Lahjawi-D2D model highlights that certain dialects consistently achieve higher scores (e.g., Qatari, Palestinian) compared to others, such as Iraqi and Libyan, which exhibit notably lower scores. Several factors could contribute to these disparities, including the quality and quantity of training data, as well as the presence of specific dialects during the pre-training phase of the *Kuwain* model . Moreover, it is observed that the model's translation capabilities are not always symmetrical. Some dialects may translate more effectively in one direction than the other. For instance, the translation score from Qatari to Iraqi is 17.21, whereas from Iraqi to Qatari, it is 6.02. This asymmetry in translation performance highlights the complexity and nuances involved in accurately capturing the linguistic variations between different dialects.

The results of the human evaluation accuracy in Figure 5a indicate that the Syrian dialect achieves the highest translation accuracy among the Arabic dialects, largely due to its large dataset and close similarity to Modern Standard Arabic and other Eastern dialects (Egyptian, Saudia, Palestinian, Jordanian, and Syrian) (see Figure 3). In contrast, although the Moroccan (Tunisia, Morocco) dialects have a large dataset, they achieve lower translation accuracy due to their divergence from Modern Standard Arabic and its most closely related dialects. Overall, the accuracy rating for this evaluation is 58%.

Figure 5b shows high fluency levels among most Arabic dialects, with the Eastern dialects showing high similarity and high fluency among them. While the Moroccan dialects show lower variation and percentages for the same reasons related to the nature of the dialect and its rarity in the basic training data in the original model. The overall fluency level, as assessed, reaches 78%.

## 7 Limitations

Our work faced significant challenges due to the complexity and diversity of Arabic dialects, which often deviate from Modern Standard Arabic in vocabulary and grammar. The lack of standardized sentence structures and written forms in many dialects complicated the training and evaluation of our models. A significant limitation is the quality and availability of Arabic dialect datasets, which are often small, unevenly distributed, and lack clear distinctions between dialects. Parallel training corpora are usually built separately for each dialect, without highlighting their similarities and differences, making it challenging to train models that accurately differentiate between them. Additionally, many translations in these datasets are rephrased rather than literal, adding complexity to both generating and evaluating precise translations. Finally, the model's tendency to generate inaccurate outputs (hallucinations), particularly in smaller models, highlighted the resource constraints in developing accurate cross-dialect translators.

## 8 Acknowledgement

This work was made possible through the support of Misraj Corporation, whose management and colleagues provided the necessary resources and technical infrastructure for this research. We express our sincere gratitude to Dr. Nada Ghneim from Arab International University for her thorough review and insightful feedback, which substantially improved this manuscript.

## References

AhmedElmogtaba Abdelmoniem Ali Abdelaziz, Ashraf Hatim Elneima, and Kareem Darwish. 2024. LLM-based MT data creation: Dialectal to MSA translation shared task. In *Proceedings of the 6th Workshop on Open-Source Arabic Corpora and Processing Tools (OSACT) with Shared Tasks on Arabic LLMs Hallucination and Dialect to MSA Machine Translation @ LREC-COLING 2024*, pages 112--116, Torino, Italia. ELRA and ICCL.

Muhammad Abdul-Mageed, AbdelRahim Elmadany, Chiyu Zhang, El Moatez Billah Nagoudi, Houda Bouamor, and Nizar Habash. 2023. NADI 2023: The fourth nuanced Arabic dialect identification shared task. In *Proceedings of ArabicNLP 2023*, pages 600--613, Singapore (Hybrid). Association for Computational Linguistics.

Muhammad Abdul-Mageed, Amr Keleg, AbdelRahim Elmadany, Chiyu Zhang, Injy Hamed, Walid Magdy, Houda Bouamor, and Nizar Habash. 2024. NADI 2024: The fifth nuanced Arabic dialect identification shared task. In *Proceedings of The Second Arabic Natural Language Processing Conference*, pages 709--728, Bangkok, Thailand. Association for Computational Linguistics.

Roqayah Al-Ibrahim and Rehab M. Duwairi. 2020. Neural machine translation from jordanian dialect to modern standard arabic. In *2020 11th International Conference on Information and Communication Systems (ICICS)*, pages 173--178.

Mansour Al Sulaiman, Abdullah M Moussa, Sherif Abdou, Hebah Elgibreen, Mohammed Faisal, and Mohsen Rashwan. 2022. Semantic textual similarity for modern standard and dialectal arabic using transfer learning. *PloS one*, 17(8):e0272991.

Salwa Saad Alahmari. 2024. Sirius_Translators at OSACT6 2024 shared task: Fin-tuning arat5 models for translating Arabic dialectal text to Modern Standard Arabic. In *Proceedings of the 6th Workshop on Open-Source Arabic Corpora and Processing Tools (OSACT) with Shared Tasks on Arabic LLMs Hallucination and Dialect to MSA Machine Translation @ LREC-COLING 2024*, pages 117--123, Torino, Italia. ELRA and ICCL.

Manan AlMusallam and Samar Ahmad. 2024. Alson at NADI 2024 shared task: Alson - a finetuned model for Arabic dialect translation. In *Proceedings of The Second Arabic Natural Language Processing Conference*, pages 764--768, Bangkok, Thailand. Association for Computational Linguistics.

Hanin Atwany, Nour Rabih, Ibrahim Mohammed, Abdul Waheed, and Bhiksha Raj. 2024. OSACT 2024 task 2: Arabic dialect to MSA translation. In *Proceedings of the 6th Workshop on Open-Source Arabic Corpora and Processing Tools (OSACT) with Shared Tasks on Arabic LLMs Hallucination and Dialect to MSA Machine Translation @ LREC-COLING 2024*, pages 98--103, Torino, Italia. ELRA and ICCL.

Houda Bouamor, Nizar Habash, and Kemal Oflazer. 2014. A multidialectal parallel corpus of Arabic. In *Proceedings of the Ninth International Conference on Language Resources and Evaluation (LREC'14)*, pages 1240--1245, Reykjavik, Iceland. European Language Resources Association (ELRA).

Houda Bouamor, Nizar Habash, Mohammad Salameh, Wajdi Zaghouani, Owen Rambow, Dana Abdulrahim, Ossama Obeid, Salam Khalifa, Fadhl Eryani, Alexander Erdmann, and Kemal Oflazer. 2018. The MADAR Arabic dialect corpus and lexicon. In *Proceedings of the Eleventh International Conference on Language Resources and Evaluation (LREC 2018)*, Miyazaki, Japan. European Language Resources Association (ELRA).

Anastasiia Demidova, Hanin Atwany, Nour Rabih, and Sanad Sha'ban. 2024. Arabic train at NADI 2024 shared task: LLMs' ability to translate Arabic dialects into Modern Standard Arabic. In *Proceedings of The Second Arabic Natural Language Processing Conference*, pages 729--734, Bangkok, Thailand. Association for Computational Linguistics.

Wiem Derouich, Sameh Kchaou, and Rahma Boujelbane. 2023. ANLP-RG at NADI 2023 shared task: Machine translation of Arabic dialects: A comparative study of transformer models. In *Proceedings of ArabicNLP 2023*, pages 683--689, Singapore (Hybrid). Association for Computational Linguistics.

Mohamed Faheem, Khaled Wassif, Hanaa Bayomi, and Sherif Abdou. 2024. Improving neural machine translation for low resource languages through non-parallel corpora: a case study of egyptian dialect to modern standard arabic translation. *Scientific Reports*, 14.

Murhaf Fares. 2024. AraT5-MSAizer: Translating dialectal Arabic to MSA. In *Proceedings of the 6th Workshop on Open-Source Arabic Corpora and Processing Tools (OSACT) with Shared Tasks on Arabic LLMs Hallucination and Dialect to MSA Machine Translation @ LREC-COLING 2024*, pages 124--129, Torino, Italia. ELRA and ICCL.

Michael Ibrahim. 2024. CUFE at NADI 2024 shared task: Fine-tuning llama-3 to translate from Arabic dialects to Modern Standard Arabic. In *Proceedings of The Second Arabic Natural Language Processing Conference*, pages 769--773, Bangkok, Thailand. Association for Computational Linguistics.

Saméh Kchaou, Rahma Boujelbane, and Lamia Hadrich-Belguith. 2020. Parallel resources for Tunisian Arabic dialect translation. In *Proceedings of the Fifth Arabic Natural Language Processing Workshop*, pages 200--206, Barcelona, Spain (Online). Association for Computational Linguistics.

Abdullah Khered, Ingy Abdelhalim, Nadine Abdelhalim, Ahmed Soliman, and Riza Batista-Navarro. 2023. UniManc at NADI 2023 shared task: A comparison of various t5-based models for translating Arabic dialectical text to Modern Standard Arabic. In *Proceedings of ArabicNLP*

*2023*, pages 658--664, Singapore (Hybrid). Association for Computational Linguistics.

Karima Meftouh, Salima Harrat, Salma Jamoussi, Mourad Abbas, and Kamel Smaili. 2015. Machine translation experiments on PADIC: A parallel Arabic DIalect corpus. In *Proceedings of the 29th Pacific Asia Conference on Language, Information and Computation*, pages 26--34, Shanghai, China.

Zinah J Mohammed Ameen and Abdulkareem Abdulrahman Kadhim. 2023. Deep learning methods for arabic autoencoder speech recognition system for electro-larynx device. *Advances in Human-Computer Interaction*, 2023(1):7398538.

Hamdy Mubarak. 2018. Dial2msa: A tweets corpus for converting dialectal arabic to modern standard arabic. *OSACT*, 3:49.

Omer Nacar, Serry Sibaee, Abdullah Alharbi, Lahouari Ghouti, and Anis Koubaa. 2024. ASOS at NADI 2024 shared task: Bridging dialectness estimation and MSA machine translation for Arabic language enhancement. In *Proceedings of The Second Arabic Natural Language Processing Conference*, pages 748--753, Bangkok, Thailand. Association for Computational Linguistics.

Hashem Sellat, Shadi Saleh, Mateusz Krubiński, Adam Pospíšil, Petr Zemánek, and Pavel Pecina. 2023. UFAL parallel corpus of north levantine 1.0. LINDAT/CLARIAH-CZ digital library at the Institute of Formal and Applied Linguistics (ÚFAL), Faculty of Mathematics and Physics, Charles University.

Neha Sengupta, Sunil Kumar Sahu, Bokang Jia, Satheesh Katipomu, Haonan Li, Fajri Koto, William Marshall, Gurpreet Gosal, Cynthia Liu, Zhiming Chen, Osama Mohammed Afzal, Samta Kamboj, Onkar Pandit, Rahul Pal, Lalit Pradhan, Zain Muhammad Mujahid, Massa Baali, Xudong Han, Sondos Mahmoud Bsharat, Alham Fikri Aji, Zhiqiang Shen, Zhengzhong Liu, Natalia Vassilieva, Joel Hestness, Andy Hock, Andrew Feldman, Jonathan Lee, Andrew Jackson, Hector Xuguang Ren, Preslav Nakov, Timothy Baldwin, and Eric Xing. 2023. Jais and jais-chat: Arabic-centric foundation and instruction-tuned open generative large language models. *Preprint*, arXiv:2308.16149.

Mohamed Ali Sghaier and Mounir Zrigui. 2020. Rule-based machine translation from tunisian dialect to modern standard arabic. *Procedia Computer Science*, 176:310--319. Knowledge-Based and Intelligent Information Engineering Systems: Proceedings of the 24th International Conference KES2020.

Khaled Shaalan, Sanjeera Siddiqui, Manar Alkhatib, and Azza Abdel Monem. 2019. Challenges in arabic natural language processing. In *Computational linguistics, speech and image processing for Arabic language*, pages 59--83. World Scientific.

Roua Torjmen and Kais Haddar. 2024. Translation from tunisian dialect to modern standard arabic: Exploring finite-state transducers and sequence-to-sequence transformer approaches. *ACM Trans. Asian Low-Resour. Lang. Inf. Process.*

## A Configuration of Supervised Fine-Tuning

**Lahjawi** models are a fine-tuned adaptation of an in-house small language model *Kuwain 1.5B* with 8 Nvidia A100 80G GPUs. We employ the AdamW optimizer, with each batch consisting of 512 samples. We adopt $8 \times 10^{-6}$ as the maximum learning rate based on the model architecture. A cosine scheduler is employed for learning rate adjustment, with a weight decay of 0.1. We train for one epoch using a variety of experiments discussed in section 5.

## B Dialect-to-MSA Translation Examples (Lahjawi-D2MSA)

| Dialect | Original Dialect Sentence | Lahjawi-D2D output |
|---|---|---|
| UAE | لا لو تسويلي عشاء، أنا مب طالع من هني إلين ما أعرِف سالفة الذهب | لا لو تحضرين لي عشاء، أنا لن أخرج من هنا حتى أعرف قصة الذهب |
| SYR | ياخي مين سائل كلو مو فرقانة معو المهم انو تجي البضاعة لعندو ويا دار ما دخلك شر | من الذى يسأل و الذى يجيب و الذى يصله هذا من خلال المهم ان تاتى البضاعه اليه . و بالتالى فان من يسأل شر و من لا يسأل شر . |
| LY | ما نبي نمشي للشغل تواء الجو حامي وحاسس روحي محتاج قعدة قدام المكيف ونشرب شاهي بالنعناع. | لا أريد الذهاب إلى العمل الآن. الجو حار جدا. أتطلع إلى الحصول على استراحة من البرد. |
| IRQ | ممكن اعرف شنو هذا الهاشتاگ لان طبيت عليه ما افتهمت شي | هل من الممكن أن تخبرني ما هذا الهاشتاغ لأنني لم أفهمه |
| ALG | هادا كيتمان عفسه سهيله نفهموها غير حنا هه | هذا كيتمان على سهيلة فهموها نحن فقط |
| JOR | البطاريه فلسعت والكهربا في حد مزعلها منا اشبكلي كابل ياخي | البطارية ضعيفة و الكهرباء مقطوعة هل من الممكن ان تزودني بالكابل |
| EGY | ايه دا يعني ايه يعني انا كمان كام شهر لما اعدي التلاتين مش هابقي طفله | نعم ماذا يعني؟ يعني أنني عندما أصل إلى الثلاثين لن أكون طفلة |
| TUN | قداش كثروا ولاد و بنات الدار الكبيره الليله | كم عدد أطفال و بنات المنزل الكبير الليلة؟ |
| PAL | بتعرف انك نكد؟ خذ امسك و مابديش احكي معك زيح هيك امشي | هل تعرف انك نكد؟ امسك و لا تريد ان تتحدث معي دعني اذهب |
| KSA | اعرف ان الأشياء اللي اسويها غلط بس كمان اسويها وما اهتم | أعلم أن ما أفعله خطأ ولكنى أفعله مرة أخرى ولا أهتم |
| OMN | واحد يسأل دلوع : وش اكثر نوع يعجبك من 'الابل'؟ رد الدلوع : تستعبط أكيد آيباد يقولون دفنوه والدلة ناشبة براسه هههههه | سأل شخص دلوع ما هو أكثر نوع تحبه من ابل؟ رد الدلوع: لا تستعجب، تستعبط، بالتأكيد آيباد، يقولون أنه تم دفنه و ربطه في شجرة و يقال أنه حي، ما هذا الهراء؟ |
| MOR | الإنسان إبن بيئته، مافيها باس استنشقو الجو اللي فيه النكْير و شد لي نقطع ليك | الإنسان ابن بيئته، لا يمكن أن تغيره، استنشق فقط الهواء و أقطع لك مثلا |
| LBN | راكبه مواصلات مع شوية متخلفين حرفيا!! | راكب حافلة مع بعض المتخلفين حرفيا! |
| YEM | طالما وما فيش موعد مع حد نام على الجهة التي تريحك دون وجع راس وقلق من الموعد هههههههه | طالما ولا يوجد موعد مع احد نام على الجهة التي تريحك دون الم وقلق من الموعد |
| SDN | الفي معتقل موقف شندي بتطلع بكرا باذن الله فلو في زول عندو زول مفقود يجي بكرا ٢٦/١٢ الساعة ٧:٠٠ صباحاً | في معتقل موقف شندي تخرج غدا بإذن الله، فلو كان هناك شخص عنده شخص مفقود يأتي غدا 26/12/2012 الساعة 7:00 صباحا |
| QAT | شف عذر اخلق بأيّة طريقة كذبة بيضا او حقيقة .. المهم أنك تجي وغير هذا ما أبي | شف عذراً إخلق بأي طريقة، كذبة بيضاء أو حقيقة، المهم أنك تأتي، وغير هذا لا أريده. |

Table 4: Examples of Dialect to Modern Standard Arabic (Lahjawi-D2MSA) Translations.

## C Dialect-to-Dialect Translation Examples (Lahjawi-D2D)

| Dialect-to-Dialect | Lahjawi-D2D output |
|---|---|
| EGY to JOR | شو القصة؟ كل ما خلصت شغل لسا في مليون اشي تاني، بديت أتشتت. |
| EGY to PAL | شو؟ كل ما خلص شغل رح أكتشف شغلات جديدة، بس ما بقدر. بصراحة، ما بقدر أشتغل أكتر. |
| EGY to LBN | شو في؟ كل هلق لما بتخلص شي بتلاقي مليون شي تاني ناطرك، فما حدا عم بيقدر يركز هون. |
| EGY to SYR | شو القصة؟ لما بخلص شغل واحد بتكون عندي كم شغل تانية لازم أكملها، ما بعرف إذا كنت عم شوف شغلات تانية. |
| EGY to SDN | كيف هو؟ انا دائما بخسر حاجة ما حقتي، ما عارف السبب. |
| EGY to LY | شن القصة؟ كل ما خلصت حاجة أكتشفت حاجة أكبر منها. مش قادر ركز. |
| EGY to TUN | شنيا القصة؟ كل ما نحل حاجة نلقاها أخرى، ديما نطيح من عيني. |
| EGY to MOR | شنو كاي؟ كل ما تنهي شي حاجة تيحصل شي وحدا أخر ب شكل عام، و تنعرف بلي معندناش حل غير ندور. |
| EGY to ALG | واش راه يصرا، دوما وين نخلص حاجة نقددها نخلص حاجة اكبر. الانسان ما لقيتوش نفسه يسوي. |
| EGY to QAT | شنو؟ كل ما خلصت شي احصل في دوشتي غير مليون شي ثاني، ما اقدر اتم تركيزي. |
| EGY to OMN | شو؟ كلما خلصت شي لقيته زيادة، ما عرفت اذا كان هالشي مهم او لا. |
| EGY to KSA | أيش؟ كل ما خلصت حاجة كان يأتيني شيء أكبر منها، حتى وصلت لشيء مستحيل أعرف أتعامل معه. |
| EGY to IRQ | شنو رأيك؟ اذا سويت كل شي، راح اوصل الى مليون شيء آخر، ما اكدر اهتم بهي. |
| EGY to YEM | طيب، ما قصتك؟ انت دائما تبسر كل شي، والكل يقول لك ان تبسر غير هذا. انسان مثلك لازم يفلس. |

Table 5: Translation from Egyptian Dialect to Other Dialects for this Sentence: "هو إيه الحكاية؟ كل ما أقوم أخلص حاجة ألاقي مليون حاجة تانية مستنياني، بجد الواحد مش عارف يركز."

| Dialect-to-Dialect | Lahjawi-D2D output |
|---|---|
| SYR to JOR | امبارح رحت على سوق اخضرت كتير، وكلو خضرا و ما في حدا اشترى، كلو زعلان . |
| SYR to PAL | امبارح رحت على محل أبو جميل و اشتريت شوية خضروات زينين و غاليين، كلو ولا اشي، وبس في ناس كتير بيخافوا و يشتروا منهم. |
| SYR to LBN | مبارح رحت على أبو جميل جبت شوية خضرا، عنجد الأسعار كتير نار و كل شي غالي و ما حدا عم يشتري . مبلاة الناس و زعلانين . |
| SYR to EGY | امبارح رحت عند ابو جميل جبت شوية خضروات، الحقيقة ان الاسعار رهيبة، وكله محجوز. |
| SYR to SDN | البارح عند بائع الخضروات، عندي خضروات، كويس جدا، و خلاه غالي، ما في زول بيبيع زي دا. |
| SYR to LY | البارح نرفعو لعند سيده حسن و نجيبو شوية خضره، هدا هو الغلا و الفشـار قاعدين غالينـا، و كل واحد يسال الاخر. |
| SYR to TUN | البارح نجري عند بو خاطر باش اشتري شوية خضرة، أما الأمر باين باهي، كل شيء غالي شوية، باهي، الناس الكل توا لاهيها الفايدة متاع لا حديقة. |
| SYR to MOR | البارح مشيت عند خو جميل باش نجيب شوية ديال العشب، ولكن العشب غالي بزاف و ما كاين حتى واحد غادي يشتريه و كانو كلشي تيغضب. |
| SYR to ALG | البارح نروح عند بابا جميل نجيب شوية خضرة، كيما نقول بالأخص الكاجو والأسماك، ولكن الناس كل هابطة عندهم الغضب. |
| SYR to QAT | امبارح رحت ابو جميل عشان اشتري خضروات، والله الاسعار واجد غالية ومافيه احد يشتري، كلهم ساكتين. |
| SYR to OMN | انا رحت الى ابو ظبي عشان اشوف بعض الخضار، صدقني الاسعار عالية، وكل شي غالي في هاذي الأيام. |
| SYR to KSA | من امس رحت لشارع ابو جميل واشريت شوية خضروات، بس والله الاسعار تهيلت، ومافيه احد يشتري، وحنا. |
| SYR to IRQ | البارح جانت راحه عند ابو سامي بجيب شوية خضروات، بس شنو كلش غالي ما واحد يشتريه. |
| SYR to YEM | البارح اشلت ل السوق لاشلاح شوية خضروات، لكن الصعوبه ان كلها غاليه وماكانش ممكن اشتريها الان لانه هيه حاله غلاء الاسعار. |

Table 6: Translation from Syrian Dialect to Other Dialects for this Sentence: مبارح رحت لعند أبو جميل نجيب شوية خضرة، لك والله الأسعار نار، وكل شي غالي وما في حدا عم يشتري.

# Lost in Variation : An Unsupervised Methodology for Mining Lexico-syntactic Patterns in Middle Arabic Texts

**Julien Bezançon**
STIH, CERES,
Sorbonne Université

**Rimane Karam**
Orient & Méditerranée, CERES,
Sorbonne Université
LiPoL, Ifpo

**Gaël Lejeune**
STIH, CERES,
Sorbonne Université

28 rue Serpente 75006 Paris, France
firstname.lastname@sorbonne-universite.fr

## Abstract

Although Modern Standard Arabic and some dialects of Arabic have been extensively studied in NLP, Middle Arabic is still very much unknown to the field. However, Middle Arabic presents challenges not addressed by current NLP tools. In particular, it is characterized by variation since it mixes standard features, colloquial ones, as well as features that belong to neither of the two. Here, we introduce a methodology to identify, extract and classify variations of 13 manually retrieved formulas. These formulas come from the nine first booklets of SĪRAT AL-MALIK AL-ẒĀHIR BAYBARṢ, a corpus of Damascene popular literature written in Middle Arabic and composed of 53,843 sentences. In total, we classified 20,386 sequences according to their similarity with the original formulas on multiple linguistic layers. We noticed that the variations in these formulas occur in a lexical, morphological and graphical level, but in opposition, the semantic and syntactic levels remain strictly invariable.

## 1 Introduction

As described in Guellil et al. (2019), three main types of Arabic have been covered by NLP research: Classical Arabic, Modern Standard Arabic (MSA) and dialects (Egyptian, Gulf, ...). While Classical Arabic has been the subject of only a few works, MSA and dialects have been the focus of a fair number of studies. This is not the case for Middle Arabic, which, to the best of our knowledge, has not been studied from a NLP perspective.

However, Middle Arabic study in NLP is interesting on its own. Middle Arabic is "distinguished by its linguistically (and therefore stylistically) mixed nature, as it combines standard and colloquial features with others of a third type, neither standard nor colloquial" (Lentin, 2008). As a result, Middle Arabic texts tend to have a wide range of possible variations for a given structure (Zack and Schippers, 2012). By studying Middle Arabic in NLP, we would be able to produce and process new resources which take into account numerous varieties of Arabic simultaneously. This would be useful for better understanding text processing in Arabic, as Arabic texts are rarely written with a single variety of Arabic (Katz and Diab, 2011).

Studying a corpus of Middle Arabic can be challenging for both linguists and NLP experts, being of mixed nature and prone to variation, as discussed in Section 2.1. For instance, formulas like "فز واثب على الاقدام" ("he leaped jumping on his feet") can also be written as "نهض واثب على الاقدام" ("he got up jumping on his feet") or with the graphical variation "فذ واثب على الاقدام" (*fḏḏ* instead of *fzz*). This challenge is compounded by other difficulties specific to Arabic processing in NLP, including orthographic ambiguity, morphological richness and orthographic noise (Habash, 2010).

Here, we aim to provide a new methodology to study a corpus with multiple varieties of Arabic. Our goal is the identification of all possible variations for a given formula. To do so, we introduce a corpus of Middle Arabic, SĪRAT AL-MALIK AL-ẒĀHIR BAYBARṢ, composed of 53,843 sentences along with 13 formulas that were manually retrieved by a linguist expert and whose variations we want to study. We plan to use token alignment techniques, lexico-syntactic patterns as well as similarity measures in order to extract and rank each possible variation of a given formula.

We find that our study is similar to the ones dealing with multiword expressions (MWEs) in NLP. MWEs are generally seen as conventionalized and idiomatic sequences (Sag et al., 2002). In MWE processing, the identification task, whose goal is to identify MWEs in a text, shares a lot of similarities with the work we try to achieve (Constant et al., 2017). For this reason, we plan to use the methodology presented in (Bezançon and Lejeune, 2023),



*Proceedings of The 4th Workshop on Arabic Corpus Linguistics (WACL-4)*, pages 25–37
January 20th, 2025. 

created for the identification and the extraction of MWEs and unfrozen MWEs, i.e. MWEs which have undergone lexical, syntactic and/or semantic changes.

We first introduce the notion of Middle Arabic in Section 2. We then introduce the corpus and the formulas we used to test our methodology in Section 3. Those formulas correspond to short and frequently occurring instances in our corpus. Hereafter, we show the different steps that led to the identification and extraction of those formulas and their look-alikes in Section 4. Finally, we discuss the variations we observe between the original formulas and their newly-found variations in Section 5.

## 2 Middle Arabic: a non standardized language

### 2.1 Definition

Arabic is usually perceived as a two-sided language: standard on the one hand, and colloquial on the other. This linguistic situation, called diglossia, was widely theorized by Charles Ferguson: the "high" variety refers to the standard, whereas the "low" stands for the dialects (Ferguson, 1959). The linguistic reality of Arabic is actually not as binary and hermetical, and Ferguson himself acknowledged the existence of intermediate varieties. Further research has defined these varieties that lay between the two poles of diglossia under the term Middle Arabic (Blau, 1982). Middle Arabic can thus be described as a set of intermediate registers that mixes both standard and colloquial features, and also has features of its own, that are not standard nor colloquial and that belong to a third pole (Larcher, 2001).

A whole area of Arabic literature has been written in Middle Arabic, and it was shown that it had nothing to do with poor language skills in *fuṣḥā* (Classical Arabic). We have examples of texts written by the same scholars both in perfect *fuṣḥā* and in Middle Arabic; and popular literature is, for a large part, written in some varieties of Middle Arabic, just as the THOUSAND AND ONE NIGHTS (Lentin, 2012). The Damascene version of SĪRAT BAYBARṢ, which we work on, is another example, and one should keep in mind that even though the text seems close to Levantine dialects, not only does it have standard features, but it also has very specific features that belong to neither of the two poles. For instance, the relative pronoun *allaḏī* in its masculine singular form remains invariable regardless of the gender and number of its antecedent (Lentin, 2012).

Thus, Middle Arabic can be distinguished by its mixed nature: it combines features from both standard and dialects. Given this situation, it makes it complex to use either standard or dialect tools such as part-of-speech taggers on a Middle Arabic corpus. Middle Arabic being a mixed, hybrid set of varieties of Arabic that tends to play on the linguistic continuum, it creates an important amount of linguistic variation throughout the text. Isolating manually all the variations of the same formulas in our corpus can be difficult given the language of the text and the size of the corpus. A closer look into Arabic NLP research could help us develop an automatic approach on Middle Arabic texts that might be expanded to other languages with frequent variations.

### 2.2 NLP Tools and Resources

MSA and Dialects Arabic studies are potentially the most useful for this work as explained in Section 2.1. On the one hand, there is a wide variety of tools used to process data in MSA, like segmenters (Abdelali et al., 2016) and morphosyntactic taggers (Zalmout et al., 2018; Pasha et al., 2014). On the other, we can find tools specific to each dialect, like Egyptian (Zalmout et al., 2018; Samih et al., 2017) or Gulf (Alharbi et al., 2018; Khalifa et al., 2017), but there are also tools that can handle several dialects simultaneously (Darwish et al., 2018; Al-Shargi et al., 2016).

To our knowledge, there are no NLP tools dedicated to Middle Arabic. This can be a problem for a language marked by linguistic variation such as Middle Arabic, that has standard as well as dialect features, but also features of its own that are neither of the two. Faced with this challenge, we plan to use CAMELTOOLS (Obeid et al., 2022) as a substitute to label our corpus in Section 4.1. It is a multi-dialect morphological disambiguation tool covering MSA as well as Egyptian, Gulf, and Levantine. While it is unlikely that this tool will identify and tag correctly Middle Arabic features, we suppose that tagging MSA and dialectal Arabic ones is at reach.

| Vol. | # Tokens | # Sent. | T/S | TTR |
|---|---|---|---|---|
| 1 | 94,315 | 5,679 | 16.61 | 16.41 |
| 2 | 100,408 | 6,482 | 15.49 | 15.00 |
| 3 | 118,986 | 6,093 | 19.53 | 15.23 |
| 4 | 92,744 | 4,389 | 21.13 | 16.20 |
| 5 | 105,081 | 5,562 | 18.89 | 15.15 |
| 6 | 106,817 | 6,515 | 16.40 | 14.46 |
| 7 | 119,921 | 7,504 | 15.98 | 15.09 |
| 8 | 82,691 | 5,235 | 15.80 | 17.12 |
| 9 | 107,972 | 6,384 | 16.91 | 14.89 |
| **All** | 928,935 | 53,843 | 17.25 | 07.06 |

Table 1: Statistics for each volume (**Vol.**) of the SĪRAT BAYBARṢ corpus. In addition to the number of tokens and sentences (**Sent.**), we give the average sentence size in tokens (**T/S**) and the Type Token Ration (**TTR**).

## 3 Dataset description

### 3.1 Corpus

SĪRAT AL-MALIK AL-ẒĀHIR BAYBARṢ is a popular prose epic cycle from the Ottoman period. It is a text designed above all for performance since it used to be told by *hakawātī*-s, storytellers of the Levant, who memorized and recited the stories in cafés or homes, by heart or with the help of booklets. For this project, we are using the Damascene version of SĪRAT BAYBARṢ (Anonymous, 2000–2021). This composite corpus consists of a set of booklets of manuscripts written down by many different scribes between the 18th and the 20th century, and gathered afterwards by three storytellers from Damascus [1]. We decided to focus on the first 90 booklets of the Abu Ahmad manuscript, named after the storyteller who compiled it. It is normally composed of 183 booklets, but only the first 90 have been digitalized so far. In the edited version (Anonymous, 2000–2021), they have been segmented into 9 volumes of 10 booklets each. Table 1 shows various statistics for each volume. We notice that the Type-to-Token Ratio (TTR) is very low for the whole corpus (7.06 %), which can indicate that a lot of constructions are repeated over and over.

Another particularity should be noted regarding the language of SĪRAT BAYBARṢ, in addition to it being mostly close to the Damascene dialect. Some characters are made fun of and portrayed as caricatures in their way of speaking, either because they come from another country or because they represent the enemy. These two layers of variation combined - Middle Arabic and idiolects within the SĪRA - complexify any kind of statistics on this text, especially given the absence of tools to explore Middle Arabic to our knowledge.

[1] https://lipol.hypotheses.org/1310

### 3.2 Formulas

We are looking for sequences within the SĪRAT BAYBARṢ that occur regularly in specific contexts. As shown by the work of J. P. Guillaume which is very close to ours linguistic-wise (Guillaume, 2004), each occurrence of a given sequence bears the same meaning despite the linguistic variations, without denoting a narrative progression in the story. For instance, these sequences can indicate a sudden change of a character's mood, or be used as opening or closing sequences in a situation, whether it is a new day dawning, the night falling, a poem declamation or even battle scenes for example. The formulation, regularity and context of these sequences make them easy to be noticed by the reader (or the listener, in a performance situation) regardless of the variations. As described in Section 2.1, Middle Arabic is characterized by linguistic variation, and these sequences are no exception. In a way, they are similar to MWEs, as they are conventionalized in our corpus and tend to have similar, almost fixed forms.

The works of Milman Parry on the Homeric style could help define these sequences. Parry described "a group of words which is regularly employed under the same metrical conditions to express a given essential idea" under the term formula (Parry, 1930). His corpus of reference is the Homeric poems, a versified text. Although it has come down to us written, it is deeply rooted in the oral tradition. As we said before in Section 3.1, orality is an important element in our corpus as it was also destined to a performance. As for the versification part, we can argue that although written in prose, our corpus is still punctuated by sequences that have a very close usage to Homer's "as soon as early rosy-fingered Dawn appeared" for "when it was morning". Moreover, these formulas in SĪRAT BAYBARṢ happen to be used in the context of *sajʿ* (rhymed prose). They do not follow versification rules, but they do not strictly belong to prose either, especially because they tend to provoke other rhyming formulas in a row. Despite the lack of versification constraints, we can assume that other types of constraints, either linguistic or stylistic, impact the formulas in SĪRAT BAYBARṢ. Their core concept consists in their regularity and in the importance of expressing an idea "without second thought" (Parry, 1930), which fits our corpus. Formulas are a landmark, for the poet / scribe as well as for the listener / reader, and their presence in the text with so many variations might tell something about the language. We aim to see how these variations occur within a formula, with the hypothesis that they do not happen randomly but that they rather follow some pattern.

Thirteen frequently occurring sequences were found by a linguist expert who is also very familiar with the SĪRAT BAYBARṢ corpus. Those sequences correspond to formulas in our corpus. We base our experiment on them. For intelligibility reasons, we chose to present three of them in order to give detailed results and examples:

1. غضب غضباً شديد
   *(ġḍb ġḍban šdīd)*
   "he got very angry"
2. لما سمع فلان من فلان ذلك الكلام
   *(lmmā smʿ flān mn flān ḏlk al-klām)*
   "when A heard those words from B"
3. قلب الضيا بعينه ظلام
   *(qlb aḍ-ḍyā b-ʿynh ẓlām)*
   "the light in his eye turned into darkness"

(1) denotes a very strong feeling (namely anger) resulting from a situation or an action taken by another character. (2) appears very often after a character has said something that affected another character, whatever type of impact it is (positive or negative), which leads most of the time to an action by the latter character or a sudden change of mood. (3) denotes a sudden and abrupt change of mood, resulting often from what a character has just said. In fact, the last two formulas frequently follow one another. Our goal is, for each formula, to automatically find similar sequences that exhibit only slight variations. For instance, for (1), we aim to find similar sequences like (a.), (b.) and (c.).

a. غضبوا غضباً شديد
   *(ġḍb**ū** ġḍban šdīd)*
   "they got very angry"

b. غضبان غضبا شديد
   *(**ġḍbān** ġḍbā šdīd)*
   "he is very angry"

c. وفرح فرحاً شديد
   *(**w-frḥ frḥan** šdīd)*
   "and he got very happy"

| | |
|---|---|
| sentence: | "فقال لى : والله ، انا احبك حباً شديد ." |
| id: | "27434" |
| tokens: | ["فقال", "لى", ":", "والله", ",", "انا", "احبك", "حباً", "شديد", "."] |
| pos tags: | ["verb", "prep", "punc", "noun_prop", "punc", "pron", "verb", "noun", "noun_prop", "punc"] |
| lemmas: | ["قال", "لِ", ":", "اللَّه", ",", "أَنا", "أَحَبّ", "حُبّ", "شَدِيد", "."] |

Table 2: Example of an entry of the SĪRAT BAYBARṢ corpus.

These three variants give an idea of what types of variation are possible within the same formula. They can be morphological and impact the verb such as *ġḍbū* in (a.) in place of *ġḍb* in the original formula. The variations can also be graphic and guide the presence or absence of some letters or diacritics, such as in (b.). The double vowel marker of the *tanwīn* (nunation, i.e. the mark of indefiniteness) is absent in *ġḍbā* even though the *ʾalif* is written, whereas (a.) indicates it in *ġḍban*. Finally, these variations can occur at a lexical level, changing completely the lexeme while preserving the structure of the sequence, as shown in (c.) where the verb *ġḍb* used in a. and b. (to get angry) becomes *frḥ* (to get happy).

## 4 Methodology

### 4.1 Processing Middle Arabic

We used CAMELTOOLS (Obeid et al., 2022) to (i) tokenize the corpus, (ii) get POS tags, (iii) get lemmas and (iv) segment it into sentences. Table 2 shows an entry of the corpus. The scripts we used to process the SĪRAT BAYBARṢ corpus are available in a dedicated GitHub repository[2]. CAMELTOOLS was chosen for its ability to handle different dialects of Arabic. Indeed, most Arabic morphosyntactic taggers have been designed to annotate Modern Standard Arabic only, as stated by Obeid et al. (2022); Darwish et al. (2018). We could have tried to use CAMELTOOLS's Levantine tool in conjunction with standard Arabic tools, to cover both the Damascene and the standard features of our corpus. Unfortunately, except for the online demo version of CAMELTOOLS, which only allows us to enter very few words in the input bar, the Levantine model was not available.

[2] https://github.com/JulienBez/ASMR

| Layer | Formula | Sequence | Score |
|---|---|---|---|
| Tok. | قلب الضيا بعينه ظلام | قلب الضيا فى وجهه ظلام | 0.67 |
| Lem. | قَلْب الضيا عَيْن ظَلام | قَلْب الضيا فِي وَجْه ظَلام | 0.67 |
| Pos. | noun noun_prop noun noun | noun noun_prop prep noun noun | 0.95 |

Table 3: Searched formula and found sequence side by side for each linguistic layer, with a cosine similarity score.

| | | | | |
|---|---|---|---|---|
| قلب | الضيا | - | - | بعينه ظلام |
| قلب | الضيا | فى | وجهه | - ظلام |

Table 4: Example of alignment at token level.

To roughly evaluate the quality of the annotation of CAMELTOOLS, we manually annotated 71 sentences for a total of 1,037 annotated tokens. Both the annotator and CAMELTOOLS had to choose between 5 tags for each token: noun, preposition, numeral, punctuation or verb. The precision of CAMELTOOLS on those tokens was 91.99 %, which can be considered low, since we drastically reduced the complexity of the tag set. The performance of the part-of-speech tagging and lemmatization is probably not as reliable as it would be for an MSA text. For instance, as table 2 shows, "شديد" (*šdīd*) is analysed as a "noun_prop" whereas it is an adjective. However, we did not expect perfect results, and we think it provides a basis that will be useful for different purposes.

### 4.2 Sequence Association

Our first step was to associate each sentence of our corpus with the formulas it resembles. We did a fuzzy matching between each sentence of our corpus and each of the manually chosen formulas by creating vectors and calculating cosine distance scores. If the distance between a formula and a sentence was too high (> to 0.9), we didn't associate them. By doing so, we only associate sentences and formulas with a minimum commonality of elements. For instance, the sentence "غضب غضبا شديد" ("he got very angry") was associated with the formula "انا احبك حباً شديد" ("I love you very much") with a cosine distance score of 0.87. Additionally, each sentence can be associated with more than one formula.

### 4.3 Candidates Ranking

For each sentence, we want to know if it contains at least one of the formulas it has been associated with, *in extenso* or with slight variations. We adapted the code and methodology presented in (Bezançon and Lejeune, 2023) for Arabic. The author's goal was to find unfrozen multiword expressions, i.e. multiword expressions which have been modified to some degree (for instance "may the force be with you" becoming "may the peace be with you"). This methodology was created to find both exact matches with a given sequence and closely related matches, i.e. matches that show a slight degree of variation and can therefore be linked to the original sequence. In the remainder of this subsection, we describe the different steps used to find and rank candidates based on their similarity to the formula they were associated with:

**Alignment** For each sentence, we aligned it with its associated formula to highlight their common tokens. As an example, we give in table 4 the alignment between the sentence "قلب الضيا فى وجهه ظلام" ("the light in his face turned into darkness") and the formula "قلب الضيا بعينه ظلام" ("the light in his eye turned into darkness"). This alignment shows us that the word "بعينه" has been replaced by the words "فى وجهه" in the sentence. Those alignments were made with BIOPYTHON[3], as this package's alignment process proposes all possible alignments between two sequences.

**Segmentation** We used the alignments to isolate common sequences between a sentence and a formula. Those sequences correspond to the longest subsequence of words that begin and end with the same words with a minimal number of misalignments (i.e. the minimal edit distance at token level). For instance, in the alignment presented in table 4, the complete sentence would be isolated since it (i) begins with the same word as the formula (قلب) and (ii) end with the same word (ظلام). A sentence can have more than one sequence with a formula.

[3] https://biopython.org/

| Sequence | Transliteration | Translation | Score | Freq |
|---|---|---|---|---|
| غضب غضباً شديد | ġḍb ġḍban šdīd | he got very angry | 0.89 | 7 |
| وغضب غضبا شديد | w-ġḍb ġḍbā šdīd | and he got very angry | 0.89 | 2 |
| عرنوس غضبا شديد | <f-ġḍb> ʿrnūs ġḍbā šdīd | so ʿArnūs <got> very angry | 0.81 | 1 |
| وغضب غضباً شديد | w-ġḍb ġḍban šdīd | and he got very angry | 0.78 | 6 |
| فغضب غضباً شديد | f-ġḍb ġḍban šdīd | so he got very angry | 0.78 | 3 |
| غضبان غضبا شديد | ġḍbān ġḍbā šdīd | he is very angry | 0.74 | 1 |
| وغضبت غضباً شديد | w-ġḍbt ġḍban šdīd | and she got very angry | 0.63 | 1 |
| احبك حباً شديد | aḥbk ḥban šdīd | I love you very much | 0.46 | 1 |
| الاسلام قتالاً شديد | <w-qātlt> l-islām qtālan šdīd | <and> the muslims <fought> very hard | 0.46 | 1 |
| وفرح فرحاً شديد | w-frḥ frḥan šdīd | and he got very happy | 0.31 | 1 |

Table 5: Some ranked sequence candidates for the formula "غضب غضباً شديد" ("he got very angry"). We show sequences with a high score as well as sequences with a lower similarity score on purpose.

**Similarity Measurement** We vectorized each sequence with its associated formula before calculating a cosine similarity score between them. The higher the score, the closer the sequence and the formula tend to be. Therefore, a score of 1 indicates a perfect match, while a score of 0 informs us that there is no common element between them. This measure is performed at different levels, as shown in the next paragraph.

**Ranking** We ranked each sequence according to its similarity with the formula. This ranking relies on several linguistic features (tokens, POS tags and lemmas) by calculating an average score from the cosine similarity obtained with each feature. Thus, the alignment, segmentation and measurement steps were repeated for every additional linguistic feature. Table 3 shows the sequence "قلب الضيا فى وجهه ظلام" ("the light in his face turned into darkness") compared with its associated formula with respect to the different linguistic layers we spoke off.

### 4.4 Results

The results take the form of a ranking for each formula we searched for. Table 5 shows the ranking obtained for the formula "غضب غضباً شديد" (1). In total, we found and ranked 20,386 sequences, including 7,329 with a cosine similarity above 0.5. Figure 1 shows the distribution of found sequences according to their score. We find that the higher the score, the fewer the corresponding sequences. Thus, only 813 sequences have a score of 0.7 or more. To evaluate the quality of our ranking, we used an intra cluster similarity score. This score

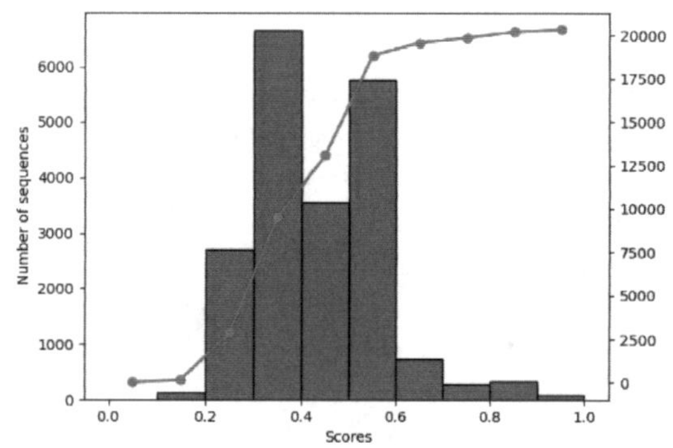


Figure 1: Distribution of found sequences according to their score for every formula we searched for. The red line shows the cumulative number of sequences found.

is obtained by computing the mean of a cosine similarity matrix created from a list of sequences $s$, as shown in Equation 1. The higher the intra-cluster score, the closer the sequences.

$$s_1, s_2, ..., s_n \Rightarrow \begin{pmatrix} s_1.s_1 & s_1.s_2 & ... & s_1.s_n \\ ... & ... & ... & ... \\ s_n.s_1 & s_n.s_2 & ... & s_n.s_n \end{pmatrix} \quad (1)$$

For each formula, we calculated the intra-cluster score of every sequence related to it with a score $\geq X$, $X$ being equal to 1. We progressively lowered $X$ to include more sequences from our ranking and to calculate the progression of the intra-cluster scores. Figure 2 is the result of this process. We observe that the lower $X$, the lower the intra cluster score. This fact could indicate that, for a given formula, our ranking seems to put the most

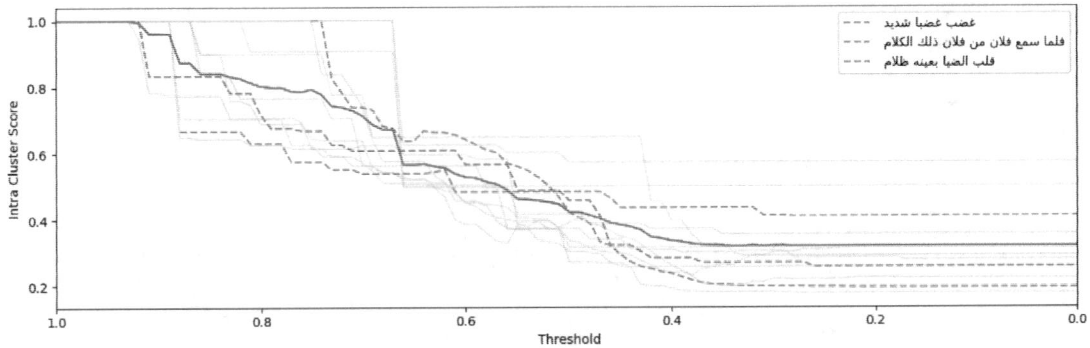


Figure 2: Progression of the intra cluster score (y-axis) for each formula, according to $X$ (x-axis). The doted lines represent the formulas we focused on in this paper. Other formulas are shown in gray. The red line is the mean intra-cluster score for every formula.

similar sequences to this formula at the top while putting the less relevant ones at the bottom. We also mapped the vectors of every sequence found for each formula in a two-dimensional vectorial space. Figure 3 shows three formulas as an example. Sequences with a high score are represented by red dots, while sequences with a low score are represented by blue dots. The formulas are represented by a black dot. We observe that sequences with a high score tend to be closer to formulas than sequences with a low score. In the remainder of this paper, we propose an analysis of the results we obtained for a selected set of formulas.

## 5 Discussion

The variations we observed appear mainly on three levels : graphical, morphological and lexical. On the graphical level, we noticed that some letters and diacritics are not always indicated. For instance, the *hamza* in *ḍyāʾ* (3) is most of the time absent, despite it being written in some variants of the same formula. This feature was already described by Lentin in (Lentin, 2008) : "final *hamza* is generally absent". This graphical flexibility is also visible within the preposition *fī*, sometimes written without the two points of the *yāʾ*, as well as the double vowels of the *tanwīn* in (1) which are not systematically indicated. On a morphological level, one of the most variable elements is the verb, which can be conjugated at any person and in any number or gender, as in (2) where *smʿ* depends on the subject, and can become *smʿt* or *smʿū* . It is also the case in (3) where *ġḍb* can be *ġḍbū* as well as *ġḍbt*. We also found many variants of 3 with *ʿynīh* in the dual form instead of *ʿynh* (see 7). Finally, variations can occur on a lexical level, either on verbs or nouns that are synonyms or describe a very close image, preserving the meaning of the formula. In (3) *ʿyn* ("eye") becomes *wjh* ("face"), and *qlb* ("turned to") can be replaced by *ṣār* ("became"), as well as *ġḍb* ("to get angry") by *frḥ* ("to get happy") in (1). For the last two, one could argue that they are not synonyms. In fact, as we will show in the next paragraphs, they still belong to the same lexical field (emotions, for instance): they do not affect the core meaning of the formula, and the landmark effect that we explained in 3.2 is preserved.

Nevertheless, some of these variations do change completely the meaning of the formula, to the point of consisting of another formula. For instance, if *smʿ* (to hear) and *fhm* (to understand), a verb that we found in one of the variants of the formula (2), are exchangeable, it is because the meaning of the two verbs - at least in this context - is very close; whereas the variant with *frġ mn* in "فلما فرغ من ذلك الكلام" ("and when he had said those words") affects way too much the formula, and thus consists in another formula. Indeed, we noticed that the formula (2) is systematically used in the context of dialog, right after one character has said something that affects another character. In opposition, the same formula with *frġ* has its own specific context: it is only used after a character has recited a poem. Following the same logic, *ġḍb* can be substituted by *frḥ* in (1), because both indicate emotions or feelings that overwhelm a character. The variant with *qātl* "وقاتلت الاسلام قتالاً شديد" ("the muslims fought very hard"), which does not denote an emotion, gives another meaning to the

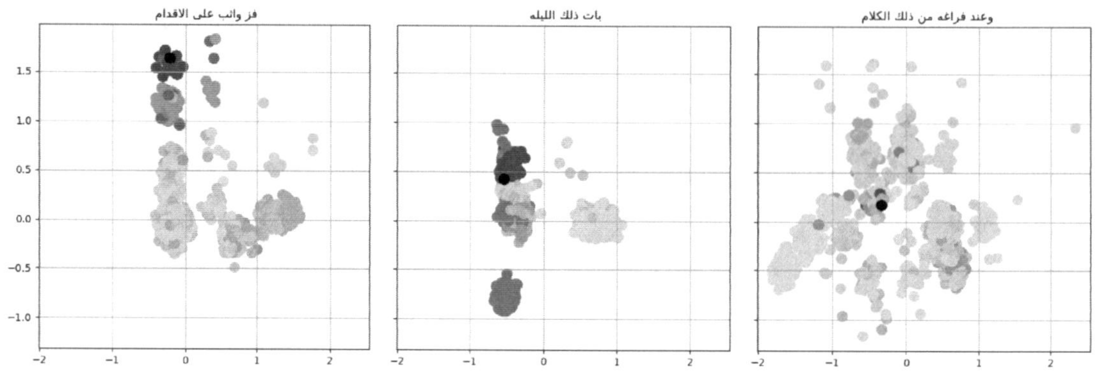


Figure 3: Distribution of found sequences for three formulas on a two-dimensional vectorial space. Red dots correspond to sequences with high scores in our ranking, while blue dots correspond to sequences with low scores. Black dots represent our formulas.

formula. In fact, it has its own context of use, which is the battle scenes that happen within the SĪRA. All these examples show that linguistic variation in our corpus and within the specific context of the formulas do not occur randomly. Some variants pass the threshold of comprehension, which indicates that they no longer belong to the same formula. The fact that they have their own context of use supports this idea.

In fact, some elements are strictly invariable, and they all happen to be syntactic and semantic. The syntactic structure of the formula stays unchanged: in (1), the *mafʿul muṭlaq* structure is constant in all the variants of the formula, regardless of any graphical, lexical or morphological changes. We can also note that there is at least one static word in each formula: a word that never changes graphically, morphologically or lexically, with a fixed position in the formula, and which is hardly ever used in unrelated found sequences. For instance, *šdīd* occurs 75 times within the formula (1), and only 8 outside of it; *ẓlām* has 47 occurrences within the formula (3), and only 5 outside of it. The formulas also follow a semantic pattern: as we explained in the previous paragraph, (2) has a specific context of occurrence which cannot be replaced by another without changing a strong parameter in the formula (as when *smʿ* becomes *frġ*). In (1), regardless of the lexical changes, all the variants of the formula describe a very strong feeling, whether it is anger (*ġḍb*), joy (*frḥ*), love (*ḥbb*) or torment (*ʿḏb*). When the lexical variation exceeds this meaning, as in the variant with *qātl* ("to kill"), the semantic level is not reached, and this meaning shift leads to an unfreezing process, as defined by (Mejri, 2009). Although we did not find any variant that underlines an unfreezing process in formula (3), such as in (1) and (2), we can guess that any lexical variation that involves a meaning shift will not be considered as part of the same formula.

## 6 Conclusion

In this paper, we presented a methodology for the identification and extraction of formulas likely to be subject to variations in a Middle Arabic corpus. We extracted 20,386 sequences resembling these formulas. We ranked those sequences according to their similarity with the searched formulas on various linguistic layers. In total, 813 segments with a score of 0.7 or more were found.

This process helped us get an overview of the variants of each formula. We noticed that some elements of a formula can easily vary whereas others are strictly invariable. Variations may occur at the lexical, morphological and graphical level but never on a syntactic nor semantic level. If any kind of variation happens on the last two levels mentioned, it changes completely the essence of the formula, consisting in another formula of another type which is used in its own specific context.

In future work, we aim to build improved NLP tools for processing Middle Arabic. It would help us to analyze more formulas, than the set we studied in this paper. We also plan to work with linguists experts in Damascene in order to annotate a sample of the sequences found. This would help us to propose further analysis of the performances of the methodology we presented here. We hope this work will be helpful for further research on non-standard Arabic variants.

## Acknowledgements

We would like to thank the ANR LiPoL program [ANR 19-CE27-0024] for making this corpus available.

## References

Ahmed Abdelali, Kareem Darwish, Nadir Durrani, and Hamdy Mubarak. 2016. Farasa: A fast and furious segmenter for Arabic. In *Proceedings of the 2016 Conference of the North American Chapter of the Association for Computational Linguistics: Demonstrations*, pages 11–16, San Diego, California. Association for Computational Linguistics.

Faisal Al-Shargi, Aidan Kaplan, Ramy Eskander, Nizar Habash, and Owen Rambow. 2016. Morphologically annotated corpora and morphological analyzers for Moroccan and sanaani yemeni Arabic. In *Proceedings of the Tenth International Conference on Language Resources and Evaluation (LREC'16)*, pages 1300–1306, Portorož, Slovenia. European Language Resources Association (ELRA).

Randah Alharbi, Walid Magdy, Kareem Darwish, Ahmed AbdelAli, and Hamdy Mubarak. 2018. Part-of-speech tagging for Arabic Gulf dialect using Bi-LSTM. In *Proceedings of the Eleventh International Conference on Language Resources and Evaluation (LREC 2018)*, Miyazaki, Japan. European Language Resources Association (ELRA).

Anonymous. 2000–2021. *Sīrat al-Malik al-Ẓāhir Baybarṣ ḥasab al-riwāya al-šāmiyya*. éd. G. Bohas, S. Diab, I. Hassan, K. Zakharia, Damas and Beyrouth, Presses de l'Ifpo.

Julien Bezançon and Gaël Lejeune. 2023. Reconnaissance de défigements dans des tweets en français par des mesures de similarité sur des alignements textuels. In *30e Conférence sur le Traitement Automatique des Langues Naturelles, TALN*, pages 56–67, Paris, France. ATALA.

Joshua Blau. 1982. The state of research in the field of the linguistic study of middle arabic. In *Études de Linguistique Arabe*, pages 187–203. Brill.

Mathieu Constant, Gülşen Eryiğit, Johanna Monti, Lonneke van der Plas, Carlos Ramisch, Michael Rosner, and Amalia Todirascu. 2017. Survey: Multiword Expression Processing: A Survey. *Computational Linguistics*, 43(4):837–892. Place: Cambridge, MA Publisher: MIT Press.

Kareem Darwish, Hamdy Mubarak, Ahmed Abdelali, Mohamed Eldesouki, Younes Samih, Randah Alharbi, Mohammed Attia, Walid Magdy, and Laura Kallmeyer. 2018. Multi-Dialect Arabic POS Tagging: A CRF Approach. In *Proceedings of the Eleventh International Conference on Language Resources and Evaluation (LREC 2018)*, Miyazaki, Japan. European Language Resources Association (ELRA).

Charles A. Ferguson. 1959. Diglossia. *WORD*, 15(2):325–340.

Imane Guellil, Houda Saâdane, Faical Azouaou, Billel Gueni, and Damien Nouvel. 2019. Arabic natural language processing: An overview. *Journal of King Saud University - Computer and Information Sciences*, 33(5):497–507.

Jean-Patrick Guillaume. 2004. Les scènes de bataille dans le roman de baybars: considérations sur le" style formulaire" dans la tradition épique arabe. *Arabica*, pages 55–76.

N.Y. Habash. 2010. *Introduction to Arabic Natural Language Processing*. Synthesis digital library of engineering and computer science. Morgan & Claypool Publishers.

Graham Katz and Mona Diab. 2011. Introduction to the special issue on arabic computational linguistics. *ACM Transactions on Asian Language Information Processing*, 10(1).

Salam Khalifa, Sara Hassan, and Nizar Habash. 2017. A morphological analyzer for Gulf Arabic verbs. In *Proceedings of the Third Arabic Natural Language Processing Workshop*, pages 35–45, Valencia, Spain. Association for Computational Linguistics.

Pierre Larcher. 2001. Moyen arabe et arabe moyen. *Arabica*, 48(Fasc. 4):578–609.

Jérôme Lentin. 2012. Reflections on middle arabic. *High vs Low and Mixed Varieties: Domain, Status and Function across Time and Languages, edited by Gunvor Mejdell and Edzard Lutz*, pages 32–51.

Jérôme Lentin. 2008. *Middle Arabic*. Volume 3 of (Versteegh et al., 2008).

Salah Mejri. 2009. Figement, défigement et traduction. Problématique théorique. In *figement, défigement et traduction (Fijación, desautomatización y traducción)*, pages 153–163. Universidad de Alicante.

Ossama Obeid, Go Inoue, and Nizar Habash. 2022. Camelira: An Arabic multi-dialect morphological disambiguator. In *Proceedings of the 2022 Conference on Empirical Methods in Natural Language Processing: System Demonstrations*, pages 319–326, Abu Dhabi, UAE. Association for Computational Linguistics.

Milman Parry. 1930. Studies in the epic technique of oral verse-making. i. homer and homeric style. *Harvard Studies in Classical Philology*, 41:73–147.

Arfath Pasha, Mohamed Al-Badrashiny, Mona T Diab, Ahmed El Kholy, Ramy Eskander, Nizar Habash, Manoj Pooleery, Owen Rambow, and Ryan Roth. 2014. Madamira: A fast, comprehensive tool for morphological analysis and disambiguation of arabic. In *Lrec*, volume 14, pages 1094–1101.

Ivan A. Sag, Timothy Baldwin, Francis Bond, Ann Copestake, and Dan Flickinger. 2002. Multiword Expressions: A Pain in the Neck for NLP. In *Computational Linguistics and Intelligent Text Processing*, Lecture Notes in Computer Science, pages 1–15, Berlin, Heidelberg. Springer.

Younes Samih, Mohammed Attia, Mohamed Eldesouki, Ahmed Abdelali, Hamdy Mubarak, Laura Kallmeyer, and Kareem Darwish. 2017. A neural architecture for dialectal Arabic segmentation. In *Proceedings of the Third Arabic Natural Language Processing Workshop*, pages 46–54, Valencia, Spain. Association for Computational Linguistics.

Kees Versteegh et al. 2008. *Encyclopedia of Arabic Language and Linguistics*, volume 3. Brill.

Liesbeth Zack and Arie Schippers. 2012. *Middle Arabic and Mixed Arabic: Diachrony and Synchrony*. Brill, Leiden, The Netherlands.

Nasser Zalmout, Alexander Erdmann, and Nizar Habash. 2018. Noise-robust morphological disambiguation for dialectal Arabic. In *Proceedings of the 2018 Conference of the North American Chapter of the Association for Computational Linguistics: Human Language Technologies, Volume 1 (Long Papers)*, pages 953–964, New Orleans, Louisiana. Association for Computational Linguistics.

## Appendix

In this Appendix, we show 3 additional Tables. Table 6 shows the 13 formulas we based our work on. Tables 7 and 8 are two additional ranking for the formulas "قلب الضيا بعينه ظلام" and "فلما سمع فلان من فلان ذلك الكلام". Figure 4 and 5 shows the distribution of found sequences for all formulas on a two-dimensional vectorial space.

About the Levantine feature of CAMELIRA: The Levantine module was made available a few days before the conference deadline. We therefore did not have the opportunity to use it in this work.

About the transliteration: the SĪRAT BAYBARṢ corpus is not vocalized (with a few rare exceptions) and we have no record nor any kind of testimony on how the text was read aloud. Therefore, we chose to follow the transliteration system used by other researchers on Middle Arabic, which consists of not assuming the short vowels, because we simply do not know and have no indication on how they were supposed to be pronounced in such a mixed variety of Arabic. For instance, the world "غضب", transliterated as *ġaḍiba* for standard texts, is transliterated as *ġḍb* in the present paper.

For our experiment, we used *sci-kit learn*'s vectorization features with the following parameters:

- $CountVectorizer$
- $ngram\_range = (1, 1)$
- $encoding = "utf-8"$
- $lowercase = True$
- $stop\_words = None$
- $analyzer = lambda\ x : x.split(" ")$

| Formula | Transliteration | Translation |
|---|---|---|
| قلب الضيا بعينه ظلام | qlb aḍ-ḍyā bʿynh ẓlām | the light in his eye turned into darkness |
| غضب غضباً شديد | ġḍb ġḍbā šdīd | he got very angry |
| فلما سمع فلان من فلان ذلك الكلام | f-lmmā smʿ flān mn flān ḏlk al-klām | when A heard from B those words |
| فز واثب على الاقدام | fz wāṯb ʿlā al-aqdām | he leaped jumping on his feet |
| بات ذلك الليله | bāt ḏlk al-lylh | he slept that night |
| اصبح الصباح | aṣbḥ aṣ-ṣbāḥ | it became morning |
| اظلم الظلام | aẓlm aẓ-ẓlām | it became night |
| دقت طبول الانفصال | dqqt ṭbūl al-anfṣāl | the drums of separation rumbled |
| وعند فراغه من ذلك الكلام | w-ʿnd frāġh mn ḏlk al-klām | when he had said those words |
| اما سمعت ما قال الشاعر | amā smʿt mā qāl aš-šāʿr | haven't you heard what the poet said |
| اما سمعت الشاعر حيث قال | amā smʿt aš-šāʿr ḥyṯ qāl | haven't you heard the poet when he said |
| وأنشد وقال | w-ʾnšd w-qāl | he chanted and said |
| أشاد يسجع نفسه بهذه الأبيات | ʾšād ysjʿ nfsh b-hḏh al-ʾbyat | he praised, rhyming himself with these verses |

Table 6: The 13 formulas we based our work on.

| Sequence | Transliteration | Translation | Score | Freq |
|---|---|---|---|---|
| قلب الضيا بعينه ظلام | qlb aḍ-ḍyā bʿynh ẓlām | the light in his eye turned into darkness | 1.0 | 21 |
| قلب الضيا بعينيه ظلام | qlb aḍ-ḍyā bʿynīh ẓlām | the light in his eyes turned into darkness | 0.92 | 6 |
| قلب الضيا بعينيه ظلام | qlb aḍ-ḍyā bʿynīh ẓlām | the light in his eyes turned into darkness | 0.92 | 6 |
| قلب الضيا بعينها ظلام | qlb aḍ-ḍyā bʿynhā ẓlām | the light in her eye turned into darkness | 0.92 | 2 |
| قلب الضيا فى عينيه ظلام | qlb aḍ-ḍyā fī ʿynīh ẓlām | the light in his eyes turned into darkness | 0.84 | 1 |
| صار الضيا بعينه ظلام | ṣār aḍ-ḍyā bʿynh ẓlām | the light in his eye became darkness | 0.8 | 2 |
| قلب الضيا بعينه طلام | qlb aḍ-ḍyā bʿynh ṭlām | the light in his eye turned into darkness | 0.8 | 1 |
| قلب الضيا فى وجهه ظلام | qlb aḍ-ḍyā fī wjhh ẓlām | the light in his face turned into darkness | 0.77 | 1 |
| قلب الضياء بعينيه ظلام | qlb aḍ-ḍyāʾbʿynīh ẓlām | the light in his eyes turned into darkness | 0.73 | 1 |
| صار الضيا بعينيه ظلام | ṣār aḍ-ḍyā bʿynīh ẓlām | the light in his eyes became darkness | 0.72 | 1 |

Table 7: Some ranked sequences for the formula "قلب الضيا بعينه ظلام" ("the light in his eyes turned into darkness").

| Sequence | Transliteration | Translation | Score | Freq |
|---|---|---|---|---|
| فلما سمع الملك من القاضى ذلك الكلام | f-lmmā smʿ al-mlk mn al-qāḍī ḏlk al-klām | when the king heard from the qāḍī those words | 0.75 | 1 |
| فلما سمع الملك منه ذلك الكلام | f-lmmā smʿ al-mlk mnh ḏlk al-klām | when the king heard from him those words | 0.74 | 3 |
| فلما سمع الملك من ابراهيم ذلك الكلام | f-lmmā smʿ al-mlk mn brāhīm ḏlk al-klām | when the king heard from Ibrahim those words | 0.73 | 2 |
| فلما سمع الملك من عماد ذلك الكلام | f-lmmā smʿ al-mlk mn ʿmād ḏlk al-klām | when the king heard from ʿImad those words | 0.73 | 1 |
| فلما سمع الملك من عيسى ذلك الكلام | f-lmmā smʿ al-mlk mn ʿysā ḏlk al-klām | when the king heard from ʿIssa those words | 0.73 | 1 |
| فلما سمع ذلك الكلام | f-lmmā smʿ ḏlk al-klām | when he heard those words | 0.72 | 6 |
| فلما سمع الملك ذلك الكلام | f-lmmā smʿ al-mlk ḏlk al-klām | when the king heard those words | 0.71 | 44 |
| فلما سمع عرنوس ذلك الكلام | f-lmmā smʿ ʿrnūs ḏlk al-klām | when the king heard from ʿrnus those words | 0.71 | 11 |
| فلما فرغ من ذلك الكلام | f-lmmā frg̣ mn ḏlk al-klām | when he had said those words | 0.69 | 1 |
| فلما فهم الملك ذلك الكلام | f-lmmā fhm al-mlk ḏlk al-klām | when the king understood those words | 0.58 | 4 |

Table 8: Some ranked sequences for the formula "فلما سمع فلان من فلان ذلك الكلام" ("when A heard those words from B").

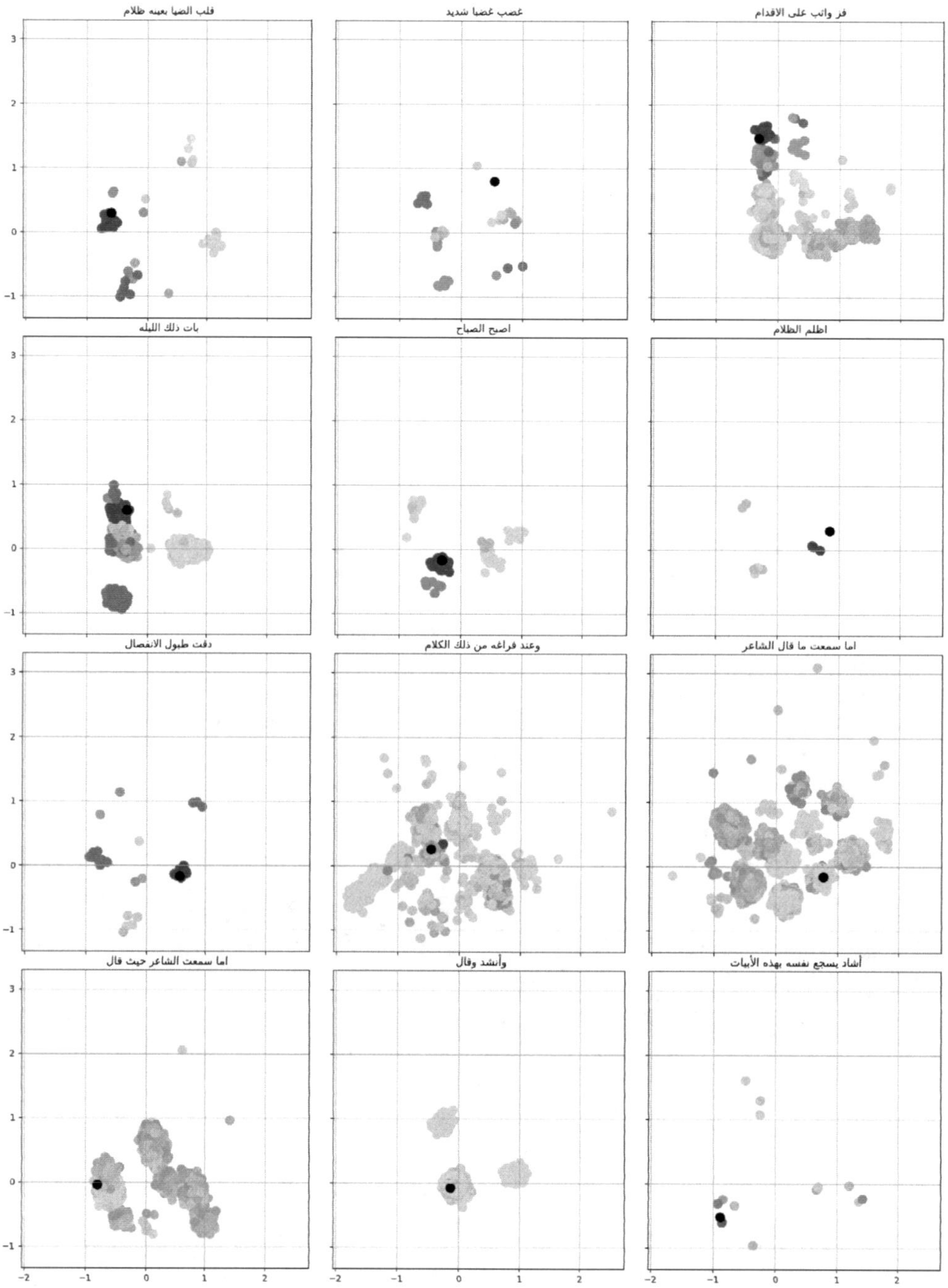


Figure 4: Distribution of found sequences for all formulas on a two-dimensional vectorial space. Red dots correspond to sequences with high scores in our ranking, while blue dots correspond to sequences with low scores. Black dots represent our formulas.

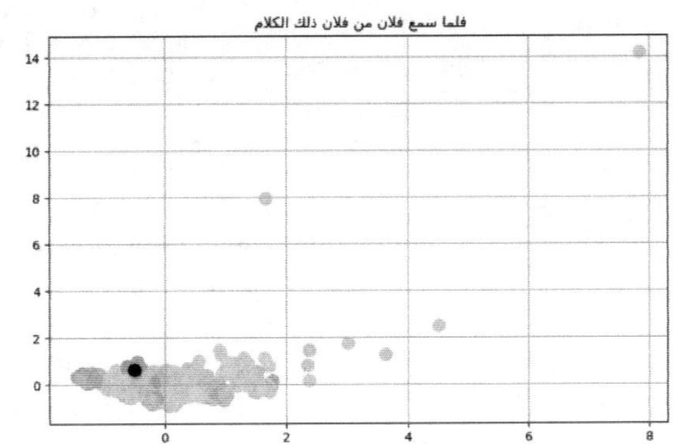


Figure 5: Distribution of found sequences for the formula فلما سمع فلان من فلان ذلك الكلام on a two-dimensional vectorial space. We separated this formula from the others because it has significant outliers.

# SADSLyC: A Corpus for Saudi Arabian Multi-dialect Identification through Song Lyrics

**Salwa Alahmari**[1,3]**, Eric Atwell**[1]**, Mohammad Alsalka**[1] **and Hadeel Saadany**[2]
[1]University of Leeds, UK,
[2]Birmingham City University and
[3]University of Hafr Al Batin, Saudi Arabia
{scssala, e.s.atwell, m.a.alsalka}@leeds.ac.uk
hadeel.saadany@bcu.ac.uk

**Abstract**

This paper presents the Saudi Arabian Dialects Song Lyrics Corpus (SADSLyC), the first dataset featuring song lyrics from the five major Saudi dialects: Najdi (Central Region), Hijazi (Western Region), Shamali (Northern Region), Janoubi (Southern Region), and Shargawi (Eastern Region). The dataset consists of 31,358 sentences, with each sentence representing a self-contained verse in a song, totaling 151,841 words. Additionally, we present a baseline experiment using the SaudiBERT model to classify the fine-grained dialects in the SADSLyC Corpus. The model achieved an overall accuracy of 73% on the test dataset.

## 1 Introduction

Through the analysis of Arabic song lyrics, one can explore the rich linguistic nuances of the Arabic language, recognise regional variations, and appreciate the artistic and literary elements present in the music. Within the structure of a song, verses often serve as the storytelling components, unravelling the plot or message, while choruses provide a recurring, emotive anchor that reinforces the song's central theme[1].

The lyrics of Arabic songs available online are categorised based on the singer's country of origin, regardless of the actual dialect of the lyrics. Taking Nancy Ajram, a famous Arabic singer, as an example[2], despite frequently singing in the Egyptian Arabic dialect, she is consistently recognised as a Lebanese singer. Thus, whether her songs are in Lebanese Arabic or not, they are invariably placed within the list of Lebanese songs on any musical platform (El-Haj, 2020). In this study, we do not rely on this classification to identify the Saudi Arabian dialect of the song lyrics. Instead, we used the songwriter's region of origin to construct the SADSLyC Corpus. We believe this approach is more accurate since it focuses on the lyrics written by the songwriter rather than the singer, who simply performs what is written.

The SADSLyC corpus consists of 1,892 Saudi Arabian songs, encompassing 31,358 sentences, and representing the five primary Saudi Arabian dialects: Najdi, Hijazi, Shamali, Janoubi,and Shargawi. In this paper, we will use the terms sentence and verse interchangeably.

The structure of this paper is as follows: Section 2 outlines related works. Section 3 describes the research methodology of this study. Section 4 provides a description of the SADSLyC corpus along with its statistical details. Section 5 presents the baseline experiment and results. Section 6 discusses the implications of the findings, addresses the limitations of the study. Finally, Section 7 provides a conclusion and suggestions for future work.

## 2 Related Work

The Habibi Corpus, developed by El-Haj (2020), is currently the only Arabic song lyrics dataset available in the literature. This corpus comprises 30,000 Arabic songs from 18 countries, covering six Arabic dialects: Egyptian, Levantine, Gulf, Maghrebi, Iraqi, and Sudanese. For dialect identification, the corpus was automatically labeled based on the nationality of the singer, providing a foundational resource for Arabic dialectal analysis in song lyrics.

Specific to the Saudi Arabian dialect, much of the prior research has focused on sentiment and emotion analysis in Saudi social media, particularly Twitter. Studies by AlMazrua et al. (2022), Almuqren and Cristea (2021), and others, such as Al-Twairesh et al. (2018), AL-Rubaiee et al. (2017), and Assiri et al. (2016), have provided valuable insights into this area. Additionally, Bayazed et al. (2020) classified Saudi tweets according to subdialects and sentiment, advancing the study of lin-

[1]https://en.wikipedia.org/wiki/Songstructure
[2]https://en.wikipedia.org/wiki/NancyAjram



*Proceedings of The 4th Workshop on Arabic Corpus Linguistics (WACL-4)*, pages 38–43
January 20th, 2025. 

guistic and emotional nuances within Saudi Arabic.

However, none of the previously mentioned studies focus on fine-grained dialects of Saudi Arabia based on geographical location. In our previous work (Alahmari et al., 2024), we employed Twitter for the Arabic dialect identification task, using ChatGPT for the identification process. We collected a small dataset from Twitter using dialectal word lists, representing the five main dialects of Saudi Arabia: Najdi, Hijazi, Shamali, Janoubi, and Shargawi.

The SADSLyC corpus stands distinct from existing literature due to its focus on a new genre, specifically Saudi song lyrics. As noted by Almuqren and Cristea (2021), the majority of Saudi corpora have primarily relied on Twitter as the sole data source.

## 3 Methodology

This section provides details on the construction of the SADSLyC corpus, including the selection of songwriters, data collection, data preprocessing, and data labeling.

### 3.1 Data Selection Criteria

Initially, we dedicated a considerable amount of time to seeking out Saudi songwriters hailing from diverse regions, representing the five primary dialects relevant to our study. Our approach to gathering information about the hometown or birthplace of each songwriter involved leveraging two main web-based resources: Wikipedia[3] and Google[4]. Typically, Wikipedia provides details about the hometown or birthplace of the songwriter. However, there were instances where the Wikipedia page for the songwriter did not exist. Furthermore, in other cases, essential information regarding the hometown or birthplace was absent. Consequently, we extended our search to include web pages such as forums, blogs, and Twitter accounts in pursuit of information about the songwriter. Additionally, we delved into YouTube, scouring TV interviews that shed light on the songwriter's hometown or birthplace. When the necessary information remained elusive from the aforementioned sources, we resorted to investigating the origin of the songwriter's family. Notably, many family names in Saudi Arabia correspond to renowned tribal names, particularly in the southern (Janoub) and northern (Shamal) regions, exemplified by well-known tribes like Alqahtani and Alshammari. Finally, when we were unable to find specific information regarding the songwriter's hometown or birthplace, we excluded the song from the list.

[3]www.wikipedia.org/

[4]www.google.com/

### 3.2 Data Collection

For the data (song lyrics) collection, we utilized the Web as Corpus method (Kilgarriff and Grefenstette, 2001). There are a large number of websites that provide textual representations of song lyrics. However, not all of them provide information about the songwriter or allow web scraping techniques.

We primarily extracted song lyrics (textual data) from three web sources: Wneen[5], Kalimat Aghani[6], and Fnanen[7]. After inspecting the HTML pages of each website, we developed Python code using the BeautifulSoup4 library[8] to scrape the website based on its HTML elements.

### 3.3 Data Preprocessing

To ensure the SADSLyC corpus is free from unwanted elements such as advertisements, spam, hashtags, or symbols, we implemented preprocessing and data-cleaning methods. This meticulous approach results in a refined corpus devoid of any noise. To achieve this, we utilised the arabicprocess[9] library in Python for cleaning and preprocessing Arabic text.

### 3.4 Data Labeling

As previously mentioned, dialect labels are assigned to the lyrics based on the songwriter's origin. For instance, renowned Saudi poet and songwriterخالد الفيصل Khalid Alfaisal[10] originates from Najd (central Saudi Arabia) and resides in Riyadh[11]. Consequently, all songs authored by him are labeled as "Najdi". Similarly, songs penned by ثريا قابل Thuraya Qabel[12], a Saudi songwriter from Hijaz (western Saudi Arabia) who resides in Jeddah[13], are labeled as "Hijazi".

As the final step, these lyrics were assigned to two native speakers from each of the five dialect regions, totaling 10 native speakers. They validated

[5]https://www.wneen.com

[6]https://www.kalimataghani.com

[7]https://fnanen.com

[8]https://pypi.org/project/beautifulsoup4/

[9]https://pypi.org/project/arabicprocess/

[10]https://en.wikipedia.org/wiki/KhalidAl-Faisal

[11]https://en.wikipedia.org/wiki/Riyadh

[12]https://en.wikipedia.org/wiki/ThurayaQabil

[13]https://en.wikipedia.org/wiki/Jeddah

the labels and ensured that the lyrics accurately represented their respective dialects.

## 4 Corpus Description

The original song lyrics are parsed into sentences based on the verses. The finalized corpus is saved in JSON format. Each song verse is assigned a unique "id" number, with the verse content stored under the "verse" field. Verses belonging to the same song are associated with the same title, writer, and dialect. Figures 1,2,3,4, and 5 show samples from the SADSLyC corpus JSON files for Najdi, Hijazi, Shamali, Janoubi, and Shargawi, respectively.

The corpus is available[14] for academic and research purposes to enrich the development of Arabic linguistic resources.

| Sub-Dialect | Sentence Count | % | #Songs |
|---|---|---|---|
| Najdi | 19481 | 62.12% | 1118 |
| Hijazi | 7359 | 23.47% | 392 |
| Janoubi | 1960 | 6.25% | 129 |
| Shamali | 1017 | 3.24% | 110 |
| Shargawi | 1541 | 4.91% | 143 |
| Total | 31358 | 100% | 1892 |

Table 1: The SADSLyC Corpus Sentence Count by Dialect

The corpus statistics in Table 1 clearly show that Najdi songs make up a significant portion of the corpus, accounting for 64.52%. The high percentage of Najdi songs can be attributed to several factors. **Firstly**, the dominance of the Najdi dialect in Saudi songs plays a significant role, as many well-known Saudi songwriters originate from Najd, further contributing to this prevalence. **Secondly**, our search for Saudi songwriters from the five regions of Saudi Arabia revealed that Shargawi songwriters tend to write in MSA rather than in the Saudi Arabian dialect, which has resulted in a limited collection of song lyrics in the Shargawi dialect. Additionally, poets from the Janoubi and Shamali regions prefer to compose Shilaat, a unique style of song that is typically performed without music. However, written sources for Shilaat are scarce, as most of them are available online in video or audio format. Consequently, we have a smaller portion of Janoubi and Shamali textual song lyrics in our corpus.

[14]https://github.com/SalwaAlahmari/SADSLyC_Corpus


```
[
  {
      "id": 1,
      "Title": "ياغالي الاثمان",
      "verse": "ياغالي الاثمان غلوك بالحيل",
      "Writer": "خالد الفيصل",
     "Dialect": "Najdi"
   },
   {
      "id": 2,
      "Title": "ياغالي الاثمان",
      "verse": "من يوم سمو بك جميل المحيا",
      "Writer": "خالد الفيصل",
     "Dialect": "Najdi"
   },
   {
      "id": 3,
      "Title": "ياغالي الاثمان",
      "verse": "شخص تمنيته على العدل والميل",
      "Writer": "خالد الفيصل",
     "Dialect": "Najdi"
   }
]
```


Figure 1: Sample of SADSLyC JSON for Najdi Dialect


```
[
{
  "id": 1,
  "Title": "جاني الاسمر",
  "Lyrics": "جاني الاسمر جاني",
  "Writer": "ثريا قابل",
 "Dialect": "Hijazi"
  },
 {
 "id": 2,
  "Title": "جاني الاسمر",
  "Lyrics": "وافتكر زماني",
  "Writer": "ثريا قابل",
 "Dialect": "Hijazi"
  },
  {
 "id": 3,
  "Title": "جاني الاسمر",
  "Lyrics": "وبعد ما نساني جاني",
  "Writer": "ثريا قابل",
 "Dialect": "Hijazi"
 }
  ]
```


Figure 2: Sample of SADSLyC JSON for Hijazi Dialect

## 5 Experiments and Results

### 5.1 Experiments

As a baseline experiment, we applied the SaudiBERT model Qarah (2024) for Saudi Arabian dialect identification using the SADSLyC corpus. To address the class imbalance in the SADSLyC corpus, as shown in Table 1, where the Najdi dialect is the dominant class and the other dialects (Hijazi, Janoubi, Shamali, and Shargawi) are underrepresented, we employed a combination of oversampling and stratified splitting. Oversampling was applied during the training phase, specifically increasing the representation of the minority dialects (Shargawi, Shamali, and Janoubi) to create a more

```
[
{
    "id": 1,
    "Title": "ياجمالك",
    "Lyrics": "الله أكبر يا جمالك",
    "Writer": "عادل مدالله الشراري",
   "Dialect": "Shamali"
  },
  {
    "id": 2,
    "Title": "ياجمالك",
    "Lyrics": "كيف يضرب بالصميم",
    "Writer": "عادل مدالله الشراري",
   "Dialect": "Shamali"
  },
  {
    "id": 3,
    "Title": "ياجمالك",
    "Lyrics": "يا حبيبي زان حالك",
    "Writer": "عادل مدالله الشراري",
   "Dialect": "Shamali"
  }
]
```


Figure 3: Sample of SADSLyC JSON for Shamali Dialect


```
[
{
    "id": 1,
    "Title": "غيمة جلوبية",
    "Lyrics": "تقول الله يطعني و اقول الله يسبق بي",
    "Writer": "سعد زهير",
   "Dialect": "Janoubi"
  },
  {
    "id": 2,
    "Title": "غيمة جنوبية",
    "Lyrics": "جنوبي نثر همه على غيمة جنوبيه",
    "Writer": "سعد زهير",
   "Dialect": "Janoubi"
  },
  {
    "id": 3,
    "Title": "غيمة جنوبية",
    "Lyrics": "احس أني إذا قالت فديتك ياعرب ربي",
    "Writer": "سعد زهير",
   "Dialect": "Janoubi"
  }
  ]
```


Figure 4: Sample of SADSLyC JSON for Jaboubi Dialect

balanced dataset. This adjustment ensures that the model receives adequate samples from each dialect, thereby enhancing its ability to learn distinguishing features from these minority classes and reducing potential bias toward the majority Najdi class.

Additionally, we used stratified splitting when dividing the dataset into training, validation, and test sets. By stratifying based on dialect labels, we ensured consistent class distribution across these subsets, preserving the original corpus proportions. This stratification guarantees that each class is adequately represented during model evaluation, providing a more reliable measure of model performance across all dialects. Combining oversampling with stratified splitting addresses the challenges of imbalanced data, resulting in a model that is better equipped to generalize across all five dialects.


```
[
{
   "id": 1,
   "Title": "تضحك الدنيا",
   "Lyrics": "لله لا يجيب الزعل بينك وبيني",
   "Writer": "احمد عبدالحق",
  "Dialect": "Shargawi"
},
{
   "id": 2,
   "Title": "تضحك الدنيا",
   "Lyrics": "وان زعلت ارضيك انا يا نور عيني",
   "Writer": "احمد عبدالحق",
  "Dialect": "Shargawi"
},
{
   "id": 3,
   "Title": "تضحك الدنيا",
   "Lyrics": "تضحك الدنيا في عيني لا رضيت",
   "Writer": "احمد عبدالحق",
  "Dialect": "Shargawi"
}
]
```


Figure 5: Sample of SADSLyC JSON for Shargawi Dialect

| Accuracy | Precision | Recall | F1 |
|---|---|---|---|
| 0.73 | 0.55 | 0.51 | 0.53 |

Table 2: The testing results of dialect identification using SaudiBERT model

### 5.2 Results

The results of the SaudiBERT model's performance are shown in Table 2, and the confusion matrix is presented in Figure 6. The model achieved an accuracy of 0.73 and an F1 score of 0.53 on the test dataset. These results indicate moderate performance, with potential for improvement in distinguishing between specific Saudi dialects. The confusion matrix reveals that SaudiBERT performs best on the Najdi dialect, with most Najdi samples correctly classified. However, it struggles to differentiate Najdi from other dialects, especially Hijazi and Shamali. Similarly, dialects like Hijazi and Shamali are frequently misclassified as Najdi, suggesting overlapping linguistic features that SaudiBERT finds challenging to separate. Shargawi was the most difficult dialect for the model to classify correctly, with frequent misclassifications into other categories. This is likely due to a combination of limited training data for this dialect and more subtle linguistic distinctions.

Overall, the findings highlight SaudiBERT's strength in identifying prominent dialects like Najdi, but also emphasize the need for further finetuning or additional data to improve its ability to capture the nuanced differences among the finer-grained Saudi dialects.

Figure 6: Confusion Matrix of Saudi Arabian dialect identification

## 6 Discussion

While the study assumes that songwriters from a given region use that region's dialect in their songs, this assumption may not always hold true. For instance, songwriters may prefer to write in Modern Standard Arabic (MSA) rather than their local dialect, such as Shargawi. Furthermore, song lyrics often incorporate multiple dialects as well as MSA. These factors could introduce limitations to the study's assumption, as they may affect the regional representation in the corpus and restrict the findings related to dialect usage.

A deep analysis of a subset of the SADSLyC corpus, based on manual human annotation, reveals dialectal overlap across all dialects, particularly between Najdi and Hijazi. For example, the sentence حنا بحد السيف الدار نحماها, which translates to "We protect our country with the edge of the sword," is labeled as Hijazi in SADSLyC. However, this sentence could be labeled as both Najdi and Hijazi, as it lacks distinctive dialectal features.

## 7 Conclusion and Future Work

To the best of our knowledge, there is currently no corpus specifically designed for Saudi Arabian song lyrics. The SADSLyC corpus will be the first collection to feature Saudi Arabian songs, representing five major dialects spoken across the country. The experimental results highlight both the strengths and limitations of SaudiBERT for dialect classification, particularly with respect to the fine-grained Saudi dialects, and underscore the need for further fine-tuning on more specialized datasets.

As part of our future research, we plan to expand the SADSLyC corpus by transcribing YouTube videos that showcase a broader range of Saudi songs and dialects.

## References

Hamed AL-Rubaiee, Renxi Qiu, Khalid Alomar, and Dayou Li. 2017. Sentiment analysis of arabic tweets in e-learning. *Journal of Computer Science*, 12(11):553–563.

Nora Al-Twairesh, Rawan Al-Matham, Nora Madi, Nada Almugren, Al-Hanouf Al-Aljmi, Shahad Alshalan, Raghad Alshalan, Nafla Alrumayyan, Shams Al-Manea, Sumayah Bawazeer, Nourah Al-Mutlaq, Nada Almanea, Waad Bin Huwaymil, Dalal Alqusair, Reem Alotaibi, Suha Al-Senaydi, and Abeer Alfutamani. 2018. Suar: Towards building a corpus for the saudi dialect. *Procedia Computer Science*, 142:72–82. Arabic Computational Linguistics.

Salwa Alahmari, Eric Atwell, and Mohammad Ammar Alsalka. 2024. Saudi arabic multi-dialects identification in social media texts. In *Intelligent Computing*, pages 209–217, Cham. Springer Nature Switzerland.

Halah AlMazrua, Najla AlHazzani, Amaal AlDawod, Lama AlAwlaqi, Noura AlReshoudi, Hend AlKhalifa, and Luluh AlDhubayi. 2022. Sa'7r: A saudi dialect irony dataset. In *Proceedinsg of the 5th Workshop on Open-Source Arabic Corpora and Processing Tools with Shared Tasks on Qur'an QA and Fine-Grained Hate Speech Detection*, pages 60–70, Marseille, France. European Language Resources Association.

Latifah Almuqren and Alexandra Ioana Cristea. 2021. Aracust: a saudi telecom tweets corpus for sentiment analysis. *PeerJ Computer Science*, 7.

Adel Assiri, Ahmed Emam, and Hmood Al-Dossari. 2016. Saudi twitter corpus for sentiment analysis. *International Journal of Computer and Information Engineering*, 10(2):272–275.

Afnan Bayazed, Ola Torabah, Redha AlSulami, Dimah Alahmadi, Amal Babour, and Kawther Saeedi. 2020. Sdct: Multi-dialects corpus classification for saudi tweets. *International Journal of Advanced Computer Science and Applications*, 11(11).

Mahmoud El-Haj. 2020. Habibi - a multi dialect multi national Arabic song lyrics corpus. In *Proceedings of the Twelfth Language Resources and Evaluation Conference*, pages 1318–1326, Marseille, France. European Language Resources Association.

Adam Kilgarriff and Gregory Grefenstette. 2001. Web as corpus. In *Proceedings of the Workshop on Comparing Corpora, 8th Conference of the European Chapter of the Association for Computational Linguistics (EACL 2001)*, Toulouse, France.

Faisal Qarah. 2024. Saudibert: A large language model pretrained on saudi dialect corpora.

# Enhancing Dialectal Arabic Intent Detection through Cross-Dialect Multilingual Input Augmentation

**Shehenaz Hossain[1], Fouad Shammary[2], Bahaulddin Shammary[1], Haithem Afli[1],**

[1]ADAPT Centre, Munster Technological University, Cork, Ireland
[2]Alef Education, Abu Dhabi, United Arab Emirates

**Correspondence:** shehenaz.hossain@mycit.ie, fouad.shammary@alefeducation.com, bahaulddin.shammary@mycit.ie, Haithem.Afli@mtu.ie

### Abstract

Addressing the challenges of Arabic intent detection amid extensive dialectal variation, this study presents a crossdialtectal, multilingual approach for classifying intents in banking and migration contexts. By augmenting dialectal inputs with Modern Standard Arabic (MSA) and English translations, our method leverages cross-lingual context to improve classification accuracy. We evaluate single-input (dialect-only), dual-input (dialect + MSA), and triple-input (dialect + MSA + English) models, applying language-specific tokenization for each. Results demonstrate that, in the migration dataset, our model achieved an accuracy gain of over 50% on Tunisian dialect, increasing from 43.3% with dialect-only input to 94% with the full multilingual setup. Similarly, in the PAL (Palestinian dialect) dataset, accuracy improved from 87.7% to 93.5% with translation augmentation, reflecting a gain of 5.8 percentage points. These findings underscore the effectiveness of our approach for intent detection across various Arabic dialects.

## 1 Introduction

Natural language understanding (NLU) powers the smart applications we use daily by helping machines grasp human intent. Yet, intent detection in Arabic is especially challenging due to the language's diversity. Spoken by over 400 million people across 22+ countries, Arabic includes both Modern Standard Arabic (MSA) for formal use and a variety of regional dialects (Al' Ammiya) for everyday speech. Each dialect presents unique challenges, from vocabulary and grammar to pronunciation, making intent detection a complex task.

This linguistic diversity poses a significant challenge for NLU systems. For example, the phrase "illegal migration" translates to الهجرة غير الشرعية (al-hijra ghayr al-shar'iyya) in MSA, but in Moroccan Arabic, it's الحريگ (al-harq), while in Tunisian Arabic, it's الحرقة (al-harqa). Without standardized spelling or structure across dialects, NLP models face a daunting task, as spelling inconsistencies and borrowed words from other languages often add extra layers of complexity.

This study introduces a novel approach that combines multilingual and multidialectal strategies to detect intent in banking (PAL dataset) and migration contexts (GPT-generated Migration dataset). Each dialectal text is translated into MSA and English to see if the structural clarity of MSA and the broader context of English enhance intent recognition. MSA adds consistency, while English captures additional meaning that might otherwise be missed.

## 2 Related Work

Multidialectal intent detection in Arabic presents unique challenges due to the diverse dialects and limited annotated data. Early research predominantly focused on MSA, but the advent of pretrained models like BERT opened new avenues for Arabic NLP. Francony et al. 2019 addressed the issue of dialect diversity by proposing a hierarchical deep learning framework. Their two-step model distinguishes MSA from dialects and further classifies dialects by region, offering a structured foundation for tasks like intent detection. Similarly, Shammary et al. 2022 explored a comparative analysis of traditional TF-IDF approaches and transformer-based models for the NADI 2022 shared task. Their findings demonstrated that while transformers are powerful, TF-IDF can be a competitive and lightweight alternative for low-resource dialects, emphasizing the value of efficient methods in resource-constrained settings. Al Hariri and Abu Farha 2024 showed that Arabic BERT models, while effective for MSA, required additional fine-tuning for dialectal Arabic. To address this, Elkordi et al. 2024 introduced contrastive learning techniques to detect intents



*Proceedings of The 4th Workshop on Arabic Corpus Linguistics (WACL-4)*, pages 44–49
January 20th, 2025. 

in different dialects, particularly in the banking sector, while Ramadan et al. 2024 developed a BERT-based ensemble model for the detection of cross-dialectal intent. One major challenge is data scarcity. Duwairi and Abushaqra 2021 addressed this issue through back-translation and paraphrasing, improving performance for low-resource dialects like Moroccan and Sudanese Arabic. Similarly, El-Makky et al. 2024 explored transfer learning to fine-tune models trained on high-resource dialects and apply them to others, enhancing generalization across dialects. To further address dialect-specific challenges, Skiredj et al. 2024 introduced the DarijaBanking dataset for Moroccan Arabic intent detection in the banking domain. The study presents BERTouch, a Darija-specific BERT model achieving state-of-the-art performance. Their findings highlight the need for domain-specific resources and multilingual approaches for effective intent detection. Shared tasks like AraFinNLP Malaysha et al. 2024a have provided benchmark datasets for multidialectal Arabic NLP. These challenges have helped researchers explore advanced techniques such as pre-trained models and data augmentation to enhance performance in intent detection for Arabic dialects. Fares and Touileb 2024 fine-tuned a T5 model and generated synthetic data in Moroccan, Tunisian, and Saudi dialects. By leveraging model ensembling, they highlighted synthetic data's role in handling dialectal variation.

## 3 Dataset

Our study draws on two primary datasets: The first is ArBanking77 (Jarrar et al. 2023) provided for the shared task 1 of the AraFinNLP 2024 (Malaysha et al. 2024b), which contains Arabic banking queries in both MSA and the Palestinian (PAL) dialect, labeled across 77 intent categories. Our analysis used only the PAL subset, which focuses on the Palestinian dialect. The second dataset was generated [1] with GPT-4, centering on Tunisian dialect text related to illegal migration. This dataset is labeled by intent strength—categorized as non-intent, weak intent, or strong intent—and each entry was meticulously validated by a native Tunisian speaker with specialized expertise in dialectal nuances and migration-related terminology, ensuring both linguistic fidelity and contextual depth.

[1]The dataset created for this research will be publicly available upon publication.

Table 1 shows the original ArBanking77 Dataset distribution.

| Dialect | Train | Dev |
|---|---|---|
| MSA | 10733 | 1230 |
| PAL | 10821 | 1234 |

Table 1: Dataset Statistics of ArBanking77

For our experiments, we split the PAL training set into 85% for training and 15% for testing, using the dev set for validation. The migration dataset was divided into 70% training, 15% validation, and 15% testing, ensuring balanced evaluation across intent strength labels.

Table 2 Shows the sample distribution in both of the datasets.

| Dataset | Total | Train | Val | Test |
|---|---|---|---|---|
| PAL | 10821 | 9197 | 1234 | 1624 |
| Migration | 2000 | 1398 | 300 | 300 |

Table 2: Dataset Distribution

## 4 Methodology

In this section, we detail our methodology for developing models capable of detecting intents in multi-dialectal banking and migration datasets. Our approach combines translation, tokenization, and model configurations designed to harness the benefits of Modern Standard Arabic (MSA) and English alongside dialectal inputs.

### 4.1 Translation

For the translation component, we utilized two open-source models via Hugging Face: Murhaf/AraT5-MSAizer[2] (Fares 2024) for Arabic dialect-to-MSA translation and Helsinki-NLP/opus-mt-ar-en[3] (Tiedemann and Thottingal 2020) for Arabic dialect-to-English translation. Both models are freely accessible on the Hugging Face platform, streamlining their integration into our workflow. AraT5-MSAizer[4], a fine-tuned version of UBC-NLP/AraT5v2-base-1024, is optimized for regional Arabic dialects (e.g., Levantine, Maghrebi, Gulf) and achieved a BLEU score of 21.79 on the OSACT 2024 test set, indicating reliable MSA translations that clarify dialectal

[2]AraT5-MSAizer on Hugging Face
[3]Helsinki-NLP/opus-mt-ar-en on Hugging Face
[4]Github.com/AraT5-MSAizer

ambiguities. Meanwhile, Helsinki-NLP/opus-mt-ar-en, part of the Opus-MT project[5] (Tiedemann 2020), is highly effective for Arabic-to-English translation, achieving a BLEU score of 49.4 on the Tatoeba test set. While primarily trained on MSA, it leverages multilingual data that may include elements of dialectal Arabic, making it useful for capturing semantic nuances in dialects. Its open-source nature and ease of deployment make it highly practical for resource-constrained settings.

### 4.2 Tokenization

To ensure consistency across data sources prior to tokenization, we pre-processed both datasets. In the PAL dataset, intents were mapped to integers(0-76), for 77 financial service-related categories, with missing or invalid entries removed, with the missing or invalid entries removed. For the Migration dataset, the intentions were categorized by strength: Non-intention (0), weak intention (1) and strong intention (2), and invalid entries were excluded. We applied specialized tokenizers to each language variant to capture the unique linguistic nuances of Arabic dialects, MSA, and English, accommodating the significant divergence of dialectal Arabic from MSA. For dialectal Arabic, we used the CAMeLBERT-Mix (bert-base-arabic-camelbert-mix)[6](Inoue et al. 2021)tokenizer derived from CAMeLBert-mix model, pretrained on a mixture of Arabic texts with different sizes and variants like MSA, DA, and classical Arabic. For MSA texts, we used MARBERT[7](Abdul-Mageed, Elmadany, and Nagoudi 2021)tokenizer derived from MARBERT, a model specifically trained on MSA and DA and proficient in capturing formal Arabic semantics. MARBERT's MSA-focused vocabulary and embeddings allowed us to standardize the input content, providing a consistent Arabic representation across both datasets. This step was particularly useful for understanding how formalized language influences intent classification in contrast to the colloquial forms in dialect. To process the English translations, we used the BERT-base model(uncased)[8](Devlin et al. 2018) tokenizer derived from BERT, a widely adopted English language model capable of extracting semantic information from English text. All inputs were tokenized with a maximum sequence length of 128 tokens using padding and truncation for consistency across input sizes.

[5]github.com/Helsinki-NLP/Opus-MT

[6]CAMeL-Lab/bert-base-arabic-camelbert-mix on Hugging Face

[7]MARBERT on Hugging Face

[8]BERT-base-uncased on Hugging Face

## 5 Model Architecture

We developed three configurations: the Dialect-Only Model (DOM), the Dialect-MSA Model (DMM) (dialect + MSA), and the Dialect-MSA-English Model (DMEM) (dialect + MSA + English). These configurations allow us to assess whether adding MSA and English translations enhances model performance.. Figure1 depicts an outline of our approach.

### 5.1 Dialect-Only Model (DOM)

This configuration uses only the original dialect input, encoded by CAMeLBERT-Mix (bert-base-arabic-camelbert-mix) for DA. The `[CLS]`[9]token (768 dimensions) is fed into a fully connected layer for classification, with dropout rates of 0.3 for the Migration dataset and 0.1 for PAL to reduce overfitting. The model outputs logits for 3 intent classes in Migration and 77 in PAL.

### 5.2 Dialect-MSA Model (DMM)

In this configuration, we combine dialect input with its MSA translation, encoded by CAMeLBERT-Mix and MARBERT respectively. The `[CLS]` tokens (768 dimensions each) are concatenated into a 1536-dimensional vector, and fed into a fully connected layer for classification. Like the DOM, dropout rates of 0.3 for Migration and 0.1 for PAL are applied to reduce overfitting, allowing the model to leverage both dialectal and formal Arabic.

### 5.3 Dialect-MSA-English Model (DMEM)

This model extends the previous configurations( 5.1 and 5.2) by incorporating the original dialect input, its MSA translation, and an English translation. CAMeLBERT-Mix encodes the dialectal Arabic, MARBERT encodes MSA, and BERT-base-uncased processes the English translation. The `[CLS]` tokens from each encoder (768 dimensions each) are concatenated into a 2304-dimensional vector, passed through a fully connected layer for classification. As with DOM and

[9]CLS tokens are special tokens placed at a beginning of each input example in a BERT model, providing a representation of the entire input for use in classification tasks(Devlin et al. 2018).

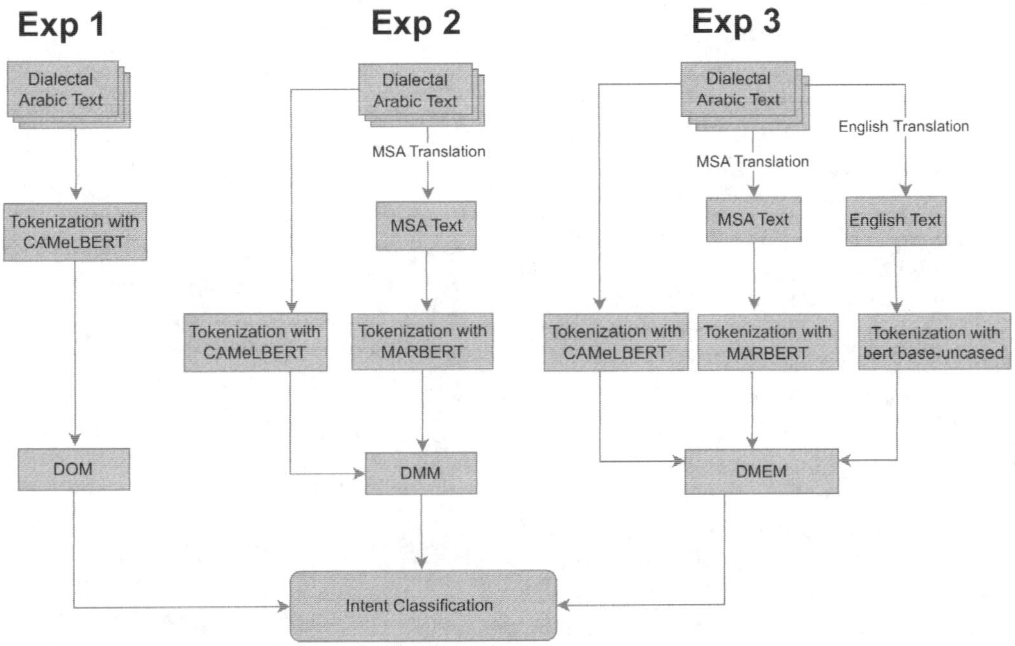


Figure 1: An outline of our approach

DMM, dropout rates are set at 0.3 for Migration and 0.1 for PAL to reduce overfitting. This multilingual configuration enables the model to leverage dialectal, formal Arabic, and English contexts, further enhancing intent classification accuracy.

## 6 Experimental Setup

We trained models on both datasets (PAL and Migration) with a batch size of 8, using the AdamW optimizer. The learning rate was set to 1e-5 for the Migration and 3e-5 for PAL, with a weight decay of 1e-4 for regularization. Cross-entropy loss was used for multiclass classification. To improve generalization with limited data in the Migration dataset (2000 samples), we applied layer freezing to the lower layers of the CAMeLBERT, MARBERT, and BERT encoders, preserving their pre-trained linguistic embeddings and focusing optimization on the task-specific upper layers. Gradient clipping with a maximum norm of 1.0 was implemented to stabilize training, which is especially beneficial in a multi-encoder setup. Early stopping with a patience of 2 epochs was applied, and all models were trained for 3 epochs to balance performance and computational efficiency.

## 7 Results and Discusssion

Table 3 and Table 4 present the performance metrics across different model configurations for the Migration and PAL datasets.

| Config | Acc | Prec | Rec | F1 |
|---|---|---|---|---|
| **DOM** | 0.433 | 0.70 | 0.43 | 0.35 |
| **DMM** | 0.843 | 0.87 | 0.84 | 0.85 |
| **DMEM** | 0.940 | 0.94 | 0.94 | 0.94 |

Table 3: Performance Metrics (Macro Average) for the Migration Dataset using DOM, DMM, and DMEM.

| Config | Acc | Prec | Rec | F1 |
|---|---|---|---|---|
| **DOM** | 0.877 | 0.88 | 0.87 | 0.87 |
| **DMM** | 0.893 | 0.89 | 0.89 | 0.89 |
| **DMEM** | 0.935 | 0.93 | 0.92 | 0.92 |

Table 4: Performance Metrics (Macro Average) for the PAL Dataset using DOM, DMM, and DMEM.

This study aimed to enhance intent classification across Arabic dialects by incorporating MSA and English translations alongside dialectal Arabic inputs. Results show that the Dialect-Only Model (DOM) provides a baseline with moderate performance (43.3% accuracy for Migration and 87.7% for PAL). Adding MSA translations in the

Dialect-MSA Model (DMM) raised accuracy to 84.3% for Migration and 89.3% for PAL, indicating that the formal structure of MSA helps clarify dialectal ambiguities. Introducing English translations in the Dialect-MSA-English Model (DMEM) further increased accuracy to 94.0% for Migration and 93.5% for PAL, where the cross-lingual context aids with domain-specific terminology in finance and migration.

While the results are promising, limitations emerge due to the MSA bias of pre-trained models like CAMeLBERT and MARBERT. These models, though trained on a mix of Arabic dialects and MSA, still favour MSA, posing challenges, particularly with the Tunisian dialect, which is underrepresented in training data. The distinct vocabulary, syntax, and colloquial phrases of Tunisian diverge significantly from MSA and other Arabic dialects, causing occasional misclassifications and reducing interpretability on migration-related topics. These findings suggest that fine-tuning models on underrepresented dialects, such as Tunisian, may improve intent classification in dialect-heavy datasets, especially those with high linguistic variability.

## 8 Conclusion and Future Work

Our findings show that adding MSA and English translations to dialectal Arabic improves intent classification. However, challenges persist due to the MSA bias in pre-trained models, impacting performance, particularly for the Tunisian dialect. Expanding training to cover more dialects could help create a more inclusive model. Additionally, fine-tuning large language models on dialectal Arabic holds promise. This approach may better capture linguistic and cultural nuances, enabling more accurate and adaptable intent classification across diverse Arabic-speaking communities.

## Acknowledgments

Data generation for the Tunisian dialect and code development for this work were assisted by GPT-3.5 Turbo and GPT-4 Omni. This research is supported by Taighde Éireann – Research Ireland through ADAPT Centre (Grant No. 13/RC/2106_P2) (www.adaptcentre.ie) at Munster Technological University.

## References

Abdul-Mageed, Muhammad, AbdelRahim Elmadany, and El Moatez Billah Nagoudi (Aug. 2021). "ARBERT & MARBERT: Deep Bidirectional Transformers for Arabic." In: *Proceedings of the 59th Annual Meeting of the Association for Computational Linguistics and the 11th International Joint Conference on Natural Language Processing (Volume 1: Long Papers)*. Online: Association for Computational Linguistics, pp. 7088–7105. DOI: 10.18653/v1/2021.acl-long.551. URL: https://aclanthology.org/2021.acl-long.551.

Al Hariri, Youssef and Ibrahim Abu Farha (Aug. 2024). "SMASH at AraFinNLP2024: Benchmarking Arabic BERT models on the intent detection." English. In: *Proceedings of The Second Arabic Natural Language Processing Conference*. The Second Arabic Natural Language Processing Conference, ArabicNLP 2024 ; Conference date: 16-08-2024 Through 16-08-2024. Association for Computational Linguistics (ACL), pp. 403–409. URL: https://arabicnlp2024.sigarab.org/.

Devlin, Jacob et al. (2018). "BERT: Pre-training of Deep Bidirectional Transformers for Language Understanding." In: *CoRR* abs/1810.04805. arXiv: 1810.04805. URL: http://arxiv.org/abs/1810.04805.

Duwairi, Rana and Feras Abushaqra (2021). "Syntactic- and morphology-based text augmentation framework for Arabic sentiment analysis." In: *PeerJ Computer Science* 7, e469. DOI: 10.7717/peerj-cs.469. URL: https://doi.org/10.7717/peerj-cs.469.

Elkordi, Hossam et al. (Aug. 2024). "AlexuNLP24 at AraFinNLP2024: Multi-Dialect Arabic Intent Detection with Contrastive Learning in Banking Domain." In: *Proceedings of The Second Arabic Natural Language Processing Conference*. Ed. by Nizar Habash et al. Bangkok, Thailand: Association for Computational Linguistics, pp. 415–421. URL: https://aclanthology.org/2024.arabicnlp-1.37.

Fares, Murhaf (May 2024). "AraT5-MSAizer: Translating Dialectal Arabic to MSA." In: *Proceedings of the 6th Workshop on Open-Source Arabic Corpora and Processing Tools (OSACT) with Shared Tasks on Arabic LLMs Hallucination and Dialect to MSA Machine Translation @*

*LREC-COLING 2024*. Ed. by Hend Al-Khalifa et al. Torino, Italia: ELRA and ICCL, pp. 124–129. URL: https://aclanthology.org/2024.osact-1.16.

Fares, Murhaf and Samia Touileb (Aug. 2024). "BabelBot at AraFinNLP2024: Fine-tuning T5 for Multi-dialect Intent Detection with Synthetic Data and Model Ensembling." In: *Proceedings of The Second Arabic Natural Language Processing Conference*. Ed. by Nizar Habash et al. Bangkok, Thailand: Association for Computational Linguistics, pp. 433–440. DOI: 10.18653/v1/2024.arabicnlp-1.40. URL: https://aclanthology.org/2024.arabicnlp-1.40.

Francony, Gael de et al. (Aug. 2019). "Hierarchical Deep Learning for Arabic Dialect Identification." In: *Proceedings of the Fourth Arabic Natural Language Processing Workshop*. Ed. by Wassim El-Hajj et al. Florence, Italy: Association for Computational Linguistics, pp. 249–253. DOI: 10.18653/v1/W19-4631. URL: https://aclanthology.org/W19-4631.

Inoue, Go et al. (Apr. 2021). "The Interplay of Variant, Size, and Task Type in Arabic Pretrained Language Models." In: *Proceedings of the Sixth Arabic Natural Language Processing Workshop*. Kyiv, Ukraine (Online): Association for Computational Linguistics.

Jarrar, Mustafa et al. (Dec. 2023). "ArBanking77: Intent Detection Neural Model and a New Dataset in Modern and Dialectical Arabic." In: *Proceedings of ArabicNLP 2023*. Ed. by Hassan Sawaf et al. Singapore (Hybrid): Association for Computational Linguistics, pp. 276–287. DOI: 10.18653/v1/2023.arabicnlp-1.22. URL: https://aclanthology.org/2023.arabicnlp-1.22.

El-Makky, Ahmed et al. (2024). "Transfer Learning for Dialect Generalization: Fine-Tuning Models on High-Resource Dialects." In: *Journal of Computational Linguistics* 50.2, pp. 123–145.

Malaysha, Sanad et al. (2024a). *AraFinNLP 2024: The First Arabic Financial NLP Shared Task*. arXiv: 2407.09818 [cs.CL]. URL: https://arxiv.org/abs/2407.09818.

– (Aug. 2024b). "AraFinNLP 2024: The First Arabic Financial NLP Shared Task." In: *Proceedings of The Second Arabic Natural Language Processing Conference*. Ed. by Nizar Habash et al. Bangkok, Thailand: Association for Computational Linguistics, pp. 393–402. DOI: 10.18653/v1/2024.arabicnlp-1.34. URL: https://aclanthology.org/2024.arabicnlp-1.34.

Ramadan, Asmaa et al. (Aug. 2024). "MA at AraFinNLP2024: BERT-based Ensemble for Cross-dialectal Arabic Intent Detection." In: *Proceedings of The Second Arabic Natural Language Processing Conference*. Ed. by Nizar Habash et al. Bangkok, Thailand: Association for Computational Linguistics, pp. 441–445. URL: https://aclanthology.org/2024.arabicnlp-1.41.

Shammary, Fouad et al. (Dec. 2022). "TF-IDF or Transformers for Arabic Dialect Identification? ITFLOWS participation in the NADI 2022 Shared Task." In: *Proceedings of the Seventh Arabic Natural Language Processing Workshop (WANLP)*. Ed. by Houda Bouamor et al. Abu Dhabi, United Arab Emirates (Hybrid): Association for Computational Linguistics, pp. 420–424. DOI: 10.18653/v1/2022.wanlp-1.42. URL: https://aclanthology.org/2022.wanlp-1.42.

Skiredj, Abderrahman et al. (2024). *DarijaBanking: A New Resource for Overcoming Language Barriers in Banking Intent Detection for Moroccan Arabic Speakers*. arXiv: 2405.16482 [cs.CL]. URL: https://arxiv.org/abs/2405.16482.

Tiedemann, Jörg (Nov. 2020). "The Tatoeba Translation Challenge – Realistic Data Sets for Low Resource and Multilingual MT." In: *Proceedings of the Fifth Conference on Machine Translation*. Online: Association for Computational Linguistics, pp. 1174–1182. URL: https://aclanthology.org/2020.wmt-1.139.

Tiedemann, Jörg and Santhosh Thottingal (Nov. 2020). "OPUS-MT – Building open translation services for the World." In: *Proceedings of the 22nd Annual Conference of the European Association for Machine Translation*. Lisboa, Portugal: European Association for Machine Translation, pp. 479–480. URL: https://aclanthology.org/2020.eamt-1.61.

# Dial2MSA-Verified: A Multi-Dialect Arabic Social Media Dataset for Neural Machine Translation to Modern Standard Arabic

**Abdullah Khered**[1,2] , **Youcef Benkhedda**[1] and **Riza Batista-Navarro**[1]
[1]The University of Manchester, UK
[2]King Abdulaziz University, Saudi Arabia
abdullah.khered@manchester.ac.uk
youcef.benkhedda@manchester.ac.uk
riza.batista@manchester.ac.uk

## Abstract

Social media has become an essential focus for Natural Language Processing (NLP) research due to its widespread use and unique linguistic characteristics. Normalising social media content, especially for morphologically rich languages like Arabic, remains a complex task due to limited parallel corpora. Arabic encompasses Modern Standard Arabic (MSA) and various regional dialects, collectively termed Dialectal Arabic (DA), which complicates NLP efforts due to their informal nature and variability. This paper presents Dial2MSA-Verified, an extension of the Dial2MSA dataset that includes verified translations for Gulf, Egyptian, Levantine, and Maghrebi dialects. We evaluate the performance of Seq2Seq models on this dataset, highlighting the effectiveness of state-of-the-art models in translating local Arabic dialects. We also provide insights through error analysis and outline future directions for enhancing Seq2Seq models and dataset development. The Dial2MSA-Verified dataset is publicly available to support further research [1].

## 1 Introduction

The rapid growth in social media users has established it as an area of interest for Natural Language Processing (NLP) research. Normalising social media texts' content is transforming informal text into a more standardised form that aligns with established linguistic conventions. This process is a challenging NLP task for morphologically rich languages such as Arabic, especially when parallel corpora for Arabic social media and their corresponding standard forms are limited (Mubarak, 2018).

Arabic, a widely spoken global language, exists in two primary forms: Modern Standard Arabic (MSA) and various regional dialects, collectively known as Dialectal Arabic (DA). MSA, the standardised form of the Arabic language, is utilised in formal contexts such as education, media, literature, and official documentation. As a linguistic bridge across the Arab world, MSA promotes a shared understanding and cultural cohesion among diverse Arab communities. In terms of grammar and vocabulary, MSA follows strict standardised rules, ensuring consistency in formal communication. Conversely, DA is the language of daily interaction, prevalent in informal settings and deeply reflective of the cultural and social identities unique to each region and community (Sadat et al., 2014).

The significant variation between Arabic dialects further complicates NLP tasks, as models trained on MSA alone may struggle with the language used on social media. Arabic users on these platforms tend to use their local informal dialect. A single Arabic word may indicate different interpretations based on the context of the sentence, between two dialects or between a dialect and MSA (Mallek et al., 2017), which shows why it is important to normalise text used in social media. Such a text often combines MSA, dialects, non-Arabic words, and unconventional spelling and may include slang, abbreviations, shortened or compound words, perhaps with grammar or spelling mistakes (Alruily, 2020). Figure 1 demonstrates the issues in Arabic social media text and their correct format.

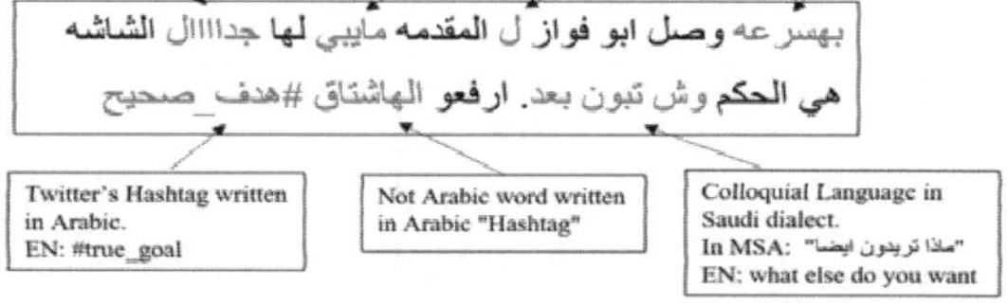


Figure 1: Examples of issues in Arabic social media text and their correct MSA/normalised forms

[1]https://github.com/khered20/Dial2MSA-Verified



*Proceedings of The 4th Workshop on Arabic Corpus Linguistics (WACL-4)*, pages 50–62
January 20th, 2025. 

The increase of unstructured text from various sources, including social media, has highlighted the need for effective preprocessing and normalisation to enhance data quality and usability. While basic preprocessing methods can still handle some issues in Figure 1, others, such as dialectal variations, syntax mistakes, ambiguity, and polysemy, require advanced techniques. To address these issues and the normalisation task, we adopted a Sequence to Sequence (Seq2Seq) technique, specifically using Neural Machine Translation (NMT) architectures. Seq2Seq models have shown promising results in handling translations across different language pairs, including from and to MSA. However, NMT models require large amounts of parallel data (i.e., pairs of sentences in two languages) for effective training. The limited availability of DA-MSA datasets poses an obstacle (Slim and Melouah, 2024). Moreover, in the context of social media, the Dial2MSA dataset (Mubarak, 2018) is currently the only publicly available resource that covers multiple regional dialects, and it has not been fully verified.

In this paper, we present Dial2MSA-Verified, which is built upon Dial2MSA (Mubarak, 2018), a Seq2Seq dataset from social media that encompasses four dialects: Egyptian (EGY), Maghrebi (MGR), Levantine (LEV), and Gulf (GLF). Our contributions to this dataset are two-fold:

- Verifying the dialects that were not verified in the original Dial2MSA dataset, specifically the LEV and GLF dialects, using three human annotators for each. The final dataset was separated into 18,991 tweets for training, 800 for validation, and 8,000 for testing, with multiple MSA references for each tweet.

- Testing and reporting the performance of different Seq2Seq translation models on each dialect of Dial2MSA-Verified, with models such as AraT5v2 (Elmadany et al., 2023) performing particularly well on the GLF dialect and slightly less effectively on other dialects.

## 2 Related Works

### 2.1 Seq2Seq DA to MSA translation

Machine Translation (MT) technology has seen significant advancements in recent years, with various approaches and techniques developed across different domains. While existing MT systems supporting Arabic have achieved moderate success, there is a growing focus on improving translation quality and developing more effective technologies, particularly through the application of NMT methods (Zakraoui et al., 2021; Bensalah et al., 2021). For DA translation, two main areas were investigated: DA-English and DA-MSA (Harrat et al., 2019). Multiple works on DA-English translation used MSA as a pivoting between DA and English to address the Out-Of-Vocabulary (OOV) issue in Arabic dialects and to improve the translation (Sawaf, 2010; Salloum and Habash, 2013; Sajjad et al., 2013; Salloum and Habash, 2014; Aminian et al., 2014). Additionally, Salloum et al. (2014) used dialect identification for MT system selection, with MSA as a pivot, to optimise translation between DA and English.

For DA-MSA, early research used rule-based MT (Al-Gaphari and Al-Yadoumi, 2010; Salloum and Habash, 2012; Hamdi et al., 2013), Statistical Machine Translation (SMT) (Salloum and Habash, 2011; Ghoneim and Diab, 2013; Meftouh et al., 2018) and hybrid approaches (Tachicart and Bouzoubaa, 2014). Later systems adapted NMT by either translating one dialect to MSA or multiple dialects to MSA. In single-DA to MSA translation, Al-Ibrahim and Duwairi (2020) employed an RNN Seq2Seq encoder-decoder model to translate the Jordanian dialect into MSA. Slim et al. (2022) applied a transductive Transfer Learning (TL) approach for translating the Algerian dialect to MSA using seq2seq models. Faheem et al. (2024) combined supervised and unsupervised NMT methods to enhance the translation from the EGY dialect to MSA. In multi-DA translation, Shapiro and Duh (2019) conducted training on transformer-based models across different Arabic varieties, including EGY and LEV dialects and MSA. Their findings indicated that leveraging multi-DA datasets can improve the translation quality for other unencountered dialects. Additionally, Baniata et al. (2021) investigated the translation between multiple dialects and MSA by employing a word-piece model to generate sub-word units for input features in the NMT transformer model.

Recently, three shared-tasks were created for DA-MSA translation: the fourth and fifth NADI shared-tasks (Abdul-Mageed et al., 2023, 2024) and OSACT DA-MSA MT shared-task (Elneima et al., 2024). Participants were allowed to use any available dataset and encouraged to create new datasets to train their models. As a result, some teams used a Large Language Model (LLM) such as ChatGPT from OpenAI to augment the training dataset (Khered et al., 2023; AlMusallam and Ahmad, 2024). Participants experimented with various NMT models, such as fine-tuning transformer-based pre-trained in Arabic models.

### 2.2 Arabic Social Media Normalisation

The social media normalisation task involves standardising various linguistic expressions in social media content. This task has attracted research attention across numerous languages and domains (ERYİĞİT and TORUNOĞLU-SELAMET, 2017; Zarnoufi et al., 2020; Aliero et al., 2023). However, these approaches cannot be applied directly to other languages or domains due to linguistic diversity (Matos Veliz et al., 2021). For Arabic, several works have tackled the issue of unstructured text in social media as part of addressing other NLP tasks. For instance, in Sentiment Analysis (SA), Rizkallah et al. (2018) translated some Saudi dialect vocabularies into MSA using the Social Analytics dynamic-link library (DLL) from "AlKhawarizmy Software" and Hegazi et al. (2021) focused on providing a single framework to handle different issues related to preprocessing Arabic tweets. Some studies used the MSA as a pivot language between the DA-English translation in social media. For example, Mallek et al. (2017) used a dictionary of non-standard words and their corresponding MSA to reduce the OOV issue in Arabic tweets, which were then translated into English using a SMT approach. Other studies were focused on normalising single DA on social media, such as Duwairi (2015), which constructed a lexicon for Jordanian DA words and their corresponding MSA. Hamada and Marzouk (2018) created a hybrid system to translate EGY to MSA in social media as part of the ALMoFseH project. They combined naive Bayesian learning to disambiguate morphological analysis, a rule-based transfer mechanism, and a dictionary look-up system. Chennafi et al. (2022) conducted experiments on various tasks within Aspect-Based SA, incorporating a Seq2Seq model for normalisation. The Seq2Seq normalisation model was trained on subsets from the PADIC (Meftouh et al., 2018) and MADAR (Bouamor et al., 2018) datasets to address the OOV issue in EGY sentences.

The Arabic social media normalisation task in previous works was concentrated on a single DA. They applied traditional MT methods to enhance the accuracy of other NLP tasks without being evaluated. Furthermore, the limited use of NMT methods is due to the lack of Seq2Seq data availability from social media platforms. In our research, we proposed a Dial2MSA-Verified, an evaluation dataset of multiple Arabic dialects in social media, by completing the verification of the Dial2MSA dataset. We experimented with various transformer-based NMT models to be evaluated on the Dial2MSA-Verified dataset.

## 3 Datasets

### 3.1 Dial2MSA Dataset

The Dial2MSA dataset comprises MSA translations of tweets from four Arabic dialects. The dataset was constructed by initially collecting 175 million Arabic tweets, from which 24,000 tweets were selected based on dialect-specific keywords: 6,000 each for EGY, MGR, LEV, and GLF dialects. The dataset's development involved two annotation tasks: first, human translators provided multiple MSA versions for each tweet; second, these translations underwent verification to remove inaccurate translations and retain only the correct ones. While all four dialects were subjected to the initial translation process, the verification step was completed only for the EGY and MGR dialects, leaving the MSA translations of the GLF and LEV dialects unverified. Table 1 provides an example of unverified MSA translations of tweets written in the GLF and LEV dialects. The colour-coding highlights translation errors: words in red are those that were not present in the original tweet, while words in orange indicate translation mistakes, such as spelling errors or the use of DA vocabulary. These MSA translations will be verified in this study as explained in Section 4.1.

| MSA (Unverified) | GLF Tweet |
|---|---|
| كيفارجع احب تويتر مثل الاول وخيم فيه 24 ساعه | سعاااااال شصار على ألتفاقية ألأمنية ؟؟؟ يقولك : عينها زرقت |
| سعال ماذا حدث في الاتفاق يقولون عينها ازرقت | |
| سعال شصار على التفاقية الأمنية يقولك عينها زرقت | |

| MSA (Unverified) | LEV Tweet |
|---|---|
| التغريدة: احنا كان عنا هيك قبل وفاة تيتا | احنا كان عنا هيك قبل وفاة تيتا 💔🥺 |
| إذا كان الوضوح من أجل الإفهام، والقوة من اجل التأثير | |
| نحن كان عندنا هكذا قبل وفاة الجدة | |

Table 1: A tweet from GLF and LEV dialects and their unverified MSA translations from Dial2MSA dataset

### 3.2 Additional Resources

While exploring potentially useful publicly available datasets, we found the following datasets to enrich the training dataset, namely the PADIC (Meftouh et al., 2018), the Multi Arabic Dialect Applications and Resources (MADAR) (Bouamor et al., 2018), the Semantic Textual Similarity (STS) (Al Sulaiman et al., 2022), and the EmiNADI dataset (Khered et al., 2023).

The PADIC (Meftouh et al., 2018) is a multilingual parallel dataset that encompasses sentences from six cities across the LEV and MGR regions, along with corresponding MSA translations. It was developed to improve statistical machine translation between these dialects and MSA.

The MADAR (Bouamor et al., 2018) dataset introduced a multilingual parallel dataset of 25 Arabic city-specific dialects and MSA.

The STS (Al Sulaiman et al., 2022) dataset assesses the semantic similarity between two sentences. It includes translations between EGY and Saudi dialects and MSA.

The EmiNADI (Khered et al., 2023) dataset was created to fill the gap of parallel corpora for the Emirati dialect in NADI 2023 shared task (Abdul-Mageed et al., 2023). It includes MSA translations of Emirati tweets from the training datasets used for NADI 2023 Subtask 1. These translations were produced using the large language model GPT 3.5 Turbo, totalling 2712 translations. Among these, 1000 translations were manually checked by native Arabic speakers to ensure quality.

## 4 Methodology

### 4.1 Dial2MSA Verification

This section demonstrates the verification phase, which includes several steps as presented in Figure 2. This process led to the creation of the Dial2MSA-Verified dataset.

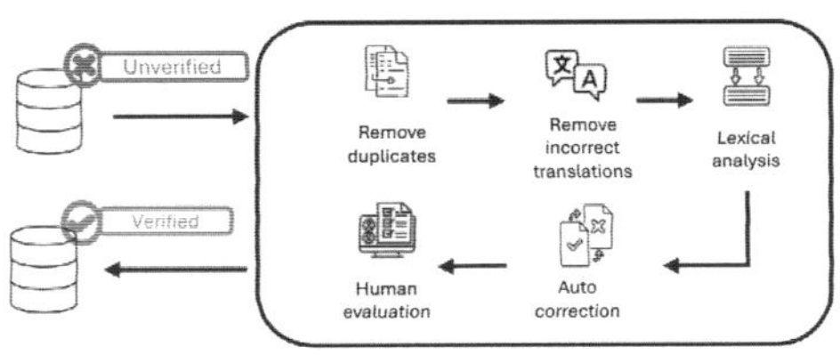


Figure 2: Dial2MSA Verification

Both the unverified GLF and LEV datasets were fed to the cleaning process. Firstly, we removed duplicated samples when a sample had the exact MSA translation. The second step is to remove the incorrectly translated samples. This was conducted by removing samples that included non-Arabic words as well as samples that included dialectal words in the MSA translations. Such words are listed in the research (Mubarak, 2018). The last step is the lexical analysis. This involves the removal of samples that have large different numbers of segments between DA and MSA pairs.

Before the cleaned samples were presented to the annotators, we utilised an Arabic auto-correction tool[2] to correct some of the mistakes automatically. Additionally, we employed GPT-4 via its API[3] to further enhance the correction process. Once these automated steps were completed, the samples were given to human annotators for final verification. We provided them to six native Arabic speakers, three of whom were native speakers of the GLF dialect and three of the LEV dialect. This review process was conducted using Label Studio [4], an open-source online tool that facilitates the annotation and labelling of data. Figure 3 illustrates the human annotation interface in Label Studio.

Figure 3: Human annotation interface in Label Studio

Each annotator had three options: 'correct MSA', 'correct MSA with modification', or 'not correct or cannot be translated'. The third option is when the provided MSA translation is in a dialect or if it is too difficult to comprehend or translate. For details

[2]https://pypi.org/project/ar-corrector/

[3]https://platform.openai.com/docs/models/gpt-4-turbo-and-gpt-4/

[4]https://labelstud.io/

on the annotation guidelines, refer to Appendix A. Table 2 presents the statistics from Dial2MSA-Verified, which includes the original Dial2MSA statistics as well as the updated statistics for GLF and LEV after completing the verification task.

| Dialect | Original Tweets | MSA (Task1) | Verified MSA (Task2) | Rem. Tweets | Avg. MSA/ Tweet |
|---|---|---|---|---|---|
| EGY | 6,000 | 30,000 | 16,355 | 5,565 | 2.94 |
| MGR | 6,000 | 18,000 | 7,912 | 4,953 | 1.6 |
| LEV | 6,000 | 18,000 | 8,301 | 5,319 | 1.56 |
| GLF | 6,000 | 18,000 | 12,775 | 5,354 | 2.39 |

Table 2: Statistics for Dial2MSA-Verified corpus after verifying the remaining (Rem.) dialects, specifically GLF and LEV in Dial2MSA (Mubarak, 2018) dataset

## 4.2 Data Preprocessing and Preparation

Arabic text on social media is usually informal (not standard) and commonly has spelling mistakes, extra characters, diacritical marks, elongations and shortened words. To reduce the noise of such text before applying the Seq2Seq normalisation models, we performed different cleaning and preprocessing methods, such as removing non-Arabic characters, mentions, links, and emojis and dealing with hashtags by including them if only they were written in Arabic. All diacritics were removed, and elongations, in which words contain repeated characters, were stripped. Finally, we removed duplicated samples found after preprocessing before training our models. Table 3 shows an example of tweets in GLF and LEV dialects before and after being preprocessed. It also presents the MSA-verified translations of the tweets.

| MSA (Verified) | GLF Tweet |
|---|---|
| كيف امتحنت؟ أليست الثانوية كلها في الأسبوع القادم؟ | user@اشلون امتحنتي مو جنه الثانوية كلها اسبوع الياي ؟ |
| كيف امتحنت؟ أليست امتحانات الثانوية كلها في الأسبوع القادم؟ | **Preprocessed Tweet** |
| كيف امتحنتي؟ أليست الثانوية كلها الأسبوع القادم؟ | اشلون امتحنتي مو جنه الثانوية كلها اسبوع الياي ؟ |

| MSA (Verified) | LEV Tweet |
|---|---|
| لقد عطلنا أسعد الله الأستاذة صفية المانع على مثل هذه الأسئلة | عطلنا!!!! 🖤🖤🖤🖤🖤🖤😱الله يسعد أ. صفيه المانع على هيك أسئله ♡😢 |
| عطلنا الله يسعد الأستاذة صفية المانع على هذه الأسئلة | **Preprocessed Tweet** |
| | عطلنا الله يسعد أ صفيه المانع على هيك أسئله |

Table 3: The original tweet from GLF and LEV dialects after applying the preprocessed methods and their verified MSA translations

## 4.3 Dataset Set Up

We collected multiple DA-MSA datasets focusing on four dialects: EGY, GLF, LEV, and MGR. To prepare the Dial2MSA-Verified dataset for model evaluation, we randomly selected 2,000 tweets for each dialect, with multiple MSA references, to test and evaluate our models. The EGY and GLF tweets have three MSA references each, while the LEV and MGR tweets have two MSA references each. From the remaining tweets in the Dial2MSA-Verified dataset, we randomly picked 200 tweets with a single MSA reference for each dialect to serve as a development set. Finally, the remaining tweets have multiple possible MSA references: EGY with 3,365 tweets and 9,099 MSA references, GLF with 3,154 tweets and 6,575 MSA references, LEV with 3,119 tweets and 4,101 MSA references, and MGR with 2,753 tweets and 3,312 MSA references. These remaining samples were combined with additional resources and will be used for training our models. Table 4 shows the training, development and testing datasets. In the Dial2MSA-Verified-test dataset, "R" indicates the number of available MSA references: 2,000 tweets in EGY and GLF have three MSA references each, and 2,000 tweets in LEV and MGR have two MSA references each.

| **Dataset** | **EGY** | **GLF** | **LEV** | **MGR** |
|---|---|---|---|---|
| Dial2MSA-V-train | 9,099 | 6,575 | 4,101 | 3,312 |
| PADIC | 0 | 0 | 12,824 | 25,648 |
| MADAR-train | 13,800 | 15,400 | 18,600 | 29,200 |
| Arabic STS | 2,758 | 2,758 | 0 | 0 |
| Emi-NADI | 0 | 2,712 | 0 | 0 |
| Total-train | 25,657 | 27,445 | 35,525 | 58,160 |
| Dial2MSA-V-dev | 200 | 200 | 200 | 200 |
| Dial2MSA-V-test | 2000 3-R | 2000 3-R | 2000 2-R | 2000 2-R |

Table 4: Dataset set up, where Dial2MSA-V (Verified) is used in the training, validation and testing datasets

## 4.4 Seq2Seq Models

Text-To-Text Transfer Transformer (T5) (Raffel et al., 2020) is an encoder-decoder Transformer-based model designed to support several NLP tasks, including machine translation. For our work, we specifically utilised the second version of **AraT5**[5] model (Nagoudi et al., 2022; Elmadany et al., 2023), which is a fine-tuned variant of T5 explicitly aimed at handling Arabic tasks. Additionally, we employed **mT5** (Xue et al., 2021), and **mT0** (Muennighoff et al., 2023), which are T5-based

[5]https://huggingface.co/UBC-NLP/AraT5v2-base-1024

models trained on a multitude of languages, including Arabic.

The Bidirectional Autoregressive Transformer (BART) (Lewis, 2019) is another model we utilised, which is developed for text generation tasks such as translation. We incorporated two derived models in our evaluation: **AraBART** (Eddine et al., 2022), and **mBART** (Liu, 2020), version mBART-large-50, which supports multiple languages for translation tasks including Arabic.

Furthermore, we used the **M2M100** model (Fan et al., 2021), version M2M100-418M, a multilingual encoder-decoder model created to facilitate many-to-many translation. It was trained on large datasets spanning 100 languages to enable direct translation between various language pairs.

### 4.5 Training Configurations

We explored two main training approaches: a joint model that integrates data from all regional dialects and an independent model that specialises in translating specific dialects.

**Joint Regional Model (J-R)**: In this setup, we combined all dialect-to-MSA translation pairs from the relevant regions for the four dialects into a single model. The resulting joint model leverages shared linguistic patterns among the dialects and is designed to translate any dialectal text into MSA, regardless of the specific dialect.

**Independent Regional Model (I-R)**: In this configuration, we developed a separate model for each regional dialect. This approach has four models, each trained exclusively to translate text from one specific dialect into MSA. A dialect identification model is used to determine which translation model should be employed for a given text.

### 4.6 Dialect Identification

We retrained an ensemble of multiple fine-tuned MARBERT (Abdul-Mageed et al., 2021) models with hyperparameter optimisations (Khered et al., 2022) and evaluated the output on the collected datasets (Table 4). More details about the configuration of the ensemble classification model are in (Khered et al., 2022). The results of the best two combination ensemble-MARBERT models and the confusion matrix of the best performing model are in Appendix B.

### 4.7 Hyperparameter Optimisation

Two Nvidia V100 GPUs were utilised and adhered to the specified configurations; all models were structured to process input and output sequences with a maximum length of 128 tokens. The learning rate was established at 5e-5, and the batch size was configured to 16. The training process was designed to run for a maximum of 20 epochs with early stopping implemented if no improvement was observed on the validation set for 3 consecutive epochs.

## 5 Evaluation and Results

In this section, we evaluate our proposed models using the Bilingual Evaluation Understudy (BLEU) (Papineni et al., 2002) and chrF++ (Popović, 2017) metrics. During training, we validated the models using the BLEU metric on the development set, selecting the checkpoint that achieved the highest BLEU score. For these optimal checkpoints, we report both BLEU and chrF++ scores on the testing set using the SacreBLEU implementation (Post, 2018). This implementation supports multi-reference evaluation for both metrics, providing a comprehensive assessment of model performance. We present results for two configurations: Joint Regional (J-R) and Independent Regional (I-R).

For the I-R configuration, dialect classification is used to select the appropriate translation model. This classification model was evaluated on the testing set of the Dial2MSA-Verified dataset using accuracy and Macro-Average F1 metrics. Additionally, we compare the results obtained when using a single reference file versus multiple reference files for the Dial2MSA-Verified-test dataset to highlight the impact of reference diversity on evaluation.

Table 5 presents the performance of all models under the I-R configuration, with each model evaluated across the four dialects. An average score (Avg) is also provided for each model to summarise overall performance. It can be seen that the AraT5

| Model | | EGY | GLF | LEV | MGR | Avg |
|---|---|---|---|---|---|---|
| mT0 | BLEU | 22.87 | 44.83 | 34.81 | 28.55 | 32.76 |
| | chrF++ | 45.35 | 64.98 | 57.66 | 53.06 | 55.26 |
| mT5 | BLEU | 23.44 | 45.35 | 35.12 | 29.02 | 33.23 |
| | chrF++ | 46.65 | 66.11 | 59.06 | 54.56 | 56.59 |
| AraT5 | BLEU | **27.80** | **47.12** | **38.94** | **32.09** | **36.49** |
| | chrF++ | **50.80** | **67.27** | **61.31** | **56.86** | **59.06** |
| mBART | BLEU | 25.38 | 45.89 | 37.71 | 31.29 | 35.07 |
| | chrF++ | 48.28 | 66.61 | 60.45 | 56.52 | 57.96 |
| AraBART | BLEU | 25.77 | 47.05 | 38.38 | 31.48 | 35.67 |
| | chrF++ | 48.26 | 66.65 | 60.31 | 56.29 | 57.88 |
| M2M100 | BLEU | 25.83 | 37.28 | 30.48 | 28.66 | 30.56 |
| | chrF++ | 49.38 | 61.94 | 55.74 | 54.19 | 55.31 |

Table 5: Performance of different models using I-R configuration

model outperforms other models across all dialects, achieving the highest average BLEU and chrF++ scores of 36.49 and 59.06, respectively. Furthermore, the mBART and AraBART also perform well, with results comparable to those of AraT5.

Similarly, Table 6 presents the performance of all models using the J-R configuration, evaluated across four dialects, along with an average score (Avg) for each model. The results indicate that the AraT5 model outperforms the other models across all four dialects, achieving an average BLEU score of 41.12 and an average chrF++ score of 62.05. Additionally, AraBART shows strong performance, with results comparable to those of AraT5.

| Model | | EGY | GLF | LEV | MGR | Avg |
|---|---|---|---|---|---|---|
| mT0 | BLEU | 27.43 | 46.02 | 37.30 | 30.95 | 35.42 |
| | chrF++ | 50.77 | 66.53 | 60.26 | 56.23 | 58.45 |
| mT5 | BLEU | 27.80 | 47.12 | 38.94 | 32.09 | 36.49 |
| | chrF++ | 50.80 | 67.27 | 61.31 | 56.86 | 59.06 |
| AraT5 | BLEU | **30.94** | **53.96** | **45.37** | **34.24** | **41.12** |
| | chrF++ | **52.94** | **70.86** | **65.40** | **58.99** | **62.05** |
| mBART | BLEU | 29.14 | 49.86 | 41.15 | 32.84 | 38.25 |
| | chrF++ | 51.75 | 68.74 | 62.85 | 57.71 | 60.26 |
| AraBART | BLEU | 29.87 | 51.38 | 43.07 | 32.95 | 39.32 |
| | chrF++ | 52.26 | 69.49 | 64.13 | 58.12 | 61.00 |
| M2M100 | BLEU | 22.58 | 40.88 | 33.45 | 27.78 | 31.17 |
| | chrF++ | 45.56 | 62.01 | 56.17 | 53.38 | 54.28 |

Table 6: Performance of different models using J-R configuration

The overall comparison between the two configurations shows that the J-R configuration outperforms the I-R configuration. This result is due to two reasons. The J-R configuration may benefit from leveraging shared linguistic patterns among similar dialects during training. Moreover, the I-R configuration depends on a dialect classification model to choose the appropriate translation model for each input. Despite the promising results of the dialect identification model (results in Appendix B), it still does not achieve perfect accuracy.

Furthermore. the use of multiple reference translations significantly enhances the evaluation of the model's performance. A single DA sentence can be translated into MSA in multiple forms due to the rich nature of Arabic morphology and syntax. Each translation can preserve the core meaning while using different vocabulary choices and sentence structures. For example, the Levantine dialectal phrase بدي أروح (I want to go), which can be translated into MSA as أرغب بالذهاب, أريد أن أغادر, or سأذهب, all conveying the same essential meaning. With more reference translations, there is a higher likelihood that the model's output will align with at least one reference, leading to a more accurate assessment.

The highest BLEU and chrF++ metrics scores are achieved when evaluating the proposed models on all available references. As shown in Table 7, the performance of the AraT5 model in the J-R configuration improves when evaluated with multiple references. For both EGY and GLF dialects, which have three MSA reference translations each, the model's performance improves when evaluated on all three references. Similarly, for the LEV and MGR dialects, which have two MSA references each, combining both references still results in better scores than using individual ones.

| | Refs. | EGY | GLF | LEV | MGR |
|---|---|---|---|---|---|
| BLEU | MSA-1 | 14.92 | 33.18 | 32.71 | 23.42 |
| | MSA-2 | 14.88 | 33.35 | 32.80 | 23.44 |
| | MSA-3 | 14.99 | 33.92 | === | === |
| | MSA-1-2 | 24.12 | 46.38 | **45.37** | **34.24** |
| | MSA-2-3 | 24.48 | 47.12 | === | === |
| | MSA-1-2-3 | **30.94** | **53.96** | === | === |
| chrF++ | MSA-1 | 41.72 | 59.97 | 57.75 | 52.23 |
| | MSA-2 | 41.04 | 60.19 | 57.75 | 52.36 |
| | MSA-3 | 41.46 | 60.62 | === | === |
| | MSA-1-2 | 48.91 | 67.09 | **65.40** | **58.99** |
| | MSA-2-3 | 48.66 | 67.33 | === | === |
| | MSA-1-2-3 | **52.94** | **70.86** | === | === |

Table 7: Comparison of BLEU and chrF++ scores using single vs. multiple MSA references (Refs.) with the J-R AraT5 model

## 6 Discussion and Analysis

### 6.1 Dialectal Challenges and Translation Quality

We provide a comprehensive example table showcasing the original tweets, their gold standard translations, and the corresponding AraT5 translations in Appendix C. Our analysis revealed notable issues in normalising Arabic in social media into MSA, particularly due to OOV tokens, many of which stem from non-Arabic origins, as well as unique expressions tied to specific dialects. In the EGY dialect, for example, several English loanwords have adapted meanings that differ from the literal sense of Arabic. The term أوفر, as seen in أنتى أوفر و هو أوفر و كلكم أوفر مش ذنبى أنى بكره, implies "too much" or "over-the-top" in English. However, the model interpreted it as "more available" (its Arabic literal meaning), resulting in translations like

أنت أوفر و هو أوفر و كلكم أوفر ليس ذنبي اني بكره.
Similarly, سكتشاتك (derived from "sketch") was misinterpreted as صمتك (your silence) due to morphological resemblance, while الشوز (from "shoes," but translated to سيارة or "car") posed similar challenges.

The J-R-AraT5 model, however, showed some accuracy in translating certain local dialect words. For instance, ازين was correctly rendered as حسن (good) in MSA, اشلون as كيف (how), and جواك in LEV as بداخلك (inside you). Despite these successes, some local expressions remained difficult. For example, اشدعوه was returned unchanged instead of the correct MSA equivalent, ماذا يحدث (what is happening), and the LEV phrase نيالك (lucky you) could not be accurately translated due to its unique connotation.

Additionally, the model showed an ability to handle other Arabised English terms frequently seen on social media. Words such as الفولورز were appropriately translated to متابعين (followers), and الفايس to فايسبوك (Facebook). It also successfully translated رتويت as اعادة تغريدة (retweet), demonstrating its adaptability to social media language.

MGR dialect posed a different set of challenges, particularly due to lexical and conjugation differences from other dialects. For example, كاتعايرو, meaning "insulting," was often misinterpreted as something related to work (عمل), while واسم (meaning "what is up" in Algerian dialect) was incorrectly translated to اسم (name). The term البيام (referring to the French BEM exam) also created difficulties, as it appears in Arabic script but is inherently non-Arabic.

LEV and EGY dialects featured unique dialectal words that the model struggled to translate accurately, even though direct MSA equivalents exist. Words like شخابيط (doodles), امبارح (yesterday), and انتخة (laziness) were challenging for the model, perhaps due to morphological or contextual ambiguities that made it difficult for the model to identify the correct translations.

### 6.2 Model Performance and Recommendations

While the model performed effectively with some dialect-specific terms, it often struggled with borrowed words and region-specific vocabulary across all dialects. Improvements in translation quality could be achieved by expanding dialect-specific datasets to include common foreign-origin terms, as well as by integrating context-sensitive embeddings to reduce ambiguity for polysemous words. Additionally, applying more nuanced preprocessing techniques could help account for regional lexical and morphological variations, enabling models to capture the linguistic richness and contextual relevance of Arabic dialects.

## 7 Conclusion and Future Work

This work introduced Dial2MSA-Verified, an extension of the Dial2MSA dataset that involves the verification of previously unverified dialects. We enriched the training data by incorporating Seq2Seq datasets from various domains. We conducted a comprehensive model evaluation using multi-reference evaluation, demonstrating improved performance compared to single-reference evaluations. Our findings indicate that models trained in the J-R configuration outperformed those in the I-R configuration. This improvement is due to the inherent similarities between dialects, allowing dialects to be learned from one another. Additionally, the I-R configuration relied on dialect identification for model selection, which affected translation performance. Overall, AraT5 outperformed other models, achieving an average BLEU score of 41.12 and a chrF++ score of 62.05.

In future work, we plan to expand the training data, focusing on the social media domain, as the limited availability remains an obstacle. Additionally, we plan to explore the possibility of improving the normalisation performance by leveraging more advanced models, data augmentation techniques and transfer learning techniques.

## 8 Limitations

While the Dial2MSA-Verified dataset offers comprehensive coverage of multiple dialectal regions, it still lacks representation for other Arabic dialects, such as Sudanese and Yemeni dialects. This gap may limit the model's ability to generalise effectively across all Arabic-speaking regions. Moreover, models trained with Seq2Seq datasets from varied domains might experience difficulties when applied to domain-specific texts, potentially affecting translation accuracy in social media contexts. Lastly, the reliance on dialect identification for model selection in some configurations poses a limitation, as incorrect identification can impact translation performance.

## 9 Ethical Considerations

This study adhered to ethical guidelines by ensuring data confidentiality and compliance with data protection regulations. Datasets were anonymised, and annotators provided informed consent for voluntary participation. Measures were taken to minimise potential biases by selecting diverse dialectal data and involving annotators from different dialect regions to ensure fairness and accuracy in data verification.

## Acknowledgments

We thank the annotators who verified the two dialects in the Dial2MSA-Verified dataset. Additionally, we acknowledge the University of Manchester for providing access to their High-Performance Computing (HPC) cluster, the Computational Shared Facility (CSF), which was used for the training process. We extend our gratitude to the Ministry of Education in Saudi Arabia and King Abdulaziz University for their continued support.

## References

Muhammad Abdul-Mageed, AbdelRahim Elmadany, and El Moatez Billah Nagoudi. 2021. ARBERT & MARBERT: Deep bidirectional transformers for Arabic. In *Proceedings of the 59th Annual Meeting of the Association for Computational Linguistics and the 11th International Joint Conference on Natural Language Processing (Volume 1: Long Papers)*, pages 7088–7105, Online. Association for Computational Linguistics.

Muhammad Abdul-Mageed, AbdelRahim Elmadany, Chiyu Zhang, El Moatez Billah Nagoudi, Houda Bouamor, and Nizar Habash. 2023. Nadi 2023: The fourth nuanced arabic dialect identification shared task. *Preprint*, arXiv:2310.16117.

Muhammad Abdul-Mageed, Amr Keleg, AbdelRahim Elmadany, Chiyu Zhang, Injy Hamed, Walid Magdy, Houda Bouamor, and Nizar Habash. 2024. Nadi 2024: The fifth nuanced arabic dialect identification shared task. *Preprint*, arXiv:2407.04910.

G. H. Al-Gaphari and M. Al-Yadoumi. 2010. A method to convert sana'ani accent to modern standard arabic. *International Journal of Information Science and Management (IJISM)*, 8(1):39–49.

Roqayah Al-Ibrahim and Rehab M Duwairi. 2020. Neural machine translation from jordanian dialect to modern standard arabic. In *2020 11th International Conference on Information and Communication Systems (ICICS)*, pages 173–178. IEEE.

Mansour Al Sulaiman, Abdullah M. Moussa, Sherif Abdou, Hebah Elgibreen, Mohammed Faisal, and Mohsen Rashwan. 2022. Semantic textual similarity for modern standard and dialectal arabic using transfer learning. *PLOS ONE*, 17(8):1–14.

Abubakar Aliero, Sulaimon Bashir, Hamzat Aliyu, Amina Tafida, Bashar Kangiwa, and Nasiru Dankolo. 2023. Systematic review on text normalization techniques and its approach to non-standard words. *International Journal of Computer Applications*, 185:975–8887.

Manan AlMusallam and Samar Ahmad. 2024. Alson at NADI 2024 shared task: Alson - a fine-tuned model for Arabic dialect translation. In *Proceedings of The Second Arabic Natural Language Processing Conference*, pages 764–768, Bangkok, Thailand. Association for Computational Linguistics.

Meshrif Alruily. 2020. Issues of dialectal saudi twitter corpus. *The International Arab Journal of Information Technology*, 17:367–374.

Maryam Aminian, Mahmoud Ghoneim, and Mona Diab. 2014. Handling oov words in dialectal arabic to english machine translation. In *Proceedings of the EMNLP'2014 Workshop on Language Technology for Closely Related Languages and Language Variants*, pages 99–108.

Laith H. Baniata, Isaac. K. E. Ampomah, and Seyoung Park. 2021. A transformer-based neural machine translation model for arabic dialects that utilizes subword units. *Sensors*, 21(19).

Nouhaila Bensalah, Habib Ayad, Abdellah Adib, and Abdelhamid Ibn El Farouk. 2021. Transformer model and convolutional neural networks (cnns) for arabic to english machine translation. In *International Conference On Big Data and Internet of Things*, pages 399–410. Springer.

Houda Bouamor, Nizar Habash, Mohammad Salameh, Wajdi Zaghouani, Owen Rambow, Dana Abdulrahim, Ossama Obeid, Salam Khalifa, Fadhl Eryani, Alexander Erdmann, and Kemal Oflazer. 2018. The madar arabic dialect corpus and lexicon. In *International Conference on Language Resources and Evaluation*.

Mohammed ElAmine Chennafi, Hanane Bedlaoui, Abdelghani Dahou, and Mohammed A. A. Al-qaness. 2022. Arabic aspect-based sentiment classification using seq2seq dialect normalization and transformers. *Knowledge*, 2(3):388–401.

Rehab M. Duwairi. 2015. Sentiment analysis for dialectical arabic. In *2015 6th International Conference on Information and Communication Systems (ICICS)*, pages 166–170.

Moussa Kamal Eddine, Nadi Tomeh, Nizar Habash, Joseph Le Roux, and Michalis Vazirgiannis. 2022. Arabart: a pretrained arabic sequence-to-sequence model for abstractive summarization. *arXiv preprint arXiv:2203.10945*.

AbdelRahim Elmadany, El Moatez Billah Nagoudi, and Muhammad Abdul-Mageed. 2023. Octopus: A multitask model and toolkit for arabic natural language generation. *Preprint*, arXiv:2310.16127.

Ashraf Hatim Elneima, AhmedElmogtaba Abdelmoniem Ali Abdelaziz, and Kareem Darwish. 2024. Osact6 dialect to msa translation shared task overview. In *Proceedings of the 6th Workshop on Open-Source Arabic Corpora and Processing Tools (OSACT) with Shared Tasks on Arabic LLMs Hallucination and Dialect to MSA Machine Translation@ LREC-COLING 2024*, pages 93–97.

GÜLŞEN ERYİĞİT and DİLARA TORUNOĞLU-SELAMET. 2017. Social media text normalization for turkish. *Natural Language Engineering*, 23(6):835–875.

Mohamed Atta Faheem, Khaled Tawfik Wassif, Hanaa Bayomi, and Sherif Mahdy Abdou. 2024. Improving neural machine translation for low resource languages through non-parallel corpora: a case study of egyptian dialect to modern standard arabic translation. *Scientific Reports*, 14(1):2265.

Angela Fan, Shruti Bhosale, Holger Schwenk, Zhiyi Ma, Ahmed El-Kishky, Siddharth Goyal, Mandeep Baines, Onur Celebi, Guillaume Wenzek, Vishrav Chaudhary, et al. 2021. Beyond english-centric multilingual machine translation. *Journal of Machine Learning Research*, 22(107):1–48.

Mahmoud Ghoneim and Mona Diab. 2013. Multiword expressions in the context of statistical machine translation. In *Proceedings of the Sixth International Joint Conference on Natural Language Processing*, pages 1181–1187.

Salwa Hamada and Reham Marzouk. 2018. *Developing a Transfer-Based System for Arabic Dialects Translation*, pages 121–138.

Ahmed Hamdi, Rahma Boujelbane, Nizar Habash, and Alexis Nasr. 2013. The effects of factorizing root and pattern mapping in bidirectional tunisian-standard arabic machine translation. In *Proceedings of Machine Translation Summit XIV: Papers*.

Salima Harrat, Karima Meftouh, and Kamel Smaili. 2019. Machine translation for arabic dialects (survey). *Information Processing Management*, 56(2):262–273. Advance Arabic Natural Language Processing (ANLP) and its Applications.

Mohamed Osman Hegazi, Yasser Al-Dossari, Abdullah Al-Yahy, Abdulaziz Al-Sumari, and Anwer Hilal. 2021. Preprocessing arabic text on social media. *Heliyon*, 7(2).

Abdullah Khered, Ingy Abdelhalim, Nadine Abdelhalim, Ahmed Soliman, and Riza Theresa Batista-Navarro. 2023. Unimanc at nadi 2023 shared task: A comparison of various t5-based models for translating arabic dialectical text to modern standard arabic. In *Proceedings of ArabicNLP 2023*, pages 658–664.

Abdullah Salem Khered, Ingy Yasser Hassan Abdou Abdelhalim, and Riza Batista-Navarro. 2022. Building an ensemble of transformer models for Arabic dialect classification and sentiment analysis. In *Proceedings of the Seventh Arabic Natural Language Processing Workshop (WANLP)*, pages 479–484, Abu Dhabi, United Arab Emirates (Hybrid). Association for Computational Linguistics.

M Lewis. 2019. Bart: Denoising sequence-to-sequence pre-training for natural language generation, translation, and comprehension. *arXiv preprint arXiv:1910.13461*.

Y Liu. 2020. Multilingual denoising pre-training for neural machine translation. *arXiv preprint arXiv:2001.08210*.

Fatma Mallek, Billal Belainine, and Fatiha Sadat. 2017. Arabic social media analysis and translation. *Procedia Computer Science*, 117:298–303. Arabic Computational Linguistics.

Claudia Matos Veliz, Orphée De Clercq, and Veronique Hoste. 2021. Is neural always better? smt versus nmt for dutch text normalization. *Expert Systems with Applications*, 170:114500.

Karima Meftouh, Salima Harrat, and Kamel Smaïli. 2018. PADIC: extension and new experiments. In *7th International Conference on Advanced Technologies ICAT*.

Hamdy Mubarak. 2018. Dial2msa: A tweets corpus for converting dialectal arabic to modern standard arabic. *OSACT*, 3:49.

Niklas Muennighoff, Thomas Wang, Lintang Sutawika, Adam Roberts, Stella Biderman, and Teven et al. Le Scao. 2023. Crosslingual generalization through multitask finetuning. In *Proceedings of the 61st Annual Meeting of the Association for Computational Linguistics (Volume 1: Long Papers)*, pages 15991–16111, Toronto, Canada. Association for Computational Linguistics.

El Moatez Billah Nagoudi, AbdelRahim Elmadany, and Muhammad Abdul-Mageed. 2022. AraT5: Text-to-text transformers for Arabic language generation. In *Proceedings of the 60th Annual Meeting of the Association for Computational Linguistics (Volume 1: Long Papers)*, pages 628–647, Dublin, Ireland. Association for Computational Linguistics.

Kishore Papineni, Salim Roukos, Todd Ward, and Wei-Jing Zhu. 2002. Bleu: a method for automatic evaluation of machine translation. In *Proceedings of the 40th Annual Meeting of the Association for Computational Linguistics*, pages 311–318, Philadelphia, Pennsylvania, USA. Association for Computational Linguistics.

Maja Popović. 2017. chrF++: words helping character n-grams. In *Proceedings of the Second Conference on Machine Translation*, pages 612–618, Copenhagen, Denmark. Association for Computational Linguistics.

Matt Post. 2018. A call for clarity in reporting BLEU scores. In *Proceedings of the Third Conference on Machine Translation: Research Papers*, pages 186–191, Belgium, Brussels. Association for Computational Linguistics.

Colin Raffel, Noam Shazeer, Adam Roberts, Katherine Lee, Sharan Narang, Michael Matena, Yanqi Zhou, Wei Li, and Peter J. Liu. 2020. Exploring the limits of transfer learning with a unified text-to-text transformer. *Journal of Machine Learning Research*, 21(140):1–67.

Sandra Rizkallah, Amir Atiya, Hossam ElDin Mahgoub, and Momen Heragy. 2018. Dialect versus msa sentiment analysis. In *The International Conference on Advanced Machine Learning Technologies and Applications (AMLTA2018)*, pages 605–613. Springer.

Fatiha Sadat, Farnazeh Kazemi, and Atefeh Farzindar. 2014. Automatic identification of arabic dialects in social media. SoMeRA '14, page 35–40, New York, NY, USA. Association for Computing Machinery.

Hassan Sajjad, Kareem Darwish, and Yonatan Belinkov. 2013. Translating dialectal arabic to english. In *Proceedings of the 51st Annual Meeting of the Association for Computational Linguistics (Volume 2: Short Papers)*, pages 1–6.

Wael Salloum, Heba Elfardy, Linda Alamir-Salloum, Nizar Habash, and Mona Diab. 2014. Sentence level dialect identification for machine translation system selection. In *Proceedings of the 52nd Annual Meeting of the Association for Computational Linguistics (Volume 2: Short Papers)*, pages 772–778.

Wael Salloum and Nizar Habash. 2011. Dialectal to standard arabic paraphrasing to improve arabic-english statistical machine translation. In *Proceedings of the first workshop on algorithms and resources for modelling of dialects and language varieties*, pages 10–21.

Wael Salloum and Nizar Habash. 2012. Elissa: A dialectal to standard arabic machine translation system. In *International Conference on Computational Linguistics*.

Wael Salloum and Nizar Habash. 2013. Dialectal arabic to english machine translation: Pivoting through modern standard arabic. In *Proceedings of the 2013 Conference of the North American Chapter of the Association for Computational Linguistics: Human Language Technologies*, pages 348–358.

Wael Salloum and Nizar Habash. 2014. Adam: Analyzer for dialectal arabic morphology. *Journal of King Saud University-Computer and Information Sciences*, 26(4):372–378.

Hassan Sawaf. 2010. Arabic dialect handling in hybrid machine translation. In *Proceedings of the 9th Conference of the Association for Machine Translation in the Americas: Research Papers*, Denver, Colorado, USA. Association for Machine Translation in the Americas.

Pamela Shapiro and Kevin Duh. 2019. Comparing pipelined and integrated approaches to dialectal Arabic neural machine translation. In *Proceedings of the Sixth Workshop on NLP for Similar Languages, Varieties and Dialects*, pages 214–222, Ann Arbor, Michigan. Association for Computational Linguistics.

Amel Slim and Ahlem Melouah. 2024. Low resource arabic dialects transformer neural machine translation improvement through incremental transfer of shared linguistic features. *Arabian Journal for Science and Engineering*, pages 1–17.

Amel Slim, Ahlem Melouah, Usef Faghihi, and Khouloud Sahib. 2022. Improving neural machine translation for low resource algerian dialect by transductive transfer learning strategy. *Arabian Journal for Science and Engineering*, 47(8):10411–10418.

Ridouane Tachicart and Karim Bouzoubaa. 2014. A hybrid approach to translate moroccan arabic dialect. In *2014 9th International Conference on Intelligent Systems: Theories and Applications (SITA-14)*, pages 1–5.

Linting Xue, Noah Constant, Adam Roberts, Mihir Kale, Rami Al-Rfou, Aditya Siddhant, Aditya Barua, and Colin Raffel. 2021. mT5: A massively multilingual pre-trained text-to-text transformer. In *Proceedings of the 2021 Conference of the North American Chapter of the Association for Computational Linguistics: Human Language Technologies*, pages 483–498, Online. Association for Computational Linguistics.

Jezia Zakraoui, Moutaz Saleh, Somaya Al-Maadeed, and Jihad Mohamed Alja'am. 2021. Arabic machine translation: A survey with challenges and future directions. *IEEE Access*, 9:161445–161468.

Randa Zarnoufi, Hamid Jaafar, and Mounia Abik. 2020. Machine normalization: Bringing social media text from non-standard to standard form. *ACM Trans. Asian Low-Resour. Lang. Inf. Process.*, 19(4).

## A Annotation Guidelines

### Overview

Thank you for agreeing to assist us with verifying Modern Standard Arabic (MSA) translations. One at a time, you will be presented with tweets in the [Gulf/Levantine] dialect and their MSA translations. Your task is to verify these MSA translations.

### Instructions

You will be using a tool called Label Studio. Before starting, you will be shown examples of correct translations and tested to ensure you are prepared for this task. This preparation helps to maintain high quality in the work.

### Your Role

You will verify the MSA translations of [Gulf/Levantine] dialect tweets. For each translation, you have the following three choices:

- **Correct MSA**: Select this option if the translation is accurate and requires no changes.
- **Correct MSA with Modification**: Choose this option if the translation is partially correct and requires corrections. Please specify the corrected translation in the textbox.
- **Not Correct or Cannot be Translated**: Use this option if the translation contains significant errors, remains in dialect, or is too difficult to understand or translate.

When reviewing translations, ensure that the MSA translation accurately conveys the original meaning of the tweet. Check for spelling and grammatical correctness as well as proper sentence structure in the MSA translation.

## B DA Identification Results and Model Performance Metrics

| Model | Accuracy | Macro-Average F1 |
|---|---|---|
| Ensemble-MARBERT-1 | 96.95 | 96.942 |
| Ensemble-MARBERT-2 | 96.224 | 96.215 |

Table 8: Results for DA identification based on the ensemble of best two combinations of MARBERT models

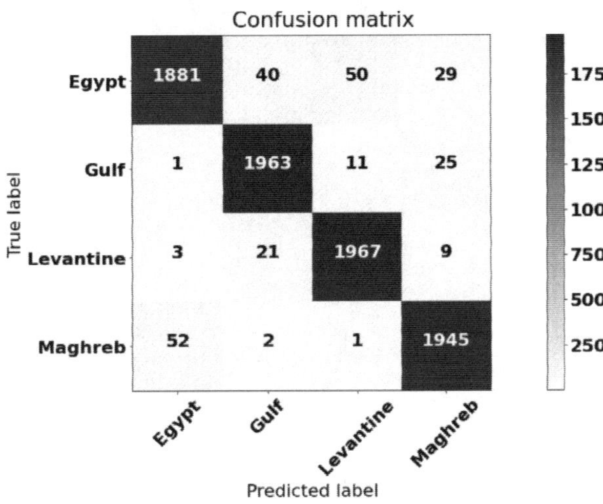


Figure 4: Confusion matrix for the best-performing ensemble model of DA identification

# C Comparative Analysis of J-R AraT5 Predictions and Gold MSA References

| DA | Cleaned Tweet | AraT5 Prediction | Gold MSA References |
|---|---|---|---|
| EGY | أنتى **أوفر** و هو **أوفر** و كلكم **أوفر** مش ذنبى أنى بكره<br>You're over, he's over, and all of you are over. It's not my fault that I hate. | أنت أوفر و هو أوفر و كلكم أوفر ليس ذنبى انى بكره<br>You're over, he's over, and all of you are over. It's not my fault that I hate. | ردود افعالك وافعالك وافعالكم كلم زائده جدا وليس ذنبى انى لا أحبه<br>انت غير طبيعية مثله ومثل الجميع ما ذنبي انا غدا<br>انت متكبرة وانت متكبر ليس ذنبي اني اكره |
| GLF | 'مرة حلوة **سكتشاتك** احس اني ابغا امسك الدفتر اقلب فيه<br>Your sketches are really nice, I feel like flipping through a notebook. | جميل جدا صمتك أشعر أنني أريد أن أمسك الدفتر وأقلب فيه<br>Your silence is so beautiful, it makes me feel like I want to pick up the notebook and flip through it. | رسوماتك رائعة أشعر أنني أريد أن أمسك الدفتر و أقلب صفحاته<br>رسوماتك جميلة جدا أشعر أني أريد أن أمسك الدفتر وأقلب فيه<br>رائعة جدا سكتشاتك أشعر أنني أريد أن أمسك الدفتر وأقلب فيه |
| EGY | بكام **الشوز** دى لو سمحت ؟؟ ب 299 يافندم يا راجل قول 300 كدا كدا مش هشترى<br>How much is this shoes, please? It's 299, sir. Come on, say 300, I'm not going to buy it anyway. | بكم هذه السيارة من فضلك ؟ ب 299 يا سيدي قل 300 هكذا لن أشترى<br>How much is this car, please? It's 299, sir. Come on, say 300, that way I won't buy it | بكم هذا الحذاء اذا سمحت؟؟ سعر 299 يلمحترم قل 300 فى الحالتين لن اشترى<br>ما سعر هذا الحذاء من فضلكك؟؟ 299 جنيه .. لماذا لا تقول 300 في اي حال ان ان اشتري<br>كم سعر هذا الحذاء من فضلك ب 229 ياسيدي يارجل قل 300 انا لن اشتري |
| GLF | **انزين** شصار عل **مدريديه** مالهم حس؟؟<br>Okay, what happened to the Madrid fans? Why are they silent? | حسنا ماذا حدث للمدنيين؟ هل هم بلا حس؟<br>Okay, what happened to the civilians? Are they silent? | ماذا حدث لأنصار مدريد لماذا هم صامتون؟<br>حسنا ماذا حدث للمدريدية لم نسمع لهم صوت<br>حسنا ما الذي حدث للمدريديين لم نعد نراهم؟ |
| GLF | **اشلون** الوصل معاك ونت بسرعه تزعل<br>How can there be a connection with you when you quickly get upset? | كيف الوصل معك وأنت بسرعة تغضب؟<br>How can there be a connection with you when you quickly get upset? | كيف يكون الوصال معك وأنت بسرعة تغضب؟<br>كيف يكون الوصال معك وأنت سريع الغضب؟<br>كيف يكون وصالك وأنت سريع الزعل؟ |
| LEV | لانك انت نظيف وطيب من **جواك** عشان **هيك** الكل بحبك ياحصتنا<br>Because you're clean and good-hearted from the inside, that's why everyone loves you, my dear. | لأنك أنت نظيف وطيب من داخلك لذلك الجميع يحبك يا حصتنا<br>Because you're clean and good-hearted from the inside, that's why everyone loves you, my dear. | لأنك نظيف وطيب من داخلك لذلك الجميع يحبك يا نصيبنا<br>لأنك نظيف وطيب من داخلك لذلك الجميع يحبك يا حصتنا |
| GLF | **اشدعوه** اشلون جي فجاه كلكم اتكلمون<br>How come suddenly all of you are talking? | أشدعوه كيف جاء فجأة كلكم تتكلمون<br>How come suddenly all of you are talking? | ماذا يحدث جميعا قمتم بالتحدث فجأة<br>ماذا حدث؟ فجأة جميعكم تتحدثون<br>ماذا جرى فجأة جميعكم تتحدثون |
| LEV | **نيالك** إحنا معطلين اليوم مشان في عيد للمسيحية<br>Lucky you, we're off today because there's a Christian holiday. | يا إلهي نحن نعطل اليوم لأجل عيد المسيحية<br>Oh my God, we are off today for the Christian holiday. | هنيئا لك نحن اليوم في عطله بسبب وجود عيد للمسيحيين<br>من حسن حظك أنك في عطلة اليوم لأن هناك عيد للمسيحيين |
| EGY | لو بنخاف على بعض قد ما بنخاف على **الفولورز** بتوعنا<br>If only we cared about each other as much as we care about our followers. | لو نخاف على بعضنا بقدر ما نخاف على متابعيننا<br>If only we cared about each other as much as we care about our followers. | ياليتنا نخاف على بعض قدر خوفنا على فولورزنا<br>لو اننا نحرص علي غيرنا كما نحرص عل متابعينا<br>يا ليتنا نهتم ببعض علي قدر اهتمامنا بالاتباع الذين عندنا |
| MGR | إلا **الفايس** لا ما نعرفت واش بيه علاش علاش<br>Except for Facebook, I don't know what's wrong with it why why | إلا الفايسبوك لا أعرف لماذا لماذا لماذا<br>Except for Facebook, I don't know why why why | ماعدا الفيس بوك لاعرف ماذا به لماذا<br>الى الفايس لا اعرف مابه هكذا |
| LEV | حبايبي بليز **رتويت** للفيديو مشان يوصل يلا بليز<br>Guys, please retweet the video so it reaches more, please. | يا أحبابي من فضلك قم بإعادة التغريد للفيديو لكي يصل هيا من فضلك<br>Guys, please retweet the video so it reaches more, please. | أرجو منكم يا أحبابي إعادة نشر الفيديو حتى يصل هيا أرجوكم<br>أحبائي من فضلكم إعادة تغريد للفيديو ليصل هيا من فضلكم |
| MGR | علاش **كاتعايرو** ف فرنسا وهي مخدمة ليكم النص ديال الشعب ف<br>Why do you criticize France when it's providing jobs for half of your population? | لماذا تعملون في فرنسا وهي تعمل لكم نصف الشعب في فرنسا<br>Why do you work in France while it works for you, half of the population in France? | لماذا معايرة فرنسا فهي قامت بتشغيل نصف شعبكم<br>لماذا تسبون فرنسا و هي تمهن لكم نصف الشعب |
| MGR | علاش **واسم** درتلك هذ حقد ولا اسم<br>Why, what did I do to you, was this hatred or what? | لماذا و اسم فعلت لك هذا حقد أم اسم<br>Why and name, did I do this to you, was it hatred or name? | لماذا ماذا فعلت لك هل هذا حقد او اسم<br>لماذا ماذا فعلت لك هذا حقد ام ماذا |
| MGR | صحاب **البيام** لي راهم معانا شحال جبتو معدل<br>The participants of the BEM exam with us, what score did you achieve? | أصحاب البيام الذين معنا كم حصلوا على معدل<br>The participants of the BEM exam with us, what score did they achieve? | أصحاب البيام الموجودين معنا كم المعدل الذي حصلتم عليه<br>أصحاب المتوسطة المتواجدون معنا كم تحصلتم على المعدل |
| EGY | ياريت متتكلمش الا بالصح متجاملش حد خليك زى ما انت **شخابيط**<br>Please only speak the truth and don't flatter anyone. Stay as you are, scribbles. | اتمنى لا تتكلم الا مع الناس ولكن لا تجامل احد كن كما انت شخابيط<br>I hope you only talk to people without flattering anyone. Be yourself, scribbles. | من فضلك لا تتكلم الا بالصح لا تجامل شخص استمر كما انت شخابيط<br>اتمنى ان لا تتكلم الا بما هو صواب ولا تجامل احدا وان تظل هكذا مثل ما انت عليو نقش<br>ليتنا لا نتكلم إلا بالصواب لا تجامل أحد ظل مثلما أنت هوامش |

Table 9: Comparison of J-R AraT5 predictions and gold MSA references across the four dialects in the Dial2MSA-Verified dataset. Bold words highlight challenging dialect terms discussed in the paper's discussion section.

# Web-Based Corpus Compilation of the Emirati Arabic Dialect

**Yousra A. El-Ghawi**
Widebot AI
yousraghawi@gmail.com

## Abstract

This paper displays some initial efforts conducted in the compilation pursuits of Arabic dialectal corpora in the form of raw text, the end purpose of which is to fine-tune existing Arabic large language models (LLM) to better understand and generate text in the Emirati dialect as instructed. The focus of the paper is on the process of compiling corpora from the web, which includes the exploration of possible methods, tools and techniques specific to web search, as well as examples of genres and domains to explore. The results of these efforts and the importance of native speaker contributions to corpus compilation for low-resource languages are also touched upon.

## 1 Introduction

The combined efforts of researchers and professionals within Arabic natural language processing (NLP) have yielded several notable achievements in the field. Of these are the continued endeavors in corpus collection for under-represented dialectal Arabic (DA). Much of the work has been notable for the Egyptian dialect, for its accessibility and abundance of popular culture and media across the Arabic-speaking regions (Elnagar et al., 2021). Other dialects remain with less resources, due to several factors including the scarcity of their usage on the web and in published works, which are the most accessible forms of corpora compilation.

Collecting appropriate and satisfactory dialectal corpora is integral to the development of suitable NLP tools for their usage in further applications. While Modern Standard Arabic (MSA) still faces existing challenges in its processing, several tools have focused on solving these issues, aided by the standard rules of MSA. DA, however, suffers from the issues being at a larger scale, with problems mostly dealing with the inconsistent orthography of the written dialects, and in some cases (such as in Egyptian, Saudi, and Jordanian), their regional variety. In addition, morphological and phonological differences are highly prominent between dialects, so there is little to no standard when it comes to processing dialects, and even less of a standard in the search for their web corpora.

LLM fine-tuning depends in its root on the availability of a large number of words serving as corpora in the dialect of choice. These corpora of mere raw text are collected and developed with multiple factors in mind, including the variety and specification of domains, the frequency of dialectal words and expressions in different contexts, and the relevance of the data to the intended applications of the language model, if they exist (Liu et al., 2024). It is defining for any corpus to be as representative and diverse as possible, as well as ensuring the validity of the data collected in a certain dialect.

Bearing the previous criteria in mind, the collection of DA corpora on the web is faced with challenges in meeting them. Such issues can be pointed out in the following:

1. The un-prescriptiveness of data, as the most used language within Arabic-speaking countries in most contexts is MSA. Dialectal usage is therefore restricted to informal settings, such as casual conversations and entertainment.

2. The un-orthographic nature of dialectal Arabic, where search results may vary greatly by a mere change of spelling or morphology. For example, when words are abbreviated into single letters, or short phrases are used with other words in-between which greatly depend on context.

3. The limited accessible genres which exist on the web for the dialect of choice, such as the issues with the Gumar corpus, created out of forum novels written in DA (Khalifa et al., 2016). The nature of DA is conversational, as stated prior, with a clear lack of formal or published usage of the dialect.

For this paper, there will be an exploration of the different methods used to search for and col-



*Proceedings of The 4th Workshop on Arabic Corpus Linguistics (WACL-4)*, pages 63–67
January 20th, 2025. 

| Source | Genre | Type |
|---|---|---|
| Al-Mal Channel | Economics | Articles |
| Coolnona | General | Blog |
| Hamdan bin Mohammed Heritage Center | Culture | Docs |
| uae.gulf7.com | General | Forum |
| Emirates reddit | General | Social |
| Baynounah TV | Culture | Subs |

Table 1: Sample of the Sources

lect a diverse Emirati corpus, with sources ranging from show and interview subtitles and children's stories to online conversations and published educational books written in the Emirati dialect meant to preserve the language. This paper serves as a documentation of the collection process only, and not the next necessary steps of cleaning, processing, and annotating raw text corpora to be suitable for LLM fine-tuning purposes.

## 2 Related Work

This section highlights some of the existing efforts in low-resource language web corpus collection as well as specific efforts within DA collection. Hoenen et al. 2020 provide a documented approach to the collection of low resource languages, including different tools and scenarios. They offer a definition to low resource languages and classifications, and multiple ways to access their web corpora. These include accessing social media as well as querying search engines, namely Google. The paper also contains a step-by-step guide to the manipulation of search queries, through single queries, multiple queries, or using operators.

Of the similar papers concerned with the same challenges and issues as this paper is the Bahrain Corpus by Abdulrahim et al., 2022, where the authors discuss the phonological and morphological challenges in the collection of DA and offer morphological annotation to a special corpus for the Bahraini dialect. Almeman and Lee, 2013 offered the same premise, using wordlists which are specific to dialects, narrowing down search results. They highlight the need for written DA corpora, as most DA is spoken rather than written online. Their process was concerned with four categories of dialects: Gulf, Egyptian, North African, and Levantine, rather than country-specific dialect corpora collection, which is the purpose of this paper.

Regarding the collection of Emirati specific corpora, efforts by AlAzzam et al., 2024 involve collecting idioms and phrases from the web. The sources included websites, social media, language blogs, and radio channels in the dialect. The main genre of interest to the researchers was the traditional and idiomatic usage of the dialect, and as such, the representativeness of the corpus was limited to a certain field of phrases used in Emirati. The paper also offers qualitative analysis of some Emirati phrases and their usages, and the data was manually gathered and extracted.

## 3 Corpus Collection Methodology

Table 1 shows a sample of the Emirati corpus sources collected to date, including tags of their genres/domains and type of source (articles, documents, forums stories, automatic/manual subtitles ...). The resulting corpora is semi-curated, where the data is manually sought, but often automatically collected. This section discusses the methods and tools used to search for and extract these resources, along with their specific challenges and possible solutions or otherwise permanent limitations.

### 3.1 Corpus Search Methods and Tools

Various tools can be utilized in the search process, explained in this section with their advantages and challenges, with possible solutions.

**Search Engines:** The most accessible form of web corpora collection. Search engines are available as diverse applications, but what mostly makes the difference is the existence of advanced search settings which make the task easier. Advanced settings which were useful in the search for Emirati web corpora include refining by region, filetype (usually DOC *or* PDF), and domain (.ae for the United Arab Emirates, or searching through specific sites like blogspot.com for blogs, and /vb/ for lightweight versions of some forums). These are different from the other helpful operators used in search querying, such as the double quotations for exact phrases, or the (-) operator to exclude specific expressions. The exclusion operator was especially useful during the search as it tackled the challenge of dialect intersection. Emirati Arabic shares multiple features with other Gulf dialects, causing the search results to often lead to pages or documents containing different dialects such as Jordanian, Kuwaiti, or Bahraini.

Of the available search engines to use online,

Google remains the most useful with diverse advanced search filters, and the "Verbatim" button for more refined searches.

**Wordlists**: For efficient usage of the exclusion operator and for the search tool overall, a wordlist of terms in Emirati as well as of the neighboring dialects. Wordlists are a beneficial resource to have access to during search endeavors and can come from different sources. For the development of wordlists, some corpus analysis skills may be useful if there does not exist a pre-compiled wordlist that is specific to the dialect.

As such, an Emirati wordlist was compiled through two methods. The first method was straightforward, using a reference book comparing between different Gulf dialects. This helped in the collection of both inclusion and exclusion wordlists to use while searching. The second method involved simple Term Frequency and N-Gram queries done through *AntConc* for a starting corpus which was formed from published books written in Emirati. The results had to be manually revised and refined to ensure the collection of helpful phrases to use in search queries. This is the process of surveying the wordlists. Afterwards, the lists may be used in individual queries or in multiple simultaneous queries using tools such as *BootCat.*

**YouTube Subtitles Search**: Most usage of DA is conversational. Therefore, videos are an incredibly rich resource for the collection of spoken Emirati. When attempting to collect the written language, YouTube offers a handy closed-captions (CC) feature which is present in most of its videos. Most of these CC are automatically generated, and some of them are manually inserted in the videos. *Filmot* is a web interface which allows searching through YouTube subtitles with a wide range of filters. It has proved immensely useful in locating and extracting DA from YouTube videos by entering a search term and setting filters if needed to locate usage of DA in a video immediately and extracting its captions. However, automatic captions, which are more prevalent, often have orthographic errors when it comes to the detection of Emirati Arabic as compared to Saudi or Egyptian Arabic.

**Manual Collection vs. Scraping**: Many sources found through search engines, mostly in the form of forums or articles, are too numerous to be collected by hand. In other times, some sources are so scarce that it is very possible to manually gather them, ensuring their validity and adherence to corpus criteria better. While scraping knowledge is greatly helpful in such tasks, with it comes the need for sound understanding of data cleaning methods. This is because many of the mentioned sources in this paper are unstructured forums and websites, without a standard form to scrape.

### 3.2 Corpus Sources and Extraction

Following querying tools and searching as per the previous methods, Emirati sources come in many forms, each with its own challenges. These sources include the following types.

**Articles**: As newspaper articles, such as columnist articles, or anonymous articles on specialized websites, such as *"The Money Channel"/ "Qanat 'Al-Mal"*.

**Blog**: Often in the form of Blogspot or WordPress websites, taking on multiple topics often within one blog, and are mostly personal.

**Documents**: Including books, study guides, or compiled stories and poetry.

**Forums**: The most common type of written dialectal use alongside formal social media. Forums served for years as organized archives of dialectal Arabic usage in conversations or think piece publishing. They also feature text other than conversations, such as stories, criticisms, and longform advice.

**Promotional**: Referring to the type of websites or accounts which use DA to promote services or products online. They are often in the form of short lines in ads or exist on the product websites.

**Social media:** Most widespread modern usages of DA exist on social media. However, access to social media posts gets harder by time due to privacy concerns. There are less location identifiers, more hashtags which are not necessarily related to DA usage and are a general unmoderated space for corpora collection. Of the more organized social media sites are Reddit and Ask.fm, offering easier access to user texts.

**Subtitles**: YouTube, Facebook, and other extracted subtitles from videos.

## 4 Search Results and Discussion

The search efforts, focused on diversity and representation, yielded 18 different sources ready for extraction, showed in Figure1. Of the genres, general texts were the most prevalent. Of these general texts, forums were easier to find, followed by blogs and subtitles. General texts do not cover a partic-

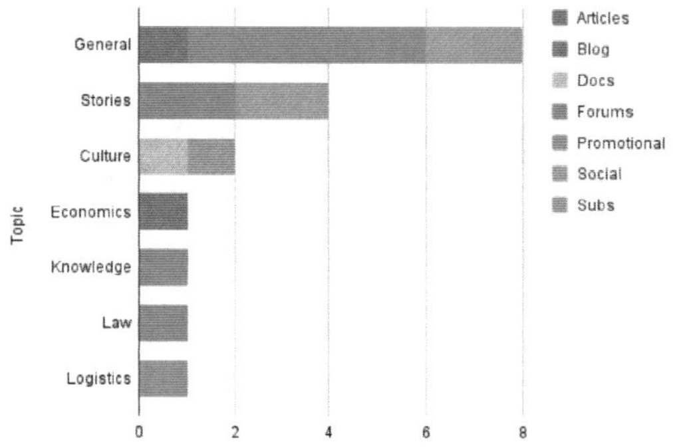


Figure 1: Corpus topics and types distribution across the available corpus.

| Source | Format | Word Count |
|---|---|---|
| Articles1 | txt | 2,500 |
| Articles2 | doc | 13,000 |
| Book1 | txt | 373,400 |
| Forum1 | csv | 272,559 |
| ForumStory1 | doc | 140,000 |
| Subtitles1 | txt | 7,000 |
| Subtitles2 | doc | 7,000 |
| Subtitles3 | csv | 3,436 |

Table 2: Pre-processing word counts of successfully extracted sources.

ular topic, and therefore do not serve well in the creation of domain-specific corpora and training specific LLMs. The resulted corpus attempted to be as diverse as possible without over-specifying the genres provided. However, there are little specific genres when dealing with dialectal corpora. This is mostly due to the nature of dialectal use in Arabic-speaking countries, where formal settings or domain expertise are usually discussed in modern standard Arabic.

Forums range in topics as they feature many users and discussions, serving the natural purpose of a social website, but they are often organized into sub-forums. For more specific topic extraction, sub-forums, Facebook groups, and Subreddits are useful options. Stories serve as the most widely available dialectal resource online. Often written in DA, they offer an informal conversational use of the language in written form, allowing the exploration of written DA in large quantities. They often come in folklore or romance genres but offer decent text to aid the understanding of how the dialect is used in multiple contexts. These two forms of data are useful in gathering insight about the nature of conversational Emirati.

The cultural resources obtained were the property of official Emirati heritage preservation institutions and contained multiple heritage-related explanation chapters written in traditional Emirati, making them very valuable resources. Blogs found were often personal, promotional, or domain-specific regarding a certain niche.

### 4.1 Extraction Limitations

Within search results, many sources were incorrectly obtained or were discarded for many reasons. PDF search, for example, was often invalid due to incorrect Arabic parsing which scrambled up letters and caused them to appear falsely in search results. Additionally, many PDF sources were difficult to extract due to limited Arabic file conversion and OCR support. Forums were difficult to gather in a proper scraping method due to their old-fashioned website nature, where users would format their posts using their own HTML knowledge, causing noisy data to be extracted. In the search within and extraction of video subtitles, many automatic captions suffered orthographic failure of the dialect due to insufficiently trained Automatic Speech Recognition models (ASR) on recognizing DA. Social media scraping efforts were not attempted, as they require extensive coding knowledge and tools, which are out of this paper's scope. Any other limitations within the search for other types of sources were largely not generalized and were specific to each source. Considering these limitations, an estimated word count of the successfully extracted sources can be found in Table2.

## 5 Conclusion

The scope of this paper was the search for Emirati Arabic sources online. While it did not touch on the cleaning and annotation efforts, it presented some of the available tools and resources which a corpus researcher may use and the process to follow when searching for Emirati representative corpora. This is done in hopes of advancing the efforts in making dialectal corpora more accessible and encourage the creation of more tools to help with the search, extraction, and processing of DA for the purpose of creating raw text datasets to train language models on these underrepresented Arabic variations.

## 6 Limitations

Preprocessing the web resources gathered in this corpus collection project is a crucial step which contains a number of obstacles due to the diverse nature and formats of the resources. Therefore, reaching an exact pre-extraction word count for the unprocessed corpus may not be achieved until websites are effectively scraped and books are accurately recognized into text. Furthermore, access to valid or formal written data (i.e: not user-generated) proved difficult at this stage of Emirati Arabic web presence.

## Acknowledgments

The researcher sincerely appreciates the reviewers' careful considerations and feedback regarding the lack of quantitative data. This paper was a preliminary insight into the availability of data and some of the methods used to collect it, and the corpus collection project is currently a work in process. The resources in the paper may be helpful in exploration of other dialects on the web.

## References

Dana Abdulrahim, Go Inoue, Latifa Shamsan, Salam Khalifa, and Nizar Habash. 2022. The Bahrain corpus: A multi-genre corpus of bahraini Arabic. In *Proceedings of the Thirteenth Language Resources and Evaluation Conference*, pages 2345–2352, Marseille, France. European Language Resources Association.

Bayan A. AlAzzam, Manar Alkhatib, and Khaled Shaalan. 2024. Towards Gulf Emirati Dialect Corpus from Social Media. In *BUiD Doctoral Research Conference 2023*, pages 273–281. Springer, Cham, Switzerland.

Khalid Almeman and Mark Lee. 2013. Automatic building of arabic multi dialect text corpora by bootstrapping dialect words. In *2013 1st International Conference on Communications, Signal Processing, and their Applications (ICCSPA)*, pages 1–6.

Ashraf Elnagar, Sane M. Yagi, Ali Bou Nassif, Ismail Shahin, and Said A. Salloum. 2021. Systematic literature review of dialectal arabic: Identification and detection. *IEEE Access*, 9:31010–31042.

Armin Hoenen, Cemre Koc, and Marc Daniel Rahn. 2020. A manual for web corpus crawling of low resource languages. *Umanistica Digitale*, 4(8).

Salam Khalifa, Nizar Habash, Dana Abdulrahim, and Sara Hassan. 2016. A large scale corpus of gulf arabic. *Preprint*, arXiv:1609.02960.

Yang Liu, Jiahuan Cao, Chongyu Liu, Kai Ding, and Lianwen Jin. 2024. Datasets for large language models: A comprehensive survey. *Preprint*, arXiv:2402.18041.

# Evaluating Calibration of Arabic Pre-trained Language Models on Dialectal Text

**Ali Al-Laith**
Copenhagen University, Denmark
alal@di.ku.dk

**Rachida Kebdani**
University of Verona, Italy
rashida-kebdani@hotmail.com

## Abstract

While pre-trained language models have made significant progress in different classification tasks, little attention has been given to the reliability of their confidence scores. Calibration, how well model confidence aligns with actual accuracy, is essential for real-world applications where decisions rely on probabilistic outputs. This study addresses this gap in Arabic dialect identification by assessing the calibration of eight pre-trained language models, ensuring their predictions are not only accurate but also reliable for practical applications. We analyze two datasets: one with over 1 million text samples and the Nuanced Arabic Dialect Identification dataset(NADI-2023). Using Expected Calibration Error (ECE) as a metric, we reveal substantial variation in model calibration across dialects in both datasets, showing that prediction confidence can vary significantly depending on regional data. This research has implications for improving the reliability of Arabic dialect models in applications like sentiment analysis and social media monitoring.

## 1 Introduction

Arabic pre-trained language models (PLMs) have advanced significantly in dialect identification and classification, with most research focusing on improving accuracy and dataset development. However, these efforts often overlook calibration—how well a model's confidence scores align with the true probability of correct predictions(Nixon et al., 2019). Calibration is crucial for Arabic dialect applications, where nuanced regional variations in language can lead to significant social and cultural implications if predictions are unreliable. In real-world applications like sentiment analysis, social media monitoring, and policy-making, accurate yet calibrated predictions are essential to support informed decision-making.

This study addresses this gap by evaluating the calibration of existing Arabic pre-trained models on dialectal text. Using 1 million text samples automatically annotated and NADI-2023 datasets, we conduct calibration analysis exclusively on cases where all eight models unanimously agree on dialect labels, focusing on high-confidence predictions. We employ metrics such as Expected Calibration Error (ECE) to measure the alignment between model confidence and accuracy, assessing the trustworthiness of these models in dialect classification.

By focusing on calibration, this work goes beyond accuracy metrics to highlight the reliability of model predictions. Calibration evaluation not only aids in model selection for high-stakes applications but also informs areas for improvement, ensuring that Arabic dialect models are both accurate and dependable in practice.

## 2 Related Work

### 2.1 Arabic Dialect Datasets

Dialectal Arabic (DA) encompasses the diverse spoken forms of Arabic used across the Arab world, differing significantly from Modern Standard Arabic (MSA) in phonology, morphology, orthography, and syntax(Bouamor et al., 2014). DA is typically divided into regional groups, including Egyptian, North African, Levantine, Gulf, and Yemeni, with each containing sub-varieties like Tunisian, Lebanese, and Saudi dialects(Zaghouani and Charfi, 2018). Given DA's prevalence in daily communication, incorporating DA resources into LLM training is crucial for creating models that understand and generate Arabic as it is spoken in real-world contexts. The MADAR Twitter corpus, used in the MADAR shared task on fine-grained Arabic dialect identification, comprises 2,980 Twitter user profiles from 21 countries, facilitating dialect identification in Twitter user profiles (Bouamor et al., 2019). The Gumar corpus, a large-scale collection of Gulf Arabic, includes 1,236 forum novels totaling around 112 million words, with manual



*Proceedings of The 4th Workshop on Arabic Corpus Linguistics (WACL-4)*, pages 68–76
January 20th, 2025. 

document-level annotations for sub-dialect information across the Gulf Cooperation Council countries: Bahrain, UAE, Kuwait, Saudi Arabia, Oman, and Qatar (Khalifa et al., 2016). Nuanced Arabic Dialect Identification (NADI) introduced different datasets for Arabic dialect identification in different level such as country or city levels(Abdul-Mageed et al., 2022, 2023a, 2024). Baimukan et al. (2022) introduced the first unified three-level hierarchical schema (region-country-city) for dialectal Arabic classification. By mapping 29 datasets to this schema, they enabled their aggregation and demonstrated its effectiveness by building language models for dialect identification.

### 2.2 Arabic Dialect Pre-trained Language Models

The development of dialect-specific BERT-based models for Arabic has emerged to address the linguistic diversity across the Arab world, resulting in several models specialized for individual dialects. SudaBERT (Elgezouli et al., 2021), for instance, focused on Sudanese Arabic, outperforming ArabicBERT (Talafha et al., 2020) in sentiment analysis (SA) for the Sudanese dialect, though ArabicBERT showed stronger performance in Modern Standard Arabic (MSA) across both SA and named entity recognition (NER). Similarly, AraRoBERTa was designed for seven dialects (Saudi, Egyptian, Kuwaiti, Omani, Lebanese, Jordanian, and Algerian), employing RoBERTa architecture with various supervision approaches (AlYami and Al-Zaidy, 2022). AraRoBERTa performed particularly well in Saudi and Egyptian dialects due to larger dataset availability, while semi-supervised training improved results for certain dialects like Egyptian and Algerian.

For the Algerian dialect, DziriBERT was trained on over a million tweets, excelling in SA, emotion classification, and topic classification tasks, with MARBERT following closely (Abdaoui et al., 2021). Haddad et al. (2023) introduced TunBERT, targeting Tunisian Arabic, performed best in SA and dialect identification but was outperformed in reading comprehension by AraBERT (Antoun et al., 2020) and GigaBERT (Safaya et al., 2020). Moroccan Arabic, or Darija, has also been addressed with models like MorrBERT (Moussaoui and El Younnoussi, 2023), DarijaBERT, and Atlas-Chat (Shang et al., 2024). MorrBERT and its RoBERTa-based counterpart MorRoBERTa achieved high accuracy in SA and dialect identification, with DarijaBERT variants showing strong performance in dialect identification, SA, sarcasm detection, and topic classification. Atlas-Chat, the latest Moroccan Arabic model, achieved notable results in sentiment analysis and translation.

In addition, AlcLAM, a model focusing on Arabic dialects in general, excelled in dialect identification and offensive language detection compared to other models (Ahmed et al., 2024). SaudiBERT (Qarah, 2024b) and EgyBERT (Qarah, 2024a), specifically trained on Saudi and Egyptian dialects respectively, showed strong performances across various tasks such as sarcasm detection, gender identification, and event detection, often surpassing established models like AraBERT, CAMeLBERT (Inoue et al., 2021), and MARBERT. This growing body of dialect-specific models demonstrates the significance of tailoring architectures and training data to regional linguistic features, leading to enhanced performance in dialect-relevant NLP tasks across the Arab world.

### 2.3 Calibration of Pre-trained Language Models

Calibrating probabilistic predictive models is essential for reliable prediction and decision-making in AI. Naeini et al. (2015) introduced Bayesian Binning into Quantiles (BBQ), a non-parametric, computationally efficient calibration method that post-processes binary classification outputs, making it compatible with various classifiers and demonstrating high accuracy in experiments on real and simulated datasets. Desai and Durrett (2020a) examined calibration in BERT and RoBERTa models for tasks like natural language inference, paraphrase detection, and commonsense reasoning, evaluating both in-domain and out-of-domain settings to account for model uncertainty. Baan et al. (2022) introduced an instance-level calibration based on human uncertainty, validated through a ChaosNLI dataset case study, which examines temperature scaling under human judgment. Neural network classification models often rely on maximum predicted probabilities as confidence scores, which typically require post-processing calibration to improve reliability. By transforming multi-class calibration into a binary surrogate task, this approach enhances calibration efficiency and significantly improves results across various neural networks for image and text classification (LeCoz et al., 2024).

Jiang et al. (2021) explored language model calibration by assessing how well models like T5,

BART, and GPT-2 match predicted probabilities to correctness likelihoods, finding them poorly calibrated on QA tasks. Calibration methods such as fine-tuning and post-hoc adjustments showed improvement in confidence accuracy across diverse datasets. Zhang et al. (2021) extended calibration in QA by combining confidence scores with input context and data augmentation, achieving 5-10% accuracy gains on reading comprehension benchmarks and opening calibration study in open retrieval settings, showing robust gains across tasks. Yang et al. (2023) benchmarked multilingual Large Language Model (LLM) calibration on QA tasks across languages, covering encoder-only, encoder-decoder, and decoder-only models (110M to 7B parameters) across high- and low-resource languages. They found that decoder-only models, like LlaMa2, benefit from in-context learning, and incorporating cheaply translated samples improves calibration, particularly for non-English languages.

For stance detection, Li and Caragea (2023) used knowledge distillation with soft labels and iterative teacher-student learning to enhance model performance, implementing dynamic temperature scaling to calibrate predictions, which improved stance detection results on three datasets.

## 3 Methodology

### 3.1 Dataset

We use two types of annotated datasets: automatically annotated data using eight Pre-trained Language Models(PLMs), limited to samples with unanimous dialect labels, and manually annotated data by human annotators.

For the automatic annotations, we compile over 1 million text samples from multiple datasets. The first source is the Arabic Dialect Identification dataset[1], with more than 360,000 labeled Arabic sentences, built by integrating arabic_pos_dialect [2], IADD (Zahir, 2022)[3], QADI (Abdelali et al., 2020)[4], and the MADAR corpus (Bouamor et al., 2018)[5]. Additionally, we select over 500,000 tweets from AraSenCorpus, a collection of 4.5 million tweets in Modern Standard Arabic and dialects (Al-Laith et al., 2021), and over 200,000 samples from a 5.5 million tweet corpus for emotion and symptom classification (Al-Laith and Alenezi, 2021). As the collected tweets were crawled from social media, the data are expected to be noisy and should be cleaned up before performing any of the NLP tasks to get better results. We apply text preprocessing steps, including the removal of URLs, hashtags, mentions, and duplicate tweets.

For manual annotations, we use the NADI 2023 dialect identification dataset (Abdul-Mageed et al., 2023b), with PLMs predicting dialects across training and development sets, totaling 15,400 samples across 14 dialects (1,100 samples per dialect).

### 3.2 Pre-trained Language Models

We use the following Pre-trained Language Models (PLMs) to conduct the Arabic dialect prediction experiments:

1. **Arabic Dialect Identification Model**[6] **(Model 1)**: The model is trained to accurately identify spoken dialects in Arabic text. It was trained using a combination of publicly available datasets and fine-tuned on their own dataset. With high accuracy in identifying Arabic dialects, the model can be utilized in a variety of applications.

2. **CAMeLBERT-MSA DID MADAR Twitter-5 Model** [7] **(Model 2)**: The model is a dialect identification (DID) model specifically designed for Arabic (Inoue et al., 2021). It was fine-tuned from the CAMeLBERT-MSA model using the MADAR Twitter-5 dataset, which includes 21 labels. This model is particularly useful for identifying different Arabic dialects in social media texts.

3. **CAMeLBERT-Mix DID NADI Model**[8]**(Model 3)**: The model is a dialect identification (DID) model that was built by fine-tuning the CAMeLBERT-Mix model. For the fine-tuning, we used the NADI Coountry-level dataset[9], which includes 21 labels.

[1]https://github.com/Lafifi-24/arabic-dialect-identification

[2]https://huggingface.co/datasets/arabic_pos_dialect

[3]https://github.com/JihadZa/IADD

[4]https://github.com/qcri/QADI

[5]https://sites.google.com/nyu.edu/madar/?pli=1

[6]https://huggingface.co/lafifi-24/arbert_arabic_dialect_identification

[7]https://huggingface.co/CAMeL-Lab/bert-base-arabic-camelbert-msa-did-madar-twitter5

[8]https://huggingface.co/CAMeL-Lab/bert-base-arabic-camelbert-mix-did-nadi

[9]https://sites.google.com/view/nadi-shared-task

4. **ADI-NADI-2023**[10] **(Model 4)**: A BERT-based model fine-tuned to perform single-label Arabic Dialect Identification (Keleg and Magdy, 2023).

5. **Arabic-MARBERT-dialect-Identification-City Model**[11] **(Model 5)**: The model is a dialect identification model that was built by fine-tuning the MARBERT model. For the fine-tuning, I used MADAR Corpus 26 dataset, which includes 26 labels(cities).

6. **Bert base arabic camelbert MSA fine-tunedArabic Dialect Identification**[12] **(Model 6)**: The model was trained on QADI dataset from (Abdelali et al., 2020).

7. **CAMeLBERT-MSA DID NADI Model**[13] **(Model 7)**: It is a dialect identification (DID) model that was built by fine-tuning the CAMeLBERT Modern Standard Arabic (MSA) model[14]. For the fine-tuning, we used the NADI Coountry-level dataset[15], which includes 21 labels.

8. **NADI-2024-baseline**[16] **(Model 8)**: A BERT-based model fine-tuned to perform single-label Arabic Dialect Identification (ADI).

### 3.3 Dialect Selection

Table 1 displays the range of dialects encompassed by each of the pre-trained language models (PLMs) discussed. Some models offer predictions of Arabic dialects at the city level, we have aligned these cities with their respective countries for a more comprehensive understanding. Since the number of labels varies across models and some dialects such as the Qatari dialect has no sample annotated by all models, we have focused our analysis on the common labels, selecting 14 out of 22 labels shared among all models' label sets.

[10] https://huggingface.co/AMR-KELEG/ADI-NADI-2023

[11] https://huggingface.co/Ammar-alhaj-ali/arabic-MARBERT-dialect-identification-city

[12] https://huggingface.co/Abdelrahman-Rezk/bert-base-arabic-camelbert-msa-finetuned-Arabic_Dialect_Identification_model_1

[13] https://huggingface.co/CAMeL-Lab/bert-base-arabic-camelbert-msa-did-nadi

[14] https://huggingface.co/CAMeL-Lab/bert-base-arabic-camelbert-msa/

[15] https://sites.google.com/view/nadi-shared-task

[16] https://huggingface.co/AMR-KELEG/NADI2024-baseline

## 4 Experiments and Results

### 4.1 Dialect Prediction Experiment

The process of dialect prediction with Hugging Face models involves loading a pre-trained model and tokenizer to numerically encode the input text, enabling model processing. The model produces logits, which are then converted into probabilities, with the highest probability determining the sample's predicted label. This approach efficiently supports tasks such as text classification and named entity recognition, offering a standardized method for leveraging pre-trained models in NLP.

After predicting dialects for each sample with all 8 selected models, we computed the majority label separately for both the automatically and manually annotated datasets. Figure 1 displays the count of models agreeing on the same label, alongside sample counts and frequencies for each dataset. In the automatically annotated dataset, 127,646 samples had full agreement across all 8 models (around 8.5%), while only 9,852 samples (approximately 0.66%) received 8 different labels, indicating minimal consensus. In the manually annotated dataset, 2,581 samples had unanimous agreement, representing around 4%, while only 10 samples (less than 0.01%) received 8 different labels, further underscoring the rarity of full disagreement.

Figure 2 provides a detailed view of the percentage of samples identified per dialect and the number of models that concurred on each label for both datasets. In the automatically annotated data, models most frequently agreed on labels with 2 to 5 models in agreement, while in the manually annotated dataset, model agreement levels were generally higher, with 4 to 8 models showing more consistent label matches. This discrepancy highlights the influence of annotation style on model consensus, with the manually annotated dataset exhibiting slightly higher overall agreement among models.

For the calibration analysis, we focus on samples that received the same label from all models (127,646 samples) from the automatically annotated dataset, while we include all samples from the manually annotated NADI-2013 dataset for model calibration analysis.

### 4.2 Expected Calibration Error (ECE)

In this experiment, we use Expected Calibration Error (ECE), a metric that measures how well the

| | Model 1 | Model 2 | Model 3 | Model 4 | Model 5 | Model 6 | Model 7 | Model 8 | Is Included? |
|---|---|---|---|---|---|---|---|---|---|
| Algeria | ✓ | ✓ | ✓ | ✓ | ✓ | ✓ | ✓ | ✓ | ✓ |
| Bahrain | ✓ | ✓ | ✓ | ✓ | ✗ | ✓ | ✓ | ✓ | ✗ |
| Djibouti | ✗ | ✓ | ✓ | ✗ | ✗ | ✗ | ✓ | ✗ | ✗ |
| Egypt | ✓ | ✓ | ✓ | ✓ | ✓ | ✓ | ✓ | ✓ | ✓ |
| Iraq | ✓ | ✓ | ✓ | ✓ | ✓ | ✓ | ✓ | ✓ | ✓ |
| Jordan | ✓ | ✓ | ✓ | ✓ | ✓ | ✓ | ✓ | ✓ | ✓ |
| KSA | ✓ | ✓ | ✓ | ✓ | ✓ | ✓ | ✓ | ✓ | ✓ |
| Kuwait | ✓ | ✓ | ✓ | ✓ | ✗ | ✓ | ✓ | ✓ | ✗ |
| Lebanon | ✓ | ✓ | ✓ | ✓ | ✓ | ✓ | ✓ | ✓ | ✓ |
| Libya | ✓ | ✓ | ✓ | ✓ | ✓ | ✓ | ✓ | ✓ | ✓ |
| MSA | ✓ | ✗ | ✗ | ✗ | ✓ | ✗ | ✗ | ✗ | ✗ |
| Mauritania | ✗ | ✓ | ✓ | ✗ | ✗ | ✗ | ✓ | ✗ | ✗ |
| Morocco | ✓ | ✓ | ✓ | ✓ | ✓ | ✓ | ✓ | ✓ | ✓ |
| Oman | ✓ | ✓ | ✓ | ✓ | ✓ | ✓ | ✓ | ✓ | ✓ |
| Palestine | ✓ | ✓ | ✓ | ✓ | ✓ | ✓ | ✓ | ✓ | ✓ |
| Qatar | ✓ | ✓ | ✓ | ✓ | ✓ | ✓ | ✓ | ✓ | ✓ |
| Somalia | ✗ | ✓ | ✓ | ✗ | ✗ | ✗ | ✓ | ✗ | ✗ |
| Sudan | ✓ | ✓ | ✓ | ✓ | ✓ | ✓ | ✓ | ✓ | ✓ |
| Syria | ✓ | ✓ | ✓ | ✓ | ✓ | ✓ | ✓ | ✓ | ✓ |
| Tunisia | ✓ | ✓ | ✓ | ✓ | ✓ | ✓ | ✓ | ✓ | ✓ |
| UAE | ✓ | ✓ | ✓ | ✓ | ✗ | ✓ | ✓ | ✓ | ✗ |
| Yemen | ✓ | ✓ | ✓ | ✓ | ✓ | ✓ | ✓ | ✓ | ✓ |

Table 1: Arabic Dialects included in our analysis.

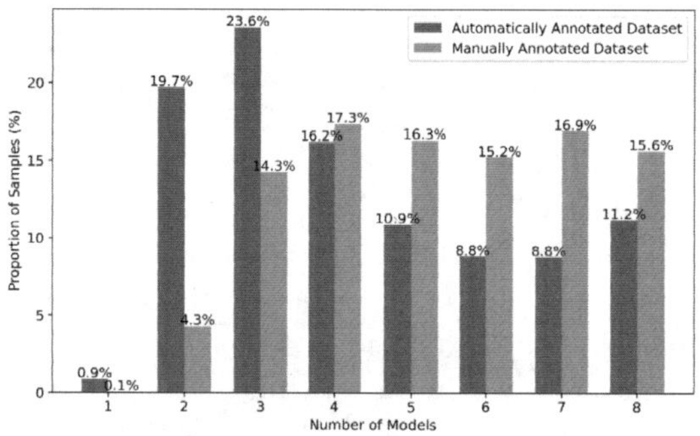


Figure 1: Sample proportion by number of models agreeing to assign the same dialect.

model's predicted probabilities reflect the true accuracy (Desai and Durrett, 2020b):

$$ECE = \sum_{k=1}^{K} \frac{|B_k|}{n} |acc(B_k) - conf(B_k)|$$

where $K = 10$ is the number of bins (confidence intervals), $|B_k|$ is the number of samples in bin $k$, $acc(B_k)$ is the accuracy in bin $k$, and $conf(B_k)$ is the average confidence in bin $k$. The ECE value reflects how well-calibrated a model's confidence estimates are, with lower ECE indicating better calibration.

#### 4.2.1 Automatically Annotated Data

ECE is used to assess the calibration quality of eight Arabic pre-trained language models on dialectal text by comparing model confidence with actual accuracy on a subset where all models agreed on the same label. ECE is calculated by binning predicted confidence scores, then measuring the discrepancy between the average confidence and accuracy within each bin. This error quantifies how closely model confidence aligns with observed accuracy, indicating whether models tend to over- or under-predict. By focusing on samples with unanimous agreement, the experiment aims to reveal calibration disparities among models that exhibit high predictive consensus, offering insights into their reliability when applied to Arabic dialect classification. It is shown that both Model 1 & 6 achieved a relatively low ECE of 0.07, as shown in Figure 3, indicating that both models are reasonably well-calibrated. In contrast, Model 4 achieves high ECE of 0.44, indicating that the model is not well-calibrated.

#### 4.2.2 Manually Annotated Data

We use the same ECE formula described in the previous section. The results of the experiment reveal significant variation in Expected Calibration Error (ECE) across the models, indicating differing levels of calibration quality. Model 4 exhibits the high-

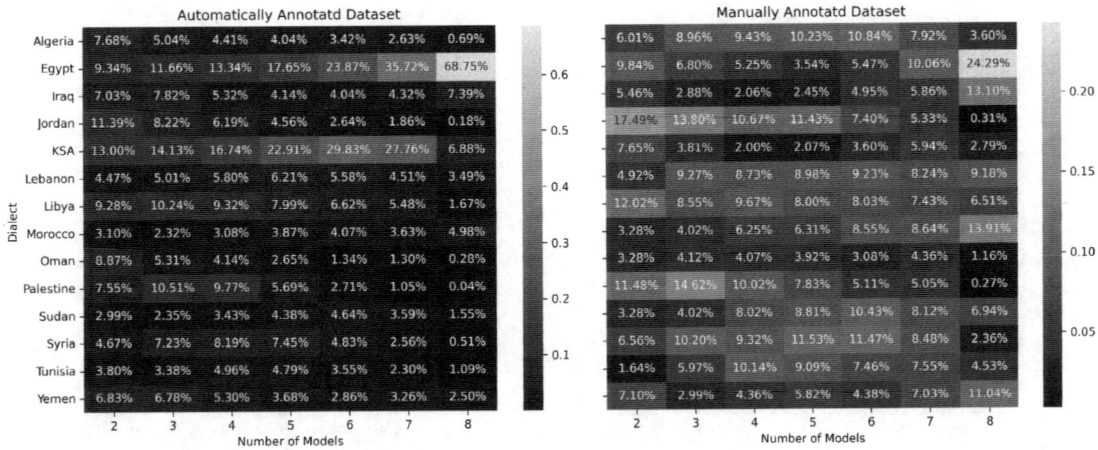


Figure 2: Sample proportion and number of models agreeing to assign the same dialect.

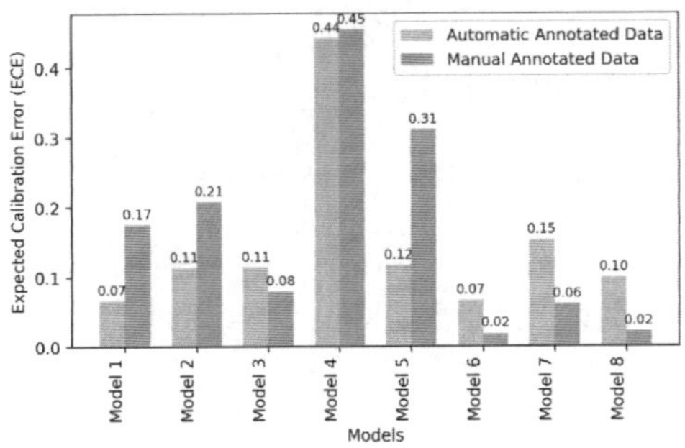


Figure 3: Expected Calibration Error (ECE) values for each model on both datasets.

est ECE at 0.45, suggesting poor calibration and a substantial gap between predicted probabilities and actual outcomes. Similarly, Models 2 and 5 show relatively high ECE values of 0.21 and 0.31, respectively, also pointing to weaker calibration. In contrast, Models 6, 7, and 8 achieve notably low ECE scores (0.02, 0.06, and 0.02), demonstrating better alignment between predictions and actual labels, indicating that these models are more reliably calibrated. Model 3 also shows moderate calibration with an ECE of 0.08. Overall, the results highlight the variance in calibration performance, with some models showing potential for practical application due to better-calibrated predictions, while others require further adjustment to improve reliability. Figure 4 shows the ECE values of each model on the NADI dataset.

## 5 Result Analysis and Discussion

The calibration analysis across models and dialects reveals distinct trends in model reliability on both automatically and manually annotated datasets. Models 1 and 8 demonstrate more consistent calibration across dialects and datasets, suggesting they are better suited for varied dialectal data and annotation styles. In contrast, Models 4 and 5 show higher calibration errors, especially on manually annotated data, indicating a greater sensitivity to the complexities introduced by human annotations. This difference underscores the potential need for fine-tuning or recalibration when applying these models to manually annotated datasets to enhance their predictive confidence.

Additionally, the calibration differences across dialects reveal that certain dialects, such as Palestinian and Sudanese, are more challenging for the models to interpret consistently, displaying higher calibration errors. This pattern suggests that these dialects might require additional data or targeted adjustments to improve model alignment. Overall, these findings emphasize the importance of considering both annotation type and dialect specificity when evaluating model calibration, as these factors can significantly impact model reliability in multilingual and multi-dialectal applications.

## 6 Limitation

This work has some notable limitations that could impact the generalizability and comprehensiveness of the findings. First, while the analysis provides insights into the calibration of eight pre-trained language models, it is constrained by the choice and availability of these models. Each model has been pre-trained on varying datasets, which may lack consistent or comprehensive coverage of spe-

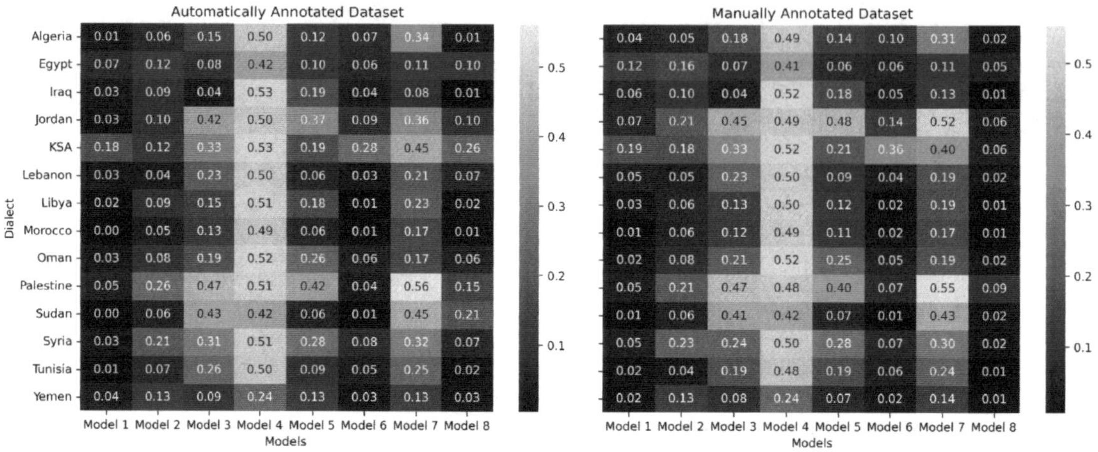


Figure 4: Expected Calibration Error (ECE) Values for Each Dialect and Model.

cific Arabic dialects, thereby limiting our ability to capture the full linguistic diversity within Arabic dialects. Consequently, the calibration results might reflect biases inherent in the pre-training datasets rather than purely dialectal features.

Second, the study relies solely on Expected Calibration Error (ECE) as the calibration metric, which, while informative, provides only a single perspective on model calibration quality. ECE does not capture all aspects of prediction reliability, such as miscalibration at different confidence levels or the potential impacts of class imbalance in dialect distribution. Integrating additional calibration metrics, like Brier Score or Maximum Calibration Error (MCE), might provide a more comprehensive evaluation of model performance across dialects.

Additionally, the study does not consider the contextual or pragmatic nuances present in real-world dialectal Arabic, as these models may not account for complex language variations or code-switching phenomena commonly seen in Arabic dialects. This limitation may impact the reliability of model predictions when applied to more dynamic or informal Arabic text data, such as social media posts, which often contain non-standard dialectal expressions.

Finally, the study focuses on calibration without incorporating linguistic or sociolinguistic factors that could influence model performance across dialects. Factors such as geographical proximity, historical language influences, and sociolinguistic prestige of certain dialects could affect model calibration in ways that ECE alone cannot capture. Future research could benefit from a more interdisciplinary approach that considers these factors, potentially enhancing model calibration for specific dialectal groups.

## 7 Conclusion and Future Work

The ECE analysis demonstrates considerable variability in model calibration performance across both automatically and manually annotated datasets for Arabic dialect prediction. Models 1, 6, and 8 exhibit relatively lower ECE scores, suggesting they maintain more reliable calibration across different dialects and annotation types. Conversely, Models 4 and 5 display notably higher calibration errors, particularly with manually annotated data, which highlights the impact of annotation style on calibration outcomes. This variability suggests that certain models are better suited to dialectal Arabic tasks, though a one-size-fits-all approach may not be feasible given the complexity of the data.

Since the data in the automatically annotated dataset was randomly sampled without balancing dialect distribution, future work can explicitly address this by exploring techniques like resampling or re-weighting to assess their impact on the reliability of the findings. We also plan to improve model calibration in Arabic dialect prediction with focus on dialect-specific calibration techniques, with a particular emphasis on dialects that exhibit higher calibration errors, such as Palestinian and Sudanese Arabic. Approaches such as fine-tuning models with dialect-specific data or applying post-hoc calibration methods may enhance model reliability for these challenging dialects. Additionally, investigating why certain models like Models 1, 6, and 8 perform better could yield insights into architectural or pre-training factors that contribute to calibration efficacy. Incorporating domain-specific knowledge on linguistic features unique to each dialect may further enhance calibration, especially for dialects with distinct phonological or lexical characteristics.

## References


Amine Abdaoui, Mohamed Berrimi, Mourad Oussalah, and Abdelouahab Moussaoui. 2021. Dziribert: a pre-trained language model for the algerian dialect. *arXiv preprint arXiv:2109.12346.*

Ahmed Abdelali, Hamdy Mubarak, Younes Samih, Sabit Hassan, and Kareem Darwish. 2020. Arabic dialect identification in the wild. *arXiv preprint arXiv:2005.06557.*

Muhammad Abdul-Mageed, AbdelRahim Elmadany, Chiyu Zhang, El Moatez Billah Nagoudi, Houda Bouamor, and Nizar Habash. 2023a. Nadi 2023: The fourth nuanced arabic dialect identification shared task. *arXiv preprint arXiv:2310.16117.*

Muhammad Abdul-Mageed, AbdelRahim Elmadany, Chiyu Zhang, El Moatez Billah Nagoudi, Houda Bouamor, and Nizar Habash. 2023b. Nadi 2023: The fourth nuanced arabic dialect identification shared task. *arXiv preprint arXiv:2310.16117.*

Muhammad Abdul-Mageed, Amr Keleg, AbdelRahim Elmadany, Chiyu Zhang, Injy Hamed, Walid Magdy, Houda Bouamor, and Nizar Habash. 2024. Nadi 2024: The fifth nuanced arabic dialect identification shared task. *arXiv preprint arXiv:2407.04910.*

Muhammad Abdul-Mageed, Chiyu Zhang, AbdelRahim Elmadany, Houda Bouamor, and Nizar Habash. 2022. Nadi 2022: The third nuanced arabic dialect identification shared task. *arXiv preprint arXiv:2210.09582.*

Murtadha Ahmed, Saghir Alfasly, Bo Wen, Jamaal Qasem, Mohammed Ahmed, and Yunfeng Liu. 2024. Alclam: Arabic dialectal language model. *arXiv preprint arXiv:2407.13097.*

Ali Al-Laith and Mamdouh Alenezi. 2021. Monitoring people's emotions and symptoms from arabic tweets during the covid-19 pandemic. *Information*, 12(2):86.

Ali Al-Laith, Muhammad Shahbaz, Hind F Alaskar, and Asim Rehmat. 2021. Arasencorpus: A semi-supervised approach for sentiment annotation of a large arabic text corpus. *Applied Sciences*, 11(5):2434.

Reem AlYami and Rabah Al-Zaidy. 2022. Weakly and semi-supervised learning for Arabic text classification using monodialectal language models. In *Proceedings of the Seventh Arabic Natural Language Processing Workshop (WANLP)*, pages 260–272, Abu Dhabi, United Arab Emirates (Hybrid). Association for Computational Linguistics.

Wissam Antoun, Fady Baly, and Hazem Hajj. 2020. Arabert: Transformer-based model for arabic language understanding. *arXiv preprint arXiv:2003.00104.*

Joris Baan, Wilker Aziz, Barbara Plank, and Raquel Fernandez. 2022. Stop measuring calibration when humans disagree. *arXiv preprint arXiv:2210.16133.*

Nurpeiis Baimukan, Houda Bouamor, and Nizar Habash. 2022. Hierarchical aggregation of dialectal data for arabic dialect identification. In *Proceedings of the Thirteenth Language Resources and Evaluation Conference*, pages 4586–4596.

Houda Bouamor, Nizar Habash, and Kemal Oflazer. 2014. A multidialectal parallel corpus of arabic. In *LREC*, pages 1240–1245.

Houda Bouamor, Nizar Habash, Mohammad Salameh, Wajdi Zaghouani, Owen Rambow, Dana Abdulrahim, Ossama Obeid, Salam Khalifa, Fadhl Eryani, Alexander Erdmann, et al. 2018. The madar arabic dialect corpus and lexicon. In *Proceedings of the eleventh international conference on language resources and evaluation (LREC 2018).*

Houda Bouamor, Sabit Hassan, and Nizar Habash. 2019. The madar shared task on arabic fine-grained dialect identification. In *Proceedings of the Fourth Arabic Natural Language Processing Workshop*, pages 199–207.

Shrey Desai and Greg Durrett. 2020a. Calibration of pre-trained transformers. *arXiv preprint arXiv:2003.07892.*

Shrey Desai and Greg Durrett. 2020b. Calibration of pre-trained transformers. In *Proceedings of the 2020 Conference on Empirical Methods in Natural Language Processing (EMNLP)*, pages 295–302, Online. Association for Computational Linguistics.

Mukhtar Elgezouli, Khalid N Elmadani, and Muhammed Saeed. 2021. Sudabert: A pre-trained encoder representation for sudanese arabic dialect. In *2020 International Conference on Computer, Control, Electrical, and Electronics Engineering (ICCCEEE)*, pages 1–4. IEEE.

Hatem Haddad, Ahmed Cheikh Rouhou, Abir Messaoudi, Abir Korched, Chayma Fourati, Amel Sellami, Moez Ben HajHmida, and Faten Ghriss. 2023. Tunbert: pretraining bert for tunisian dialect understanding. *SN Computer Science*, 4(2):194.

Go Inoue, Bashar Alhafni, Nurpeiis Baimukan, Houda Bouamor, and Nizar Habash. 2021. The interplay of variant, size, and task type in arabic pre-trained language models. *arXiv preprint arXiv:2103.06678.*

Zhengbao Jiang, Jun Araki, Haibo Ding, and Graham Neubig. 2021. How can we know when language models know? on the calibration of language models for question answering. *Transactions of the Association for Computational Linguistics*, 9:962–977.

Amr Keleg and Walid Magdy. 2023. Arabic dialect identification under scrutiny: Limitations of single-label classification. *arXiv preprint arXiv:2310.13661*.

Salam Khalifa, Nizar Habash, Dana Abdulrahim, and Sara Hassan. 2016. A large scale corpus of gulf arabic. *arXiv preprint arXiv:1609.02960*.

Adrien LeCoz, Stéphane Herbin, and Faouzi Adjed. 2024. Confidence calibration of classifiers with many classes. *Preprint*, arXiv:2411.02988.

Yingjie Li and Cornelia Caragea. 2023. Distilling calibrated knowledge for stance detection. In *Findings of the Association for Computational Linguistics: ACL 2023*, pages 6316–6329.

Otman Moussaoui and Yacine El Younnoussi. 2023. Pre-training two bert-like models for moroccan dialect: Morroberta and morrbert. In *MENDEL*, volume 29, pages 55–61.

Mahdi Pakdaman Naeini, Gregory Cooper, and Milos Hauskrecht. 2015. Obtaining well calibrated probabilities using bayesian binning. In *Proceedings of the AAAI conference on artificial intelligence*, volume 29.

Jeremy Nixon, Michael W Dusenberry, Linchuan Zhang, Ghassen Jerfel, and Dustin Tran. 2019. Measuring calibration in deep learning. In *CVPR workshops*, volume 2.

Faisal Qarah. 2024a. Egybert: A large language model pretrained on egyptian dialect corpora. *arXiv preprint arXiv:2408.03524*.

Faisal Qarah. 2024b. Saudibert: A large language model pretrained on saudi dialect corpora. *arXiv preprint arXiv:2405.06239*.

Ali Safaya, Moutasem Abdullatif, and Deniz Yuret. 2020. Kuisail at semeval-2020 task 12: Bert-cnn for offensive speech identification in social media. *arXiv preprint arXiv:2007.13184*.

Guokan Shang, Hadi Abdine, Yousef Khoubrane, Amr Mohamed, Yassine Abbahaddou, Sofiane Ennadir, Imane Momayiz, Xuguang Ren, Eric Moulines, Preslav Nakov, et al. 2024. Atlas-chat: Adapting large language models for low-resource moroccan arabic dialect. *arXiv preprint arXiv:2409.17912*.

Bashar Talafha, Mohammad Ali, Muhy Eddin Za'ter, Haitham Seelawi, Ibraheem Tuffaha, Mostafa Samir, Wael Farhan, and Hussein T Al-Natsheh. 2020. Multi-dialect arabic bert for country-level dialect identification. *arXiv preprint arXiv:2007.05612*.

Yahan Yang, Soham Dan, Dan Roth, and Insup Lee. 2023. Understanding calibration for multilingual question answering models. *arXiv preprint arXiv:2311.08669*.

Wajdi Zaghouani and Anis Charfi. 2018. Arap-tweet: A large multi-dialect twitter corpus for gender, age and language variety identification. *arXiv preprint arXiv:1808.07674*.

Jihad Zahir. 2022. Iadd: An integrated arabic dialect identification dataset. *Data in Brief*, 40:107777.

Shujian Zhang, Chengyue Gong, and Eunsol Choi. 2021. Knowing more about questions can help: Improving calibration in question answering. *arXiv preprint arXiv:2106.01494*.

# Empirical Evaluation of Pre-trained Language Models for Summarizing Moroccan Darija News Articles

**Azzedine Aftiss[1], Salima Lamsiyah[2], Christoph Schommer[2], Said Ouatik El Alaoui[1]**

Engineering Sciences Laboratory, National School of Applied Sciences, Ibn Tofail University, Kenitra, Morocco
[2] Department of Computer Science, FSTM, University of Luxembourg, Esch-sur-Alzette, Luxembourg

**Correspondence:** azzedine.aftiss@uit.ac.ma

## Abstract

Moroccan Dialect (MD), or "Darija," is a primary spoken variant of Arabic in Morocco, yet remains underrepresented in Natural Language Processing (NLP) research, particularly in tasks like summarization. Despite a growing volume of MD textual data online, there is a lack of robust resources and NLP models tailored to handle the unique linguistic challenges posed by MD. In response, we introduce **GOOD.MA_v2**, an expanded version of the **GOUD.MA** dataset, containing over 50k articles with their titles across 11 categories. This dataset provides a more comprehensive resource for developing summarization models. We evaluate the application of large language models (LLMs) for MD summarization, utilizing both fine-tuning and zero-shot prompting with encoder-decoder and causal LLMs, respectively. Our findings demonstrate that an expanded dataset improves summarization performance and highlights the capabilities of recent LLMs in handling MD text. We open-source our dataset, fine-tuned models, and all experimental code, establishing a foundation for future advancements in MD NLP. We release the code at https://github.com/AzzedineAftiss/Moroccan-Dialect-Summarization.

## 1 Introduction

Moroccan Dialect (MD), commonly known as "Darija," is the primary spoken variety of Arabic in Morocco, coexisting with Berber in some regions. Approximately 91% of Moroccans communicate in Darija [Ridouane et al., 2014]. With the rise of digital resources, MD textual data available online is rapidly growing [Labied and Belangour, 2021], creating a need for effective automatic summarization to help users extract key information efficiently. While extensive work has focused on widely spoken languages, such as English, limited research exists on MD [Tachicart and Bouzoubaa, 2022], especially in sequence-to-sequence (Seq2Seq) tasks like summarization.

Challenges in MD research include a lack of comprehensive corpora, limited linguistic resources, complex syntax that challenges NLP models, and unique vocabulary not present in standard Arabic lexicons. Although existing datasets, such as **GOUD.MA** [Issam and Mrini, 2021], offer foundational resources, the evolving nature of the MD necessitates additional, robust datasets. Motivated by these challenges, we introduce ***GOOD.MA_v2***, an expanded version of the **GOUD.MA** dataset, containing over 50,000 articles with titles across 11 categories, aiming to enhance model robustness for MD data. Additionally, we explore LLMs for summarizing MD text, analyzing various Seq2Seq models in addition to evaluating recent causal LLMs in a zero-shot prompting setting, thus contributing valuable insights into their performance on MD.

The emergence of LLMs has led to remarkable NLP advancements [Chang et al., 2024]. However, adapting these models for low-resource languages, including the MD, remains underexplored. Recent efforts have attempted to adapt Arabic-specific models (e.g., ArBERT [Antoun et al., 2020], DarijaBERT [Gaanoun et al., 2024], DziriBERT [Abdaoui et al., 2021]) and multilingual models (e.g., mBART [Liu, 2020], mT5 [Xue, 2020]) for dialectal Arabic [Khered et al., 2023, Nagoudi et al., 2021b, Smadi and Abandah, 2024, Fuad and Al-Yahya, 2022]. More recent models, such as GPT-4 [Achiam et al., 2023] and Llama 3 [Dubey et al., 2024], offer advanced NLP capabilities but have not yet been adapted to the MD.

In this paper, we conduct an empirical study of LLMs on **GOUD.MA_v2** specifically curated for abstractive summarization. We demonstrate that expanding the dataset with additional samples improves summarization performance. Our approach includes fine-tuning encoder-decoder models and adapting recent LLMs for zero-shot prompting, pro-



*Proceedings of The 4th Workshop on Arabic Corpus Linguistics (WACL-4)*, pages 77–85
January 20th, 2025. 

viding comprehensive insights into the effectiveness of LLMs for MD text summarization. Our dataset, fine-tuned models, and all code used in our experiments are open-sourced.

The main contributions of this paper are as follows:

- We expand **GOUD.MA** to **GOOD.MA_v2**, comprising over 50,000 articles with their titles across 11 categories.

- We demonstrate that increasing the MD dataset improves model performance on summarization tasks in terms of ROUGE and BERTScore evaluation metrics.

- We empirically evaluate the effectiveness of various LLMs, including Seq2Seq and causal models, for MD summarization. To the best of our knowledge, this is the first study exploring the use of pre-trained language models for MD summarization.

The rest of this paper is organized as follows: Section 2 reviews related work on Arabic text summarization, with a focus on Arabic dialect summarization. Section 3 details the dataset collection process. Section 4 describes the experimental settings, while Section 5 presents the experimental results. Finally, Section 7 discusses the conclusions and limitations of this work.

## 2 Related Work

Arabic dialect processing has gained attention due to the linguistic diversity and widespread use of dialects in the Arabic-speaking world. Unlike Modern Standard Arabic (MSA), Arabic dialects, such as Moroccan Darija, exhibit unique lexical, syntactic, and phonological variations [ALFattah, 2024], presenting challenges for NLP tasks due to limited labeled data and resources. Early work in Arabic dialect NLP focused on tasks like classification [Maghfour and Elouardighi, 2018, Al-Walaie and Khan, 2017], identification [Elaraby and Abdul-Mageed, 2018, Zaidan and Callison-Burch, 2014, Salameh et al., 2018], and translation [Zbib et al., 2012, Harrat et al., 2019]. However, studies on dialectal summarization, particularly for MD, remain sparse. Issam and Mrini [2021] introduced one of the first MD summarization datasets, with articles paired with titles as reference summaries.

Arabic text summarization has advanced with methods like clustering, minimum redundancy–maximum relevance (mRMR), and graph-based approaches [Oufaida et al., 2014, Elbarougy et al., 2020]. Deep learning techniques, such as Seq2Seq architectures with LSTMs and attention mechanisms, have also been explored [Al-Maleh and Desouki, 2020]. Recent transformer-based models, such as AraBART [Eddine et al., 2022], AraT5 [Nagoudi et al., 2021a], and AraBERT [Antoun et al., 2020], pre-trained on large Arabic corpora, have shown strong performance in Arabic summarization tasks. Additionally, multilingual models like mBART [Liu, 2020] and mT5 [Xue, 2020], pre-trained on diverse language corpora, have demonstrated cross-lingual effectiveness, making them suitable for low-resource dialects, including Moroccan Darija. Recently, models like DarijaBERT [Gaanoun et al., 2024] and DziriBERT [Abdaoui et al., 2021] have been pre-trained on North African dialectal Arabic, specifically to address Moroccan and Algerian dialects. DarijaBERT, focused on Moroccan Darija, incorporates dialect-specific vocabulary, bridging the gap between MSA and regional dialects, thus enhancing contextual understanding compared to general Arabic models. The emergence of advanced LLMs, such as GPT-4o mini [Achiam et al., 2023], Llama 3 [Dubey et al., 2024], and Mistral NeMo [team, 2024] have brought attention to their capabilities in domain-specific tasks in zero-shot or few-shot settings. These models exhibit strong reasoning and text generation capabilities without fine-tuning task-specific data. However, applying them to dialectal summarization has limitations, as their training data generally lacks comprehensive coverage of specific dialects, such as Moroccan Darija. Fine-tuning remains essential to optimize performance for dialectal tasks. Our work builds upon these prior studies by applying and comparing Arabic-specific, multilingual, and causal LLMs for MD summarization using both zero-shot and fine-tuning methods. To our knowledge, this is the first work that evaluated LLMs for Moroccan Darija abstractive summarization, contributing valuable insights to NLP research for dialectal Arabic.

## 3 *GOOD.MA_v2*: A Newspaper Corpus for Moroccan Darija Summarization

### 3.1 Dataset Description

A primary challenge in NLP tasks for low-resource languages, such as Moroccan Darija, is the scarcity of high-quality datasets. To address this gap, Issam and Mrini [2021] recently introduced a benchmark dataset specifically for summarization, sourced from the GOUD.MA website[1].

GOUD.MA, a news website established by Ahmed Najim in 2011, is a primary source of Moroccan Darija text for summarization research. Articles on this platform are primarily in Arabic, with titles in Moroccan Darija and the body text in either Modern Standard Arabic (MSA) or a mix of MSA and Darija. The dataset is derived from GOUD.MA supports summarization tasks where the article text serves as input, and the title provides a concise target summary. Table 1 presents statistical details for the GOUD summarization datasets, including train, validation, and test splits.

Furthermore, the dataset covers various categories, such as الرئيسية (Main) and آش واقع (What's Happening), with each article assigned to a single category. This classification consists of a wide range of topics, from general news to specialized subjects like media, culture, and sports. Table 2 shows the distribution of articles across categories, including translations and article counts for each.

### 3.2 Data Collection

As previously mentioned, a major challenge in Moroccan Darija NLP tasks is the scarcity of large, annotated datasets. To address this, we expanded the **GOUD.MA** dataset by scraping additional articles and summaries from the GOUD.ma website. Expanding the dataset with additional text-summary pairs helps improve model performance by capturing a broader representation of linguistic patterns, expressions, and vocabulary unique to Moroccan Darija.

We utilized the Python libraries Scrapy[2] and Selenium[3] to automatically crawl the GOUD.ma website, collecting article titles, publication dates, content, and categories. This scraping process, conducted between 2022 and October 2024, took approximately four days and resulted in a total of 50,517 articles.

We cleaned and organized the collected data into CSV format for analysis, ensuring that each article entry includes metadata such as publication date, title, content, and category. Table 2 presents the distribution of articles across categories, while Table 1 provides statistics on article and title lengths. The expanded dataset aligns closely with previous datasets in terms of length distribution and is utilized to fine-tune models, enhancing performance on MD summarization tasks.

## 4 Experiment Settings

The main objectives of this study are twofold: (1) to expand the dataset to capture evolving dialectal variations and hence improve the performance of text summarization models, and (2) to evaluate the effectiveness of large language models in summarizing Moroccan Darija text. We conducted an empirical study to assess the performance of various LLMs, including pre-trained causal models and fine-tuned Seq2Seq models, on the ***GOOD.MA_v2*** dataset. In this section, we present the implementation details and a brief description of the models used for comparison.

### 4.1 Implementation Details

In this study, we applied three categories of models for MD text summarization: Arabic-specific models (AraBERT, DarijaBERT, DziriBERT, AraBART, and AraT5), a Multilingual Model (mBART), and causal large language models (GPT-4o mini, Llama 3, and Mistral NeMo). Following the approach of Rothe et al. [2020], which leverages pre-trained language models for abstractive summarization within a Seq2Seq framework, we fine-tuned DziriBERT, DarijaBERT, and AraBERT on our summarization dataset to capture linguistic nuances specific to Moroccan dialects, utilizing the strengths of encoder-based models. For AraT5, AraBART, and mBART, which already feature Seq2Seq architectures with both encoder and decoder components, we fine-tuned them directly for MD summarization. We used a merged dataset, combining the training set of **GOOD.MA** with the expanded **GOOD.MA_v2**, for training. For validation and testing, we used the original validation and test sets from **GOOD.MA**.

Each model was fine-tuned for 20 epochs with a batch size of 20, gradient accumulation set to 8,

[1] https://www.goud.ma/
[2] https://scrapy.org/
[3] https://selenium-python.readthedocs.io/

| Dataset Split | Number of Articles | Avg. tokens per article | Avg. tokens per title |
|---|---|---|---|
| Train (GOUD.MA) | 139,288 | 238.03 | 15.137 |
| Validation (GOUD.MA) | 9,497 | 238.54 | 15.14 |
| Test (GOUD.MA) | 9,497 | 238 | 15.20 |
| Train (GOUD.MA_v2) | 189,805 | 253.54 | 16.40 |

Table 1: Summary Statistics of the **GOUD.MA** and **GOUD.MA_v2** Dataset Splits. The "Number of Articles" column indicates the total count of articles in each split. The "Avg. tokens per article" represents the average number of tokens in the articles for each split. Finally, the "Avg. tokens per title" indicates the average number of tokens in the titles of the articles.

| Category | Category Translation | Goud.MA Dataset (Number of Articles) | Goud.MA_v2 Dataset (Total Number of Articles) |
|---|---|---|---|
| الرئيسية | Main | 104,724 | 132,392 |
| آش واقع | What's happening | 98,569 | 116,297 |
| تبركيك | Gossip | 16,867 | 17,827 |
| كود سبور | Goud Sport | 13,236 | 16,083 |
| آراء | Opinions | 8,239 | 8,585 |
| ميديا وثقافة | Media and Culture | 7,579 | 8,218 |
| كودتيفي | Goud TV | 6,966 | 7,043 |
| الزين والحداكة | Beauty and Sharpness | 5,223 | 5,297 |
| جورنالات بلادي | National Newspapers | 4,549 | 4,693 |
| راس السوق | Market head | 0 | 31 |
| كود | Goud | 1 | 4 |

Table 2: Distribution of Articles by Category. The "Category" column represents the name of the category, the "Category Translation" indicates the translation of the original category into English, the "**GOUD.MA** Dataset" column shows the number of articles from the old dataset, the "**GOUD.MA_v2** Dataset" column shows the number of articles from the expanded datasets.

weight decay of 0.01, and a learning rate of 2e-5. For text generation, we used beam search with a beam width of 5, a maximum input sequence length of 256, and a maximum target sequence length of 32. All models used in our study are available on Hugging Face [Wolf et al., 2020].

For the causal LLMs, we employed zero-shot prompting to adapt these models for MD summarization. Using the `unsloth`[4] library, which supports quantization techniques and parameter-efficient fine-tuning (PEFT) methods like Low-Rank Adaptation (LoRA), we optimized the LLMs to reduce computational resources and memory usage, facilitating deployment in resource-constrained environments. For GPT-4o mini, we used openAI API[5] to generate article summaries (titles). Figures 1, 2, and 3 illustrate the prompts used for the Llama 3, GPT-4 mini, and Mistral NeMo models, respectively.

```
You are a helpful AI assistant for generating a detailed title
that highlights the main ideas and topics of the article.
Please ensure the title is written in Arabic. Format the output
as follows:

### Text:
[Content of the Current Article]
### Title:
```

Figure 1: Prompt used for Llama 3 model.

### 4.2 Model Selection Criteria

As outlined earlier, the pre-trained models used in our study are grouped into three main categories: Arabic-specific models, multilingual mod-

[4]https://huggingface.co/unsloth

[5]https://platform.openai.com/

```
Generate a concise and coherent title in Arabic that highlights the main ideas and themes of the article.

### Text:
[Content of the Current Article]
### Title:
```

Figure 2: Prompt used for GPT-4o mini model.

```
Generate a title that accurately captures the main ideas and themes of the article.

### Text:
[Content of the Current Article]
### Title:
```

Figure 3: Prompt used for Mistral NeMo model.

els, and causal language models, which are briefly described below.

**Arabic-Specific Models:** These models are pre-trained on Modern Standard Arabic (MSA) and various Arabic dialects, making them well-suited for Moroccan Darija summarization. The Arabic-specific models used in this study include:

- **AraBERT** [Antoun et al., 2020]: A BERT-based transformer encoder pre-trained on large Arabic corpora, designed for masked language modeling across MSA and Arabic dialects.

- **DarijaBERT** [Gaanoun et al., 2024]: A BERT variant specifically pre-trained on Moroccan Darija, capturing its distinctive vocabulary and linguistic features.

- **DziriBERT** [Abdaoui et al., 2021]: A BERT-based model pre-trained on Algerian dialect, which shares linguistic similarities with Moroccan Darija, enhancing its relevance to this study.

- **AraBART** [Eddine et al., 2022]: An adaptation of the BART architecture, combining a bidirectional encoder and an autoregressive decoder, suited for sequence-to-sequence tasks like summarization.

- **AraT5** [Nagoudi et al., 2021a]: A variant of the text-to-text transformer (T5) pre-trained on MSA and various Arabic dialects, supporting a range of generative tasks.

**Multilingual Models:** Pre-trained on multiple languages, these models can handle diverse linguistic structures. We employed mBART [Liu, 2020], a Seq2Seq model pre-trained on numerous languages, including Arabic, using a denoising autoencoder to enhance performance across multilingual text generation tasks.

**Causal Language Models:** We evaluate three large language models — GPT-4o mini [Achiam et al., 2023], Llama 3 [Dubey et al., 2024], and Mistral NeMo [team, 2024]— in MD summarization using zero-shot prompting.

- **GPT-4o mini** [Achiam et al., 2023]: An autoregressive LLM with strong reasoning capabilities, supporting both text and vision inputs.

- **Llama 3** [Dubey et al., 2024]: A decoder-only transformer optimized for efficiency and robust across various language tasks.

- **Mistral NeMo** [team, 2024]: A LLM built on a transformer decoder architecture with a 128k-token context window, suitable for long-form summarization tasks.

## 5 Experimental Results

In this section, we present a comparative analysis of the pre-trained language models used on the ***GOOD.MA_v2*** dataset.

### 5.1 Evaluation Measures

To evaluate the quality of the generated summaries in this study, we used two automatic evaluation metrics: ROUGE [Lin, 2004] and BERTScore [Zhang et al., 2019]. ROUGE-1 measures the unigram overlap between the reference and generated summaries, while ROUGE-2 evaluates the bigram overlap. ROUGE-L calculates the longest common subsequence (LCS) between the reference and generated summaries, providing a measure of sequence similarity. BERTScore, on the other hand, measures similarity by comparing token pairs in the reference and generated summaries using contextual embeddings from the pre-trained BERT model.

## 6 Results

The results of our experiment are presented in Table 3 and Table 4. In Table 3, we report the performance of the BERT-based models (AraBERT, DarijaBERT, and DziriBERT), which we fine-tuned following the approach by Rothe et al.

[2020]. We adapted these models for sequence-to-sequence tasks within an encoder-decoder framework. We observe that fine-tuning the models on *GOOD.MA_v2* dataset improved their performance compared to previous results reported by Issam and Mrini [2021]. This improvement supports our hypothesis that a more diverse dataset enhances model generalization, enabling them to better handle the linguistic nuances of Moroccan Darija.

The other investigated models are reported in Table 4. Among the models, mBART achieved the highest performance, likely due to its Multilingual Denoising Pretraining on a large corpus covering 50 languages, which provides robust cross-lingual representations beneficial for Moroccan Darija summarization. AraBART and AraT5 also demonstrated competitive performance, leveraging their encoder-decoder architectures that were pre-trained end-to-end on Arabic text. This architecture effectively captures input context and generates abstract summaries, making it well-suited for MD summarization given the shared vocabulary between MSA and MD.

On the other hand, the extractive summarization baselines (Lead-2, TextRank, SumRank) and causal language models (GPT-4o mini, Llama 3, Mistral NeMo) achieved comparatively lower performance. The extractive baselines struggled to produce coherent summaries, as they simply concatenate sentences in an unsupervised manner, often leading to disconnected and inconsistent outputs. Similarly, causal LLMs like GPT-4o mini and Llama 3, which were employed using zero-shot prompting, did not perform as well as fine-tuned Arabic-specific and multilingual models. This is likely due to the lack of fine-tuning, which limits their adaptability to Moroccan Darija summarization tasks.

Moreover, relying exclusively on ROUGE and BERTScore metrics may not provide a comprehensive assessment of generative models. As noted by Nguyen et al. [2024], automatic evaluation metrics like ROUGE and BERTScore primarily measure n-gram overlap or embedding similarity, which may not fully capture the creative and contextually nuanced outputs generated by large language models (LLMs). For instance, LLMs like GPT-4o-mini and Llama 3 are capable of rephrasing summaries in ways that differ from the reference text but still convey the intended meaning. For the Mistral NeMo model, we observed difficulties in understanding Arabic texts and dialects, which led to hallucinations in the resulting summaries, Additionally, during the experiment, we found that Mistral NeMo sometimes generated the summary in French or Spanish. To mitigate this, we applied post-processing to translate these summaries into Arabic using the Google Translate API[6]. This translation step may have impacted Mistral's overall performance.

To illustrate the qualitative differences across models, we provide example summaries generated by each model alongside the reference summary in Table 5.

## 7 Conclusion

In this study, we conducted an empirical evaluation of various pre-trained language models for abstractive summarization of Moroccan Darija text, comparing the performance of Arabic-specific encoder-decoder models, multilingual models, and causal language models. Our findings demonstrate that the multilingual model mBART, which is pre-trained on a diverse set of languages, generally achieved superior performance compared to the other models. The zero-shot application of causal language models, including GPT-4o mini, Llama 3, and Mistral NeMo, showed potential; however, results indicated that fine-tuning would be necessary to achieve contextually accurate and fluent summaries in MD. Moreover, while automatic evaluation metrics like ROUGE and BERTScore provided useful quantitative insights, they may not fully reflect qualitative aspects such as readability, fluency, and consistency—attributes that are crucial in summarization tasks. Future research could further explore this area by fine-tuning causal language models for MD summarization and incorporating human evaluation to gain a more comprehensive understanding of summary quality.

## References


Amine Abdaoui, Mohamed Berrimi, Mourad Oussalah, and Abdelouahab Moussaoui. 2021. Dziribert: a pre-trained language model for the algerian dialect. *arXiv preprint arXiv:2109.12346*.

Josh Achiam, Steven Adler, Sandhini Agarwal, Lama Ahmad, Ilge Akkaya, Florencia Leoni Aleman, Diogo Almeida, Janko Altenschmidt, Sam Altman, Shyamal Anadkat, et al. 2023. Gpt-4 technical report. *arXiv preprint arXiv:2303.08774*.

Molham Al-Maleh and Said Desouki. 2020. Arabic


[6]https://github.com/ssut/py-googletrans

| Models | GOOD.MA | | | | GOOD.MA_v2 | | | |
|---|---|---|---|---|---|---|---|---|
| | R-1 | R-2 | R-L | BERTScore | R-1 | R-2 | R-L | BERTScore |
| AraBERT [Antoun et al., 2020] | 23.08 | 8.98 | 22.06 | - | 28.47 | 15.78 | 25.47 | 64.79 |
| DarijaBERT [Gaanoun et al., 2024] | 19.41 | 6.64 | 18.48 | - | 27.79 | 15.53 | 24.8 | 64.24 |
| DziriBERT [Abdaoui et al., 2021] | 17.98 | 5.83 | 17.22 | - | 24.16 | 12.42 | 21.89 | 63.11 |

Table 3: The performance result of the BERT-based models (AraBERT, DarijaBERT, and DziriBERT). The first set of results are from the models fine-tuned on the **GOOD.MA** dataset as reported by Issam and Mrini [2021], and the second set of results are from the models fine-tuned on the expanded **GOOD.MA_v2** dataset.

| Models | R-1 | R-2 | R-L | BERTScore |
|---|---|---|---|---|
| Lead-2 | 17.19 | 8.67 | 15.14 | 56.66 |
| TextRank | 12.96 | 5.027 | 10.49 | 53.54 |
| SumRank | 12.47 | 4.724 | 10.44 | 54.86 |
| AraBART [Eddine et al., 2022] | 31.51 | 19.24 | 28.98 | 66.21 |
| MBart [Liu, 2020] | **33.55** | **21.56** | **30.86** | **67.21** |
| AraT5 [Nagoudi et al., 2021a] | 32.63 | 20.15 | 29.97 | 66.48 |
| GPT-4o mini [Achiam et al., 2023] | 18.05 | 7.75 | 18.9 | 60.07 |
| Llama 3 [Dubey et al., 2024] | 16.59 | 7.17 | 14.44 | 58.52 |
| Mistral NeMo [team, 2024] | 7.06 | 2.11 | 6.40 | 54.31 |

Table 4: Performance of Compared Models on the Test Set of the **GOOD.MA** Dataset. Fine-tuned models were trained on the expanded **GOOD.MA_v2** dataset.


text summarization using deep learning approach. *Journal of Big Data*, 7(1):109.

Mona Abdullah Al-Walaie and Muhammad Badruddin Khan. 2017. Arabic dialects classification using text mining techniques. In *2017 International Conference on Computer and Applications (ICCA)*, pages 325–329. IEEE.

Mohammed ALFattah. 2024. Morpho-lexical analysis of tehami arabic dialect. *Social Science and Humanities Journal (SSHJ)*, 8(06):4036–4076.

Wissam Antoun, Fady Baly, and Hazem Hajj. 2020. Arabert: Transformer-based model for arabic language understanding. *arXiv preprint arXiv:2003.00104*.

Yupeng Chang, Xu Wang, Jindong Wang, Yuan Wu, Linyi Yang, Kaijie Zhu, Hao Chen, Xiaoyuan Yi, Cunxiang Wang, Yidong Wang, et al. 2024. A survey on evaluation of large language models. *ACM Transactions on Intelligent Systems and Technology*, 15(3):1–45.

Abhimanyu Dubey, Abhinav Jauhri, Abhinav Pandey, Abhishek Kadian, Ahmad Al-Dahle, Aiesha Letman, Akhil Mathur, Alan Schelten, Amy Yang, Angela Fan, et al. 2024. The llama 3 herd of models. *arXiv preprint arXiv:2407.21783*.

Moussa Kamal Eddine, Nadi Tomeh, Nizar Habash, Joseph Le Roux, and Michalis Vazirgiannis. 2022. Arabart: a pretrained arabic sequence-to-sequence model for abstractive summarization. *arXiv preprint arXiv:2203.10945*.

Mohamed Elaraby and Muhammad Abdul-Mageed. 2018. Deep models for arabic dialect identification on benchmarked data. In *Proceedings of the Fifth Workshop on NLP for Similar Languages, Varieties and Dialects (VarDial 2018)*, pages 263–274.

Reda Elbarougy, Gamal Behery, and Akram El Khatib. 2020. Extractive arabic text summarization using modified pagerank algorithm. *Egyptian informatics journal*, 21(2):73–81.

Ahlam Fuad and Maha Al-Yahya. 2022. Araconv: Developing an arabic task-oriented dialogue system using multi-lingual transformer model mt5. *Applied Sciences*, 12(4):1881.

Kamel Gaanoun, Abdou Mohamed Naira, Anass Allak, and Imade Benelallam. 2024. Darijabert: a step forward in nlp for the written moroccan dialect. *International Journal of Data Science and Analytics*, pages 1–13.

Salima Harrat, Karima Meftouh, and Kamel Smaili. 2019. Machine translation for arabic dialects (survey). *Information Processing & Management*, 56(2):262–273.

Abderrahmane Issam and Khalil Mrini. 2021. Goud.ma: a news article dataset for summarization in moroccan

| Model | Generated Summary |
|---|---|
| Reference Summary | بعد الجفاف.. القرض الفلاحي خصص قروض إضافية بقيمة 1,5 مليار درهم للفلاحة. |
| GPT-4o mini Summary | مجموعة القرض الفلاحي تدعم الفلاحة بتدابير جديدة لمواجهة جفاف الموسم. |
| Llama 3 Summary | اتخذات مجموعة القرض الفلاحي، من بعد ما تشاورات مع وزارة الفلاحة والصيد البحري والتنمية القروية والمياه والغابات، مجموعة من التدابير اللي كتستهدف التخفيف من آثار ضعف التساق |
| Mistral Summary | أصدروا 1.5 مليار درهم للتخفيف من تأثير إكويا. |
| MBart | القرض الفلاحي خصص كريديات للفلاحة بقيمة 1,5 مليار درهم. |
| AraT5 | القرض الفلاحي خصص غلاف مالي إضافي للقروض بقيمة 1,5 مليار درهم للتخفيف من آثار ضعف الشتا. |
| AraBART | القرض الفلاحي خصص 1,5 مليار درهم لإعادة جدولة مديونية الفلاحين. |
| AraBERT | القرض الفلاحي خصص 1 ,5 مليار درهم لكريدي الفلاحي لفائدة الفلاحين الصغار. |
| DarijaBERT | القرض الفلاحي خصص 2 ,5 مليار درهم للقروض الفلاحية بقيمة 1 ,5 مليون درهم |
| DziriBERT | القرض الفلاحي خصص مليار درهم لتمويل ازمة كورونا |

Table 5: The generated summaries of the models for a given article from the test set.


darija. In *3rd Workshop on African Natural Language Processing*.

Abdullah Khered, Ingy Abdelhalim, Nadine Abdelhalim, Ahmed Soliman, and Riza Theresa Batista-Navarro. 2023. Unimanc at nadi 2023 shared task: A comparison of various t5-based models for translating arabic dialectical text to modern standard arabic. In *Proceedings of ArabicNLP 2023*, pages 658–664.

Maria Labied and Abdessamad Belangour. 2021. Moroccan dialect "darija" automatic speech recognition: a survey. In *2021 IEEE 2nd International Conference on Pattern Recognition and Machine Learning (PRML)*, pages 208–213. IEEE.

Chin-Yew Lin. 2004. Rouge: A package for automatic evaluation of summaries. In *Text summarization branches out*, pages 74–81.

Y Liu. 2020. Multilingual denoising pre-training for neural machine translation. *arXiv preprint arXiv:2001.08210*.

Mohcine Maghfour and Abdeljalil Elouardighi. 2018. Standard and dialectal arabic text classification for sentiment analysis. In *Model and Data Engineering: 8th International Conference, MEDI 2018, Marrakesh, Morocco, October 24–26, 2018, Proceedings 8*, pages 282–291. Springer.

El Moatez Billah Nagoudi, AbdelRahim Elmadany, and Muhammad Abdul-Mageed. 2021a. Arat5: Text-to-text transformers for arabic language generation. *arXiv preprint arXiv:2109.12068*.

El Moatez Billah Nagoudi, AbdelRahim Elmadany, and Muhammad Abdul-Mageed. 2021b. Investigating code-mixed modern standard arabic-egyptian to english machine translation. *arXiv preprint arXiv:2105.13573*.

Huyen Nguyen, Haihua Chen, Lavanya Pobbathi, and Junhua Ding. 2024. A comparative study of quality evaluation methods for text summarization. *arXiv preprint arXiv:2407.00747*.

Houda Oufaida, Omar Nouali, and Philippe Blache. 2014. Minimum redundancy and maximum relevance for single and multi-document arabic text summarization. *Journal of King Saud University-Computer and Information Sciences*, 26(4):450–461.

Tachicart Ridouane, Bouzoubaa Karim, and Jaafar Hamid. 2014. Building a moroccan dialect electronic dictionary (mded). In *5th International Conference on Arabic Language Processing*.

Sascha Rothe, Shashi Narayan, and Aliaksei Severyn. 2020. Leveraging pre-trained checkpoints for sequence generation tasks. *Transactions of the Association for Computational Linguistics*, 8:264–280.

Mohammad Salameh, Houda Bouamor, and Nizar Habash. 2018. Fine-grained arabic dialect identification. In *Proceedings of the 27th international conference on computational linguistics*, pages 1332–1344.

Malak Smadi and Gheith Abandah. 2024. Correcting auditory spelling mistakes in jordanian dialect using machine learning techniques. In *2024 15th International Conference on Information and Communication Systems (ICICS)*, pages 1–6. IEEE.

Ridouane Tachicart and Karim Bouzoubaa. 2022. Moroccan arabic vocabulary generation using a rule-based approach. *Journal of King Saud University-Computer and Information Sciences*, 34(10):8538–8548.

Mistral AI team. 2024. Mistral nemo. Accessed: November 2024.

Thomas Wolf, Lysandre Debut, Victor Sanh, Julien Chaumond, Clement Delangue, Anthony Moi, Pierric Cistac, Tim Rault, Rémi Louf, Morgan Funtowicz, et al. 2020. Transformers: State-of-the-art natural language processing. In *Proceedings of the 2020 conference on empirical methods in natural language processing: system demonstrations*, pages 38–45.

L Xue. 2020. mt5: A massively multilingual pre-trained text-to-text transformer. *arXiv preprint arXiv:2010.11934*.

Omar F Zaidan and Chris Callison-Burch. 2014. Arabic dialect identification. *Computational Linguistics*, 40(1):171–202.

Rabih Zbib, Erika Malchiodi, Jacob Devlin, David Stallard, Spyros Matsoukas, Richard Schwartz, John Makhoul, Omar Zaidan, and Chris Callison-Burch. 2012. Machine translation of arabic dialects. In *Proceedings of the 2012 conference of the north american chapter of the association for computational linguistics: Human language technologies*, pages 49–59.

Tianyi Zhang, Varsha Kishore, Felix Wu, Kilian Q Weinberger, and Yoav Artzi. 2019. Bertscore: Evaluating text generation with bert. *arXiv preprint arXiv:1904.09675*.

# *Dialect2SQL*: A Novel Text-to-SQL Dataset for Arabic Dialects with a Focus on Moroccan Darija

**Salmane Chafik**
Mohammed VI Polytechnic University
Ben Guerir, Morocco
chafik.salmane@um6p.ma

**Saad Ezzini**
Lancaster University
Lancaster, England
s.ezzini@lancaster.ac.uk

**Ismail Berrada**
Mohammed VI Polytechnic University
Ben Guerir, Morocco
ismail.berrada@um6p.ma

## Abstract

The task of converting natural language questions (NLQs) into executable SQL queries, known as text-to-SQL, has gained significant interest in recent years, as it enables non-technical users to interact with relational databases. Many benchmarks, such as SPIDER and WikiSQL, have contributed to the development of new models and the evaluation of their performance. In addition, other datasets, like SEDE and BIRD, have introduced more challenges and complexities to better map real-world scenarios. However, these datasets primarily focus on high-resource languages such as English and Chinese. In this work, we introduce *Dialect2SQL*, the first large-scale, cross-domain text-to-SQL dataset in an Arabic dialect. It consists of 9,428 NLQ-SQL pairs across 69 databases in various domains. Along with SQL-related challenges such as long schemas, dirty values, and complex queries, our dataset also incorporates the complexities of the Moroccan dialect, which is known for its diverse source languages, numerous borrowed words, and unique expressions. This demonstrates that our dataset will be a valuable contribution to both the text-to-SQL community and the development of resources for low-resource languages.

**Keywords** : Text-to-SQL, Low Resource Language, Moroccan Dialect

## 1 Introduction

SQL or Structured Query Language is a powerful, standardized programming language used by developers to interact with relational databases. It provides a framework for defining, manipulating, and querying data stored in a structured format, typically organized into tables. It is essential for managing the creation, retrieval, update, and deletion of data, commonly referred to as CRUD operations (Create, Read, Update, Delete). SQL is commonly used in various applications, from small systems to large-scale enterprise platforms, and is integral to desktop, web, and mobile applications alike. Mastery of SQL remains a foundational skill for software engineers and professionals working with databases and data management.

Implementing SQL queries has become significantly easier and simpler with the introduction of text-to-SQL models, which can convert natural language questions (NLQs) into executable and efficient SQL queries (Qin et al., 2022). The availability of various datasets and benchmarks, such as (Yu et al., 2019; Zhong et al., 2017), has facilitated the training, fine-tuning, and evaluation of code-based Large Language Models (LLMs) for the text-to-SQL task.

The development of such datasets and models was driven by the significant demand for text-to-SQL chatbots and integrated applications, which provide an environment for generating and executing SQL queries. These tools allow non-technical users, who may not be familiar with SQL, to interact with a deployed relational database using everyday language. Such applications have immense potential across industries that store data in structured formats and make it accessible to users via web or mobile applications. For example, in the healthcare sector, text-to-SQL integrated applications can enable doctors and other medical professionals to easily query patient records or retrieve statistics by simply asking questions like, 'How many patients had advanced-stage cancer in 2025 and survived?', all without needing SQL knowledge. This capability not only saves time but also provides crucial data insights that can inform patient care and treatment planning. Similarly, in the finance sector, a financial analyst could ask, 'What was the revenue growth for each quarter this year?' and retrieve relevant data directly from a financial database. This simplifies data analysis and allows analysts to focus on interpretation rather than query



*Proceedings of The 4th Workshop on Arabic Corpus Linguistics (WACL-4)*, pages 86–92
January 20th, 2025. 

composition.

However, previous work has primarily focused on high-resource languages, such as English and Chinese, often by translating English versions of these datasets. While translation models have significantly improved for high-resource languages, creating text-to-SQL datasets for low-resource languages or dialects remains challenging. This difficulty stems from the need for skilled software engineers who not only fully understand SQL syntax but also have a strong command of English, as most existing resources and dataset examples are in English. Additionally, cultural and linguistic differences can affect how questions are phrased, making it difficult to adapt high-resource or even multilingual text-to-SQL models to these languages and dialects.

To address these challenges, we introduce what we believe to be the first text-to-SQL dataset specifically developed for an Arabic dialect, named *Dialect2SQL*. This dataset is tailored to the Moroccan dialect, also known as Darija, which is known by its linguistic complexity. Moroccan Darija is a unique mix, incorporating vocabulary and grammatical structures from a diverse range of source languages, including Arabic, Berber, French, and Spanish. It features numerous borrowed words and distinctive expressions that set it apart from Modern Standard Arabic and other Arabic dialects, making it particularly challenging for natural language processing tasks. We believe that *Dialect2SQL* will play a significant role in advancing text-to-SQL capabilities for low-resource languages.

The paper is structured as follows. Section 2 presents a review of related work, while Section 3 provides a detailed explanation of each step involved in the construction of *Dialect2SQL*. We finish concluding the paper and suggesting potential directions for future research.

## 2 Related Work

In recent years, there has been significant progress in the field of text-to-SQL. Various studies (Qin et al., 2022; Gao et al., 2023) focused on improving the accuracy and efficiency of converting natural language questions into SQL queries, and others focused on addressing the critical needs of datasets and benchmarks.

Zhong et al. (Zhong et al., 2017) introduced the first large-scale cross-domain text-to-SQL dataset WikiSQL, composed of 80,654 examples distributed across 24,241 tables from Wikipedia in different domains. However this dataset was judged of simplicity, each question concerns only one simple table. To address this problem, 11 students from Yale University manually annotated a text-to-SQL dataset named SPIDER (Yu et al., 2019). This dataset comes with more complex queries joining multiple tables and spanning different domains and databases. However, both datasets were judged non-realistic because of the way they were created, simple database schemas, and simple questions.

To address this issue, hazoom et al. (Hazoom et al., 2021) introduced SEDE, a text-to-SQL dataset dedicated solely for training and evaluation, composed of 12,023 NLQ-SQL pairs collected from real usage on the Stack Exchange website, including a variety of real-world challenges rarely reflected in previous works. In the same context, Li et al. (Li et al., 2023) constructed another benchmark named BIRD containing 12,751 pairs, 95 databases, and spanning over 37 professional domains. This benchmark comes with more challenges to immitate real-world situation by providing long sequence schemas, One database may include up to 60 tables, and dirty values.

While these studies focused on English datasets, other works have explored datasets in additional languages. For example, Dou et al. (Dou et al., 2022) manually translated the SPIDER dataset into multiple languages, including English, German, French, Spanish, Japanese, Chinese, and Vietnamese. They conducted various experiments using multilingual models in each language to assess the impact of training large language models on the same dataset across different languages simultaneously. Additionally, they introduced a framework called SAVE (Schema Augmentation with Verification) to help close the performance gap between models trained on the English dataset and those trained on other languages.

On the other hand, Bakshandaeva et al. (Bakshandaeva et al., 2022) introduced PAUQ, the first Russian text-to-SQL dataset, which they developed based on the SPIDER dataset. They trained two baseline models, RAT-SQL (Wang et al., 2019) and BRIDGE (Lin et al., 2020), on PAUQ to assess the trade-offs between using automatically translated and manually crafted natural language questions. Their analysis highlights the strengths and limitations of each approach, offering insights into how translation quality affects model performance in multilingual text-to-SQL tasks.

Similarly, Almohaimeed et al. (Almohaimeed et al., 2024) introduced an Arabic version of the SPIDER dataset, naming it Ar-SPIDER. To explore the linguistic challenges specific to Arabic, the authors fine-tuned two base models, LGESQL (Cao et al., 2021) and S2SQL (Hui et al., 2022), using two different multilingual encoders: mBERT (Pires, 2019) and XLM-R (Conneau, 2019). Additionally, they proposed a Context Similarity Relationship (CSR) approach, which led to a significant increase in overall performance, helping to close the gap between Arabic and English language models.

Other datasets have been created from scratch to support cross-database context-dependent Text-to-SQL (XDTS) tasks. For instance, the CHASE dataset (Guo et al., 2021) includes 17,940 questions in Chinese designed specifically for XDTS. CHASE enables models to handle complex, multi-turn questions across different databases, facilitating research into both cross-database adaptability and contextual dependency in query generation. Likewise, the SeSQL dataset (Huang et al., 2022) comprises 27,012 question-SQL pairs, also in Chinese. SeSQL further enriches the resources available for training and evaluating models on XDTS tasks by providing a wide array of question types and database contexts.

Motivated by these works, our paper introduces a large-scale, cross-domain text-to-SQL dataset in the Moroccan dialect, based on the well-known BIRD dataset (Li et al., 2023).

## 3 Approach

This section explains the choice of dataset, the translation process, and presents key statistics for *Dialect2SQL*.

### 3.1 Dataset

The BIRD dataset, formally known as the BIg Bench for laRge-scale Database Grounded Text-to-SQL Evaluation (Li et al., 2023), represents one of the latest and most comprehensive resources for evaluating text-to-SQL systems. Released at the end of 2023, BIRD is designed to test the capabilities of models in generating SQL queries from natural language questions across a diverse set of domains and databases. It contains 12,751 unique question-SQL pairs, which span across 95 extensive databases in 37 distinct domains.

We chose BIRD because of the unique challenges it introduces. This dataset includes long schemas, with some databases containing up to 60 tables. It also incorporates dirty values, where natural language questions may include incomplete or abbreviated values. In such cases, the model must infer the correct values using external knowledge, a new aspect introduced by this dataset. Additionally, BIRD features complex queries that may join up to six tables in a single query and utilize various functions not seen in previous datasets.

### 3.2 Dataset Translation

To achieve an efficient translation, we use GPT-4 to translate BIRD questions of the train set into Moroccan Darija. We then ask three computer science students, one PhD student and two master's students, who are native speakers of Moroccan Darija and proficient in SQL, to edit these questions according to the following guidelines:

- The English question is translated into Darija using Arabic letters.
- Values such as names, surnames, countries, cities, company names, and movie titles remain in English.
- Numbers are written using the Hindu-Arabic numeral system, or Western Arabic numerals (1, 2, 3) rather than Eastern Arabic numerals (١، ٢، ٣).
- The context for this SQL task, which includes table-creation statements (e.g., `CREATE TABLE ...`), is not translated.

The first guideline was established because many Moroccans use Latin characters to write in Darija. To avoid confusion, we implemented this guideline. The second guideline was created because personal or company names can be written in various ways using Arabic letters. For example, the name "Wolfgang Reitherman" can be written in different forms, as shown in Table 1. The back translation to English might change a letter or two, which can lead to different results in an SQL query. The final guideline was established because the context is an SQL query that creates database tables including columns and their types, that's why it should remain in SQL (English).

A final iteration was conducted by the same PhD student to ensure the quality of the translation and adherence to the established guidelines across the entire dataset.

***Dialect2SQL*** includes four main features: **db_id**, representing the database identifier; **question**, representing the English question; **darija_question**, representing the translated question into Moroccan Darija; **SQL**, the related SQL query; and **schema**, the database schema, which includes the SQL queries for the creation of all the tables in the related database. An example is displayed in Listing 1.

### 3.3 Translation Error

To illustrate the difference between the automatic and the manual translation, we computed several metrics on automatically translated questions by comparing them to manually translated ones as references. Table 2 presents four main metrics.

- ***CER*** (Character Error Rate), measures the percentage of characters that are incorrect in the translation. Calculated as the number of character insertions, deletions, and substitutions required to convert the translation to the reference, divided by the total number of characters in the reference.

$$\text{CER} = \frac{S+D+I}{N} = \frac{S+D+I}{S+D+C}$$

  Where S is the number of substitutions, D is the number of deletions, I is the number of insertions, C is the number of correct characters, N is the number of characters in the reference (N=S+D+C).

- ***WER*** (Word Error Rate), which is similar to CER, but operates in a word level.

- ***TER*** (Translation Edit Rate), measures the number of edits (insertions, deletions, substitutions, and shifts) needed to match the translated text with the reference. It's also normalized by the length of the reference.

- ***CharacTER*** (Character Translation Edit Rate), is a variant of TER that operates at the character level.

| English name | Arabic name |
|---|---|
| Wolfgang Reitherman | وولفغانغ رايثيرمان ، وولفغانغ ريثيرمان ، وولفغانغ ريثرمان<br>ولفغانغ ريتيرمان ، وولفغاند رايثيرمان ، وولفغانغ ريثيرمن<br>وولفغانغ ريتيرمن ، ولفغنغ ريثيرمان ، وولفغانغ رايثرمان<br>وولفغنغ رايترمان ، وولفغانغ ريتيرمان ، ولفغانغ ريثيرمان |

Table 1: Different ways to write "Wolfgang Reitherman" in Darija

```
                Example

schema :
    CREATE TABLE client (
        client_id   TEXT    primary key,
        sex         TEXT,
        day         INTEGER,
        address_1   TEXT,
        address_2   TEXT,
        district_id TEXT,
            . . .
        foreign key (district_id)
            references district(district_id)
    );
            . . .

    CREATE TABLE events (
        Date received       DATE,
        Product             TEXT,
        Timely_response     TEXT,
        Consumer_disputed   TEXT,
        Client_ID           TEXT,
            . . .
        foreign key (Client_ID)
            references client(client_id)
    );
            . . .

question :
    What is the full address of the customers
    who, having received a timely response
    from the company, have dispute about that
    response?

darija_question :
    شنو هو العنوان الكامل ديال الكليان اللي، بعد ما وصلهوم
    الجواب فالوقت من الشركة، ماعجبهمش داك الجواب؟

SQL :
    SELECT
      T1.address_1,
      T1.address_2
    FROM
      client AS T1
      INNER JOIN events AS T2 ON
      T1.client_id = T2.Client_ID
    WHERE
      T2.Timely_response = "Yes"
      AND T2.Consumer_disputed = "Yes";
```

Listing 1: One example of DARIJA_BIRD

| Metric | CER | WER | TER | CharacTER |
|---|---|---|---|---|
| AVG | 0.170 | 0.234 | 0.233 | 0.168 |

Table 2: Average error rates across the translated dataset: Character Error Rate (CER), Word Error Rate (WER), Translation Edit Rate (TER), and Character Translation Edit Rate (CharacTER)

The results show that, on average, 17% of the characters in the automatically translated questions are incorrect when compared to the manually translated questions. Also, 23.40% of the words in the automatically translated questions are inaccurate compared to the manual translations. Finally, the TER score illustrates that 23.30% is the proportion of changes needed.

These metrics were computed using HuggingFace library ***Evaluate*** [1]

### 3.4 Statistics

As illustrated in Table 3, *Dialect2SQL*, which is the translated training set of BIRD, consists of 9,428 NLQ-SQL pairs spanning 69 different databases covering diverse domains, such as food, books, education, transport, crime, and more. On average, there are 137 examples per database, though some databases contain only a few dozen examples, while others contain several hundred. Similarly, the number of tables per database varies from 2 to 60, with an average of 8 tables per database. The average number of tables per database in BIRD is 7.30 due to the low complexity of the test set.

### 3.5 Baselines

Large Language Models (LLMs) have rapidely emerged as the best solution for the text-to-SQL task. They have outperformed previous solutions such as rule-based, or sketch-based methods, and traditional machine learning models, by better understanding the questions and their related schemas.

Table 4 illustrates the performance of three famous families of LLMs dedicated for code generation, StarCoder2 (Lozhkov et al., 2024), Code llama (Roziere et al., 2023), CodeT5 (Wang et al., 2021), on a subset of *Dialect2SQL* composed of 697 random questions in the Moroccan dialect.

In this evaluation, we computed three main metrics, which are defined below.

- ***BLEU*** (Bilingual Evaluation Understudy), used to evaluate the quality of a generated SQL query compared to one or more reference SQL queries. It compares the n-grams (sequences of n tokens or words) in the generated query to those in the reference queries.
- ***SQAM*** (SQL Query Analysis Metric), which divides the predicted and true queries into several clauses (SELECT, FROM, WHERE, etc.) and compares the content of each clause individually, with importance weights assigned to each clause based on its relevance.
- ***TSED*** (Tree Similarity of Editing Distance), a metric that converts both the predicted and true queries into abstract syntax trees (ASTs) and calculates the editing distance between them to capture their structural similarity.

These metrics ranges from 0 to 1, where a higher score indicates higher quality and greater similarity between the queries.

As shown in Table 4, the 7-billion-parameter variant of StarCoder2 outperforms the 7-billion-parameter variant of CodeLlama, as well as the smaller models: the 3-billion-parameter variant of StarCoder2 and the 2-billion-parameter variant of CodeT5. This demonstrates that StarCoder2, particularly in its 7-billion-parameter configuration, offers superior performance in this task compared to both similar-sized and smaller alternatives in the domain of code generation and comprehension.

## 4 Conclusion & Future Work

In this paper, we introduce a novel large-scale, cross-domain text-to-SQL dataset in the Moroccan dialect (Darija), named *Dialect2SQL*. This dataset is manually translated from the English version of BIRD, which is known for its complexity, variety, and the new challenges it introduces in mapping real-world scenarios. To ensure the quality of the dataset, we first perform an initial automatic translation using GPT-4, followed by manual editing of the automatically translated questions by three computer science students who are native speakers of Darija and proficient in SQL. This two-step process, automatic translation followed by detailed manual revision, ensures both linguistic accuracy and alignment with the technical requirements of SQL, thereby enhancing the quality and usability of the dataset.

[1] https://huggingface.co/evaluate-metric

| Database | N° examples | N° databases | N° examples / db | N° tables / db |
|---|---|---|---|---|
| BIRD | 12 751 | 95 | 134 | 7.30 |
| *Dialect2SQL* | 9 428 | 69 | 137 | 8.00 |

Table 3: *Dialect2SQL* compared to BIRD statistics

| Model | BLEU | SQAM | TSED |
|---|---|---|---|
| **Starcoder2-7b** | **0.171** | **0.403** | **0.224** |
| Codellama-7b | 0.095 | 0.323 | 0.135 |
| Starcoder2-3b | 0.086 | 0.335 | 0.031 |
| CodeT5-2b | 0.023 | 0.232 | 0.056 |

Table 4: Code based Large Language Models performance on a subset of *Dialect2SQL*

While the creation of the first text-to-SQL dataset in an Arabic dialect marks a significant step forward, our journey to improve the performance of text-to-SQL models for Arabic dialects is just beginning. First, we aim to use this dataset to develop a model capable of understanding Darija and performing effectively in the text-to-SQL task. Second, we plan to expand the dataset to include other Arabic dialects, allowing the model to cover a broader range of dialects across the Arabic-speaking world. Finally, we may leverage this dataset to create a translation model capable of translating effectively in both directions, English to Darija and Darija to English, further supporting cross-linguistic applications and bridging the gap between Darija and English-language resources.

## References


Saleh Almohaimeed, Saad Almohaimeed, Mansour Al Ghanim, and Liqiang Wang. 2024. Ar-spider: Text-to-sql in arabic. In *Proceedings of the 39th ACM/SIGAPP Symposium on Applied Computing*, page 1024–1030. ArXiv:2402.15012 [cs].

Daria Bakshandaeva, Oleg Somov, Ekaterina Dmitrieva, Vera Davydova, and Elena Tutubalina. 2022. Pauq: Text-to-sql in russian. In *Findings of the Association for Computational Linguistics: EMNLP 2022*, page 2355–2376, Abu Dhabi, United Arab Emirates. Association for Computational Linguistics.

Ruisheng Cao, Lu Chen, Zhi Chen, Yanbin Zhao, Su Zhu, and Kai Yu. 2021. Lgesql: line graph enhanced text-to-sql model with mixed local and non-local relations. *arXiv preprint arXiv:2106.01093*.

A Conneau. 2019. Unsupervised cross-lingual representation learning at scale. *arXiv preprint arXiv:1911.02116*.

Longxu Dou, Yan Gao, Mingyang Pan, Dingzirui Wang, Wanxiang Che, Dechen Zhan, and Jian-Guang Lou. 2022. Multispider: Towards benchmarking multilingual text-to-sql semantic parsing. (arXiv:2212.13492). ArXiv:2212.13492 [cs].

Dawei Gao, Haibin Wang, Yaliang Li, Xiuyu Sun, Yichen Qian, Bolin Ding, and Jingren Zhou. 2023. Text-to-sql empowered by large language models: A benchmark evaluation. (arXiv:2308.15363).

Jiaqi Guo, Ziliang Si, Yu Wang, Qian Liu, Ming Fan, Jian-Guang Lou, Zijiang Yang, and Ting Liu. 2021. Chase: A large-scale and pragmatic chinese dataset for cross-database context-dependent text-to-sql. In *Proceedings of the 59th Annual Meeting of the Association for Computational Linguistics and the 11th International Joint Conference on Natural Language Processing (Volume 1: Long Papers)*, page 2316–2331, Online. Association for Computational Linguistics.

Moshe Hazoom, Vibhor Malik, and Ben Bogin. 2021. Text-to-sql in the wild: A naturally-occurring dataset based on stack exchange data. (arXiv:2106.05006). ArXiv:2106.05006.

Saihao Huang, Lijie Wang, Zhenghua Li, Zeyang Liu, Chenhui Dou, Fukang Yan, Xinyan Xiao, Hua Wu, and Min Zhang. 2022. Sesql: Yet another large-scale session-level chinese text-to-sql dataset. (arXiv:2208.12711). ArXiv:2208.12711 [cs].

Binyuan Hui, Ruiying Geng, Lihan Wang, Bowen Qin, Bowen Li, Jian Sun, and Yongbin Li. 2022. S2sql: Injecting syntax to question-schema interaction graph encoder for text-to-sql parsers. *arXiv preprint arXiv:2203.06958*.

Jinyang Li, Binyuan Hui, Ge Qu, Jiaxi Yang, Binhua Li, Bowen Li, Bailin Wang, Bowen Qin, Rongyu Cao, Ruiying Geng, Nan Huo, Xuanhe Zhou, Chenhao Ma, Guoliang Li, Kevin C. C. Chang, Fei Huang, Reynold Cheng, and Yongbin Li. 2023. Can llm already serve as a database interface? a big bench for large-scale database grounded text-to-sqls. (arXiv:2305.03111). ArXiv:2305.03111.

Xi Victoria Lin, Richard Socher, and Caiming Xiong. 2020. Bridging textual and tabular data for cross-domain text-to-sql semantic parsing. *arXiv preprint arXiv:2012.12627*.

Anton Lozhkov, Raymond Li, Loubna Ben Allal, Federico Cassano, Joel Lamy-Poirier, Nouamane Tazi, Ao Tang, Dmytro Pykhtar, Jiawei Liu, Yuxiang Wei, et al. 2024. Starcoder 2 and the stack v2: The next generation. *arXiv preprint arXiv:2402.19173*.

T Pires. 2019. How multilingual is multilingual bert. *arXiv preprint arXiv:1906.01502*.

Bowen Qin, Binyuan Hui, Lihan Wang, Min Yang, Jinyang Li, Binhua Li, Ruiying Geng, Rongyu Cao, Jian Sun, Luo Si, Fei Huang, and Yongbin Li. 2022. A survey on text-to-sql parsing: Concepts, methods, and future directions. (arXiv:2208.13629). ArXiv:2208.13629 [cs].

Baptiste Roziere, Jonas Gehring, Fabian Gloeckle, Sten Sootla, Itai Gat, Xiaoqing Ellen Tan, Yossi Adi, Jingyu Liu, Romain Sauvestre, Tal Remez, et al. 2023. Code llama: Open foundation models for code. *arXiv preprint arXiv:2308.12950*.

Bailin Wang, Richard Shin, Xiaodong Liu, Oleksandr Polozov, and Matthew Richardson. 2019. Rat-sql: Relation-aware schema encoding and linking for text-to-sql parsers. *arXiv preprint arXiv:1911.04942*.

Yue Wang, Weishi Wang, Shafiq Joty, and Steven CH Hoi. 2021. Codet5: Identifier-aware unified pre-trained encoder-decoder models for code understanding and generation. *arXiv preprint arXiv:2109.00859*.

Tao Yu, Rui Zhang, Kai Yang, Michihiro Yasunaga, Dongxu Wang, Zifan Li, James Ma, Irene Li, Qingning Yao, Shanelle Roman, Zilin Zhang, and Dragomir Radev. 2019. Spider: A large-scale human-labeled dataset for complex and cross-domain semantic parsing and text-to-sql task. (arXiv:1809.08887). ArXiv:1809.08887.

Victor Zhong, Caiming Xiong, and Richard Socher. 2017. Seq2sql: Generating structured queries from natural language using reinforcement learning. (arXiv:1709.00103). ArXiv:1709.00103.

# AraSim: Optimizing Arabic Dialect Translation in Children and Literature with LLMs and Similarity Scores


**Alaa Bouomar**
University of Leeds
Woodhouse, Leeds LS2 9JT,
UK
od21ahb@leeds.ac.uk

**Noorhan Abbas**
University of Leeds
Woodhouse, Leeds LS2 9JT,
UK
n.h.abbas@leeds.ac.uk



## Abstract

The aim of this study is to apply advanced neural machine translation (NMT) models to translate children's stories from Modern Standard Arabic (MSA) to the Egyptian (Cairo) dialect, addressing the significant linguistic gap faced by young Arabic speakers. It utilizes state-of-the-art transformer-based models, including Claude [1]for initial translation and a fine-tuned AraT5 for back-translation and evaluation, with the aim of improving the accessibility and enjoyment of children's literature for young Egyptian readers. We assess translation quality using semantic similarity and BLEU scores. The basic AraT5 model achieved an average semantic similarity score of 0.94. Through fine-tuning on an Egyptian (Cairo) dialect-specific dataset, we enhanced these metrics, with the fine-tuned model achieving an average semantic similarity score of 0.97, representing an improvement of 3 percent. Our research has produced a high-quality parallel corpus of 130 stories, a valuable resource for future research in Arabic dialect translation. This work contributes to bridging the linguistic gap for the Arabic language between MSA and regional dialects, offering critical insights and practical solutions to enhance the educational and cultural experiences for the young Arabic speakers. The findings demonstrate significant improvements in translation accuracy and quality.



**Keywords:** Neural Machine Dialect Translation, Modern Standard Arabic, Egyptian Arabic Dialect, Children's Literature, Transformer Models, AraT5, Claude, Arabic NLP


## 1 Introduction

Modern Standard Arabic (MSA) serves as the formal and standardized form of Arabic used in written texts and formal communication across the Arab world (Obeid et al., 2020). Despite its widespread use, MSA differs markedly from the various regional dialects spoken in daily life, such as Egyptian, Gulf, Levantine, and Maghrebi Arabic (Qwaider et al., 2018). These dialects, being more prevalent in everyday conversations, informal settings, and local media, present a significant linguistic challenge for young Arabic speakers who are primarily exposed to their native dialects at home and in their communities. For children, this linguistic discrepancy could be a challenge. MSA's complex grammatical structures, extensive vocabulary, and formal style can be tough for young learners accustomed to the dialects spoken at home. This gap can affect their comprehension and enjoyment of texts written in MSA, thereby impacting their educational and cultural experiences (Al-Sulaiti et al., 2016). Addressing it is crucial for enhancing the accessibility and engagement of children's literature among young Arabic readers. This paper explores the application of advanced neural machine translation (NMT) models to bridge the linguistic gap between MSA and the Egyptian (Cairo) dialect, focusing specifically on children's literature. By employing state-of-the-art transformer-based models, including Claude for initial translation and a fine-tuned AraT5 for back-translation and evaluation, this research aims to produce high-quality translations that make children's stories more relatable and enjoyable for young Egyptian readers. The evaluation of translation quality through semantic similarity and BLEU scores further contributes to refining the models and enhancing their performance. Through this work, a high-quality parallel corpus of 130 children's stories will be developed, providing a valuable resource for future research in Arabic dialect translation. By making children's literature more accessible in the Egyptian dialect, this research not only bridge a critical linguistic divide but also enriches the educational and cultural experiences of young readers. This study offers significant insights in the field of Ara-

[1] https://claude.ai




*Proceedings of The 4th Workshop on Arabic Corpus Linguistics (WACL-4)*, pages 93–102
January 20th, 2025.

bic dialect translation and sets the stage for further exploration and innovation in this area.

## 2 Background Research

Translating between Modern Standard Arabic (MSA) and regional dialects poses significant challenges due to linguistic variations and limited annotated corpora (Bouamor et al., 2018; Al-Sulaiti et al., 2016). Various approaches have been employed, including rule-based methods, statistical machine translation (SMT), and neural machine translation (NMT) (Obeid et al., 2020; Qwaider et al., 2018). While rule-based and SMT methods have provided foundational insights, they have limitations in capturing dialectal nuances. NMT, particularly transformer models like AraT5 (Obeid et al., 2020), has emerged as a promising approach due to its ability to handle long-range dependencies and complex linguistic structures.

### 2.1 LLMs for Arabic Dialects

Large Language Models (LLMs) like GPT-4 and Bard show varying proficiency with Arabic dialects. Kadaoui et al. (2023) found that while LLMs often outperform existing commercial systems for dialects with limited datasets, they still lag behind in MSA translation. Alyafeai et al. (2023) evaluated GPT-3.5 and GPT-4 on various Arabic NLP tasks, revealing improvements in performance but highlighting challenges in consistent evaluation across dialects. Al-Thubaity et al. (2023) and Mullappilly et al. (2023) emphasized the need for specialized training and dialect-specific corpora to enhance LLMs' proficiency in handling diverse Arabic dialects. Qwaider et al. (2018) highlighted the importance of creating dialect-specific corpora for improving LLMs in Arabic dialect translation and identification tasks.

### 2.2 Additional Dialectal Datasets

Recent studies have introduced several valuable dialectal datasets to improve Arabic dialect translation models (Abdelali et al., 2024). These include the Arabic Dialectal Tweets Corpus (Qwaider et al., 2018), MADAR Parallel Corpus (Bouamor et al., 2018), CALCS Dataset (Malartic et al., 2023) focusing on conversational Arabic, and the ArzEn Corpus (Waheed et al., 2023) for Arabic-English code-switching. These resources provide a range of real-world language usage examples, covering various dialects and linguistic phenomena, which can significantly contribute to training and evaluating translation models.

### 2.3 Evaluation Challenges

Evaluating LLMs for Arabic dialects faces several challenges. The significant variation among Arabic dialects complicates the development of standardized benchmarks (Alyafeai et al., 2023). Resource limitations, particularly the scarcity of high-quality annotated data for many dialects, constrain the effectiveness of LLMs. Al-Thubaity et al. (2023) found that while GPT-4 excelled in classification tasks, it struggled with generating high-quality dialectal text. Mullappilly et al. (2023) highlighted that LLMs often lack the cultural and contextual understanding necessary for accurate interpretation of dialectal Arabic, requiring significant fine-tuning on domain-specific datasets to achieve satisfactory performance in tasks like sentiment analysis and text generation.

## 3 Design and Methodology

This study aims to translate children's stories from Modern Standard Arabic (MSA) to the Egyptian dialect, leveraging advanced neural machine translation models. The primary objectives are to evaluate the performance of these models, improve their translation quality through fine-tuning, and create a high-quality parallel corpus for future research.

### 3.1 Methodological Framework

Our approach leverages two transformer-based models: AraT5 and Claude. Claude, developed by Anthropic, performs the initial MSA to Egyptian dialect translations, capitalizing on its contextual understanding. AraT5, specifically designed for Arabic, is fine-tuned for the Egyptian dialect and used for back-translation to MSA. This dual-model approach combines Claude's robust language generation with AraT5's specialized Arabic processing capabilities, aiming to produce high-quality translations tailored to the Egyptian dialect.

### 3.2 Data Sources

**Arabic Children's Corpus:** The Arabic Children's Corpus, compiled by (Al-Sulaiti et al., 2016), was inspired by the Oxford Children's Corpus. This corpus consists of 2,950 documents and nearly 2 million words, collected manually from the web . It includes a variety of genres specifically targeted at children, featuring classic tales from "The Arabian Nights" and stories about popular fictional characters such as Goha. The corpus is of high quality and aims to facilitate studies in text classification, language use, and ideology in children's texts (Al-Sulaiti et al., 2016)

**MADAR Corpus**: The MADAR corpus is a collection of different parallel sentences covering the dialects of 25 cities or counties from the Arab World, in addition to English, French, and MSA. It was created by translating selected sentences from the Basic Traveling Expression Corpus (BTEC) (Takezawa et al., 2007) to the different dialects. The exact details on the translation process and source and target languages are described in (Bouamor et al., 2018).

### 3.3 Data Pre-processing Overview

For this study, we selected 130 stories of varying lengths from the Arabic Children's Corpus, chosen based on their moral and educational value. The preprocessing phase began with converting the collected Word documents into plain text files using automated scripts to ensure consistency across all files. Next, we employed natural language processing (NLP) tools to segment each story into individual sentences, storing them in a line-by-line format. We then used automated spell-checking tools to identify and correct spelling errors, followed by a manual review to ensure accuracy, especially for words with multiple correct forms depending on the context. As a final quality assurance measure, a subset of the cleaned and formatted data was manually reviewed by expert translators who are also native Egyptian speakers to verify the accuracy and quality of the text.

#### 3.3.1 MADAR Corpus Pre-processing:

For fine-tuning and training purposes, we utilized the MADAR (Cairo) dataset. Initially, only the dialect corpus was available, with the source MSA later found on Hugging Face. We merged these Excel files using the V-lookup function. However, upon closer inspection by an Arabic and Egyptian native speaker, we identified several inconsistencies and inaccuracies in the Cairo dialect translations. These issues ranged from minor dialectal nuances to more significant semantic discrepancies. In some cases, the dialect translation did not accurately capture the meaning of the MSA sentence:

- **MSA:** أريد ساعة مستعملة.
- **Inaccurate CAI:** عايز مع ساعة يد تانية.
- **Corrected CAI:** عايز ساعة مستعملة.

In other instances, the dialect translation missed key elements of the original sentence:

- **MSA:** أريد إجازة لمدة أسبوع واحد من فضلك.
- **Inaccurate CAI:** عايز كورس مايزيدش عن اسبوع، لو سمحت.
- **Corrected CAI:** عايز إجازة لمدة أسبوع، من فضلك.

To address these issues, we split the training corpus into two sheets, each containing approximately 4500 lines. These sheets were then reviewed by two qualified Egyptian native speakers who provided suggested translations. We used Claude to compare the original CAI dialect translations with the reviewers' translations, noting improved accuracy in the translation from MSA to Egyptian Arabic.

After addressing these inconsistencies through manual review and correction, we retrained our transformer model using the updated training corpus. This process led to a significant reduction in both training and validation loss, underscoring the critical importance of data quality in machine translation tasks. The training loss decreased from 0.0892 in the first epoch before corpus improvement to 0.0484 after improvement. Similarly, the validation loss decreased from 0.05547 to 0.0360 in the first epoch. This trend of improved performance continued throughout the training process, demonstrating the value of our rigorous data preparation and correction efforts.

### 3.4 Transformer Models

**ARAT5 Model:** Building upon the work of (Nagoudi et al., 2022), we selected the AraT5 base model (PRAli22/arat5-base-arabic-dialects-translation[2]) as our starting point. This model was selected due to its demonstrated effectiveness in handling both Modern Standard Arabic (MSA) and various Arabic dialects. Our goal was to fine-tune this model specifically for translation between MSA and the Cairo dialect.

[2] https://huggingface.co/PRAli22/arat5-arabic-dialects-translation

AraT5 employs a sequence-to-sequence (seq2seq) framework with an encoder-decoder structure. Both the encoder and decoder use self-attention mechanisms and multi-head attention layers to capture dependencies and contextual information across the entire input sequence (Vaswani et al., 2017).

**Claude Model:** Claude is an advanced large language model (LLM) developed by Anthropic, designed to understand and generate human-like text. It is based on the transformer architecture, using self-attention to efficiently process and understand text context and dependencies (Vaswani et al., 2017). The model is pre-trained on a vast corpus of text data from diverse sources, allowing it to learn a wide range of language patterns, facts, and nuances. This extensive training helps Claude generate coherent and contextually relevant text across various topics (Brown et al., 2020).

### 3.5 Rationale for Utilizing Claude for Initial Translation

The choice of Claude for the initial translation from Modern Standard Arabic (MSA) to Egyptian Cairo dialect was informed by several factors. Recent research has highlighted limitations in ChatGPT's handling of Arabic dialects. Kadaoui et al. (2023) found that while ChatGPT performed well with Classical Arabic and MSA, its accuracy dropped significantly when dealing with dialectal Arabic. Claude's architecture is optimized for better contextual understanding and linguistic nuances, which are critical for accurately translating dialects (Mullappilly et al., 2023). Moreover, Claude's training incorporated a more balanced dataset including substantial representations of various Arabic dialects, potentially making it more robust for dialect-specific tasks (Waheed et al., 2023).

We conducted experiments comparing Claude and ChatGPT, with results reviewed by a native Egyptian speaker. Claude consistently outperformed ChatGPT in dialect translation tasks. Additionally, when presented with long paragraphs, ChatGPT tended to lose coherence in line-by-line translation, while Claude maintained consistency throughout. These factors, combined with Claude's demonstrated capabilities in handling complex linguistic tasks, made it the preferred choice for our initial MSA to Egyptian dialect translations.

### 3.6 Rationale for Dialect Translation

Young readers often find MSA challenging due to its complex grammar and formal tone. Translating children's literature to their native dialect fosters greater engagement and comprehension, creating a gateway to literature, especially in the underdeveloped countries. While MSA proficiency remains critical, introducing stories in a familiar dialect can nurture a love for reading and gradually bridge the gap to MSA.

### 3.7 Evaluation Metrics

To assess the quality and accuracy of our translations, we employed two primary metrics: Semantic Similarity and BLEU (Bilingual Evaluation Understudy) Score. These metrics offer complementary insights into the performance of our translation model.

**Semantic Similarity:** We utilized cosine similarity to quantify the semantic congruence between the original MSA sentences and their translations into Egyptian Arabic. This method allows us to measure how effectively the meaning of the original text is preserved in the translation, regardless of specific lexical choices.**:**

1. **Embedding Generation**: Both the original MSA sentences and their Egyptian Arabic translations were encoded into high-dimensional vectors using the selected model. This process transforms the textual data into a format that can be mathematically compared.
2. **Cosine Similarity Calculation**: We computed the cosine similarity between the vector representations of the original and translated sentences. This yielded similarity scores ranging from -1 to 1, where:
    - A score of 1 indicates identical semantic meaning
    - A score of 0 suggests no semantic similarity
    - A score of -1 implies opposite meanings (rarely observed in translation contexts)

**BLEU Score:** BLEU (Bilingual Evaluation Understudy) is a widely used metric in machine translation that compares a candidate translation to one or more reference translations. It primarily measures the precision of n-grams (typically up to 4-grams) in the candidate translation with respect to the reference(s). We use smoothing (specifically,

method4 from SmoothingFunction) to handle cases where there are no matching n-grams, which is particularly important when evaluating short sentences.
We implemented BLEU score calculation using the Natural Language Toolkit (NLTK) library in Python, which provides a robust implementation of this metric.

1. **Data Preparation**: We loaded our translated sentences along with their original MSA versions from an Excel file. The MSA sentences served as reference translations, while the model-generated Egyptian Arabic translations were the candidates for evaluation.
2. **Tokenization**: Both reference (MSA) and candidate (Egyptian Arabic) sentences were tokenized into words using simple space-based splitting. This approach assumes that words in both MSA and Egyptian Arabic are space-separated, which is generally true for written Arabic.
3. **Score Computation**: For each sentence pair, we computed the BLEU score using the tokenized reference and candidate translations. The scores were calculated individually for each sentence, allowing for a granular analysis of translation quality across our dataset.
4. **Significance in Dialect Translation:** The BLEU score provides several key insights in the context of MSA to Egyptian Arabic translation including N-gram Precision that measures how many of the n-grams (typically up to 4-grams) in the candidate translation appear in the reference translation. This is particularly useful for assessing how well the model preserves common phrases and linguistic structures from MSA to Egyptian Arabic and Brevity Penalty for translations that are too short, which helps in identifying cases where the dialect translation might be oversimplified or incomplete compared to the MSA original.

### 3.8 Motivation for Fine-Tuning AraT5

Initial testing of AraT5 revealed areas for improvement, prompting fine-tuning to enhance accuracy. The process involved dataset preparation, train-test split, data preprocessing, and hyperparameter optimization. The dataset was split into training (80%) and testing (20%) sets, with careful attention to tokenization, sequence length, and key hyperparameters such as learning rate and batch size.

### 3.9 Manual Evaluation Criteria

To ensure translation quality, we conducted manual evaluations for translations with semantic similarity scores below 96%. The evaluation focused on the following criteria:

- **Semantic Accuracy:** Faithfulness of the translation to the original meaning.
- **Dialectal Fidelity:** Appropriateness of dialect-specific expressions.
- **Cultural Relevance:** Maintenance of cultural context and tone.

Two native Egyptian speakers with expertise in linguistics independently reviewed the translations. Discrepancies were resolved through discussion.

### 3.10 Dealing with Different Story Sizes

To address challenges with longer stories and maintain consistency, a line-by-line translation approach was implemented for all stories regardless of length. This method helped mitigate issues of repetition and irrelevant content generation in longer texts, ensured consistent methodology across the corpus, and facilitated the creation of a structured parallel corpus for future research.

## 4 Experimental Results and Discussion

This section presents the findings from the translation experiments and fine-tuning processes using the Claude and AraT5 models. The results are evaluated using semantic similarity and BLEU scores to assess the quality and accuracy of translations from Modern Standard Arabic (MSA) to the Egyptian (Cairo) dialect.

### 4.1 Dialect-Translation-(Quality Improvement through Fine-Tuning)

The initial translations generated by AraT5 demonstrated a robust contextual understanding and high-quality output, which set a strong foundation for further refinement. However, several issues, including semantic substitution errors and inconsistencies in handling dialect-specific expressions, highlighted the need for fine-tuning the AraT5 model:

**Semantic Substitution Errors**: In some instances, AraT5 replaced words with semantically unrelated terms, significantly altering the meaning of sentences. A striking example of this is:

- **Original MSA** كانَ ضفدعٌ منهمكاً في صيد البعوض بلسانهِ
- **English:** A frog was busy catching mosquitoes with its tongue
- **Claude's Egyptian:** كان في ضفدع مشغول بصيد الناموس بلسانه
- **Basic AraT5:** كان كلب مشغولا في صيد الكلاب بلسانه
- **English back-translation:** A dog was busy catching dogs with its tongue
- **Fine-Tuned AraT5:** كان الضفدع مشغولا في صيد البعوض بلسانه
- **English back-translation:** The frog was busy catching mosquitoes with its tongue

Here, the basic AraT5 model replaced "ضفدع" (frog) with "كلب" (dog), and "البعوض" (mosquitoes) with "الكلاب" (dogs). Despite the high similarity score of 97.2%, this error fundamentally changes the meaning of the sentence. However, the fine-tuned AraT5 model correctly translates the sentence, preserving the original meaning.

**Dialect-Specific Challenges**: AraT5 sometimes struggles with dialect-specific expressions or vocabulary:

- **Original MSA:** خرج الديك وأخذ يبحث على ابنه الصغير ، فوجد الصياد يركض وبيده بيضة ، أخذ الديك يركض وراءه
- **English:** The rooster went out and started searching for his little son, then he found the hunter running with an egg in his hand, so the rooster started running after him
- **Claude's Egyptian:** خرج الديك وبدأ يدور على ابنه الصغير، فلقى الصياد بيجري وفي ايده بيضة، خد الديك يجري وراه
- **Basic AraT5:** خرج الديك و يبحث عن إبنه الصغير ، وجد الكلب يركض و به بيضة ، أخذ الحمام يركض وراءه
- **English back-translation:** The rooster went out and searched for his little son, found the dog running with an egg, and the pigeon started running after him
- **Fine-Tuned AraT5:** خرج الديك و يبحث عن إبنه الصغير ، وجد الصياد يركض بداخل البيضة ، أخذ الديك يركض وراءه
- **English back-translation:** The rooster went out and searched for his little son, found the hunter running inside the egg, and the rooster started running after him

Here, the basic AraT5 model mistranslates "الصياد" (hunter) as "الكلب" (dog) and "الديك" (rooster) as "الحمام" (pigeon) in the last part. The fine-tuned AraT5 model, while still not perfect, maintains the correct translation of "الديك" (rooster) throughout the sentence.

These examples demonstrate the significant improvement in translation quality achieved by fine-tuning the AraT5 model. The fine-tuned model is better able to handle semantic preservation, maintain consistency across translations, and navigate dialect-specific challenges. While not flawless, the fine-tuned AraT5 model represents a substantial step forward in our ability to accurately convert Egyptian Arabic dialect to MSA.

### 4.2 Limitations and Considerations:

It is important to note that while these metrics provide valuable insights, they each have limitations. Semantic similarity might not capture nuances in dialect-specific expressions, while BLEU scores can sometimes undervalue semantically correct translations that use different wording than the reference. To address these limitations, we also conducted manual evaluations by Arabic language experts to ensure the quality and appropriateness of the translations, especially for dialect-specific expressions and cultural nuances that automated metrics might miss.

### 4.3 Transformer Performance Comparison

To evaluate the effectiveness of the fine-tuning process, we compared the performance of the Basic AraT5 model with the Fine-Tuned AraT5 model. The performance was measured based on the similarity score between the translated sentences and the original MSA sentences. The similarity score was calculated using the Sentence Transformer model, which computes cosine similarity scores. The key observations were as follows:

**Basic AraT5 Model:** The Basic AraT5 model shows a relatively even distribution of similarity rates across the spectrum, with a slight peak around the 96% similarity score. However, it struggles to achieve higher similarity scores consistently. The Basic AraT5 model has more occurrences at lower similarity scores (88% to 89%) compared to the Fine-Tuned AraT5 model, indicating the effectiveness of the fine-tuning process.

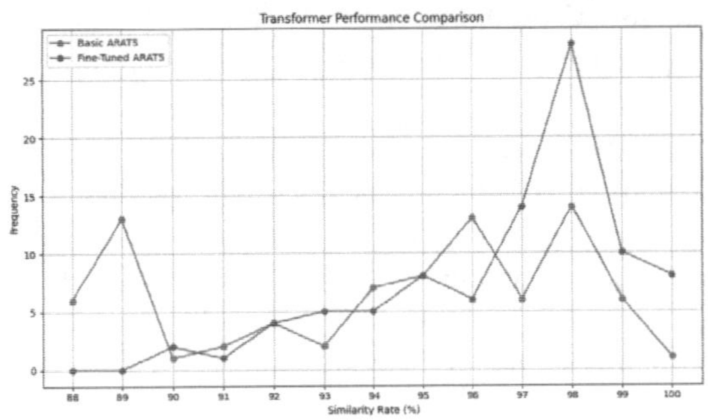


**Fig. 1.** Similarity Count Comparison between Basic AraT5 and Fine-Tuned AraT5

**Fine-Tuned AraT5 Model:** The Fine-Tuned AraT5 model demonstrates a significant improvement, with a higher frequency of translations achieving similarity scores between 96% and 100%. The peak at 98% indicates that the fine-tuning process has effectively enhanced the model's performance, resulting in translations that are closer to the original MSA sentences.

### 4.4 Fine-Tuned AraT5 Model

The AraT5 model was trained in two distinct phases, once before validating the training and testing datasets, and once after this validation. The primary aim was to observe the impact of dataset validation on the model's performance, particularly in terms of training loss and validation loss.

**BLEU Score Analysis:** The fine-tuned AraT5 model achieved a BLEU score improvement from 0.082 to 0.087. Although modest, this increase reflects the model's enhanced ability to produce linguistically accurate translations. BLEU's limitations in capturing dialectal nuances underscore the importance of complementing it with semantic similarity and manual evaluations.

### 4.5 Challenges with Long Stories and Line-by-Line Approach

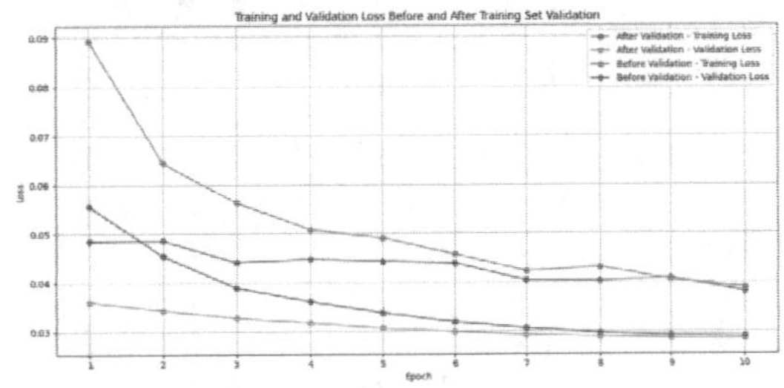


**Fig. 2.** Comparison of both training and validation losses after validating the training and testing datasets

Our research revealed challenges in translating longer children's stories from Modern Standard Arabic (MSA) to Egyptian dialect using neural machine translation models. Key issues included repetition of sentences in longer stories and generation of irrelevant content in very long stories. To address these challenges and ensure consistency, we implemented a line-by-line dialect-translation approach for all stories, regardless of length. This method maintained methodological consistency across the corpus, facilitated the creation of a parallel corpus, and preserved context in each line. It also ensured consistent corpus quality across all story lengths, improved coherence, and reduced irrelevant content. The method also better-preserved original content, enhanced control over translation quality, and proved scalable for handling stories of varying lengths.

### 4.6 Corpus Creation

We developed a high-quality parallel corpus using 130 children's stories from the Arabic Children's Corpus (Al-Sulaiti et al., 2016). Our translation process involved line-by-line translation using our fine-tuned model, followed by a selective review where human experts examined lines with semantic similarity below 96%. The resulting corpus serves as a training resource for machine translation models, an evaluation benchmark, a tool for linguistic analysis, and a unique resource for children's literature translation. To facilitate further research and development in Arabic dialect translation, we will make this corpus publicly available on GitHub[3] in Excel format. The Excel file will include a sample of the original MSA text, the translated Egyptian (Cairo) dialect text, and the corresponding semantic similarity scores for each line. This comprehensive dataset will allow researchers to analyze the relationship between the original and translated text, as well as the quality of translations as measured by semantic similarity.

## 5 Conclusion

This study has made significant progress in addressing the complex challenge of translating children's stories from Modern Standard Arabic (MSA) to the Egyptian (Cairo) dialect using advanced neural machine translation models. The study's methodology combining initial translations with Claude and fine-tuning the AraT5 model, has yielded marked improvements in translation quality, as evidenced by higher similarity and BLEU scores. The basic AraT5 model achieved an average semantic similarity score of 0.945 and through fine-tuning on an Egyptian (Cairo) dialect-specific dataset, we were able to enhance this alignment, achieving an average semantic similarity score of 0.971. The 2.6% improvement demonstrates the model's enhanced capability to understand and replicate the meanings and linguistic characteristics specific to the Egyptian (Cairo) dialect, further bridging the gap between MSA and the dialect used in everyday communication by Egyptian children. Furthermore, the BLEU score, which measures the precision of the translated output by comparing it to reference translations, also showed notable improvement by increasing from 0.0828 to 0.0867 after fine-tuning. This enhancement highlighted the fine-tuned model's ability to produce translations that are not only more semantically accurate but also more aligned with human linguistic expression. Another achievement of this study is the creation of a comprehensive parallel corpus comprising 130 children's stories in both MSA and Egyptian dialect. This corpus stands to benefit future studies and model training efforts in the field of Arabic dialect translation. The study's evaluation framework, incorporating both semantic similarity and BLEU scores, along with manual reviews, ensured a thorough assessment of translation quality while maintaining cultural and contextual accuracy. This approach has resulted in translations that are culturally resonant and linguistically. Additionally, this research contributes to enhancing the accessibility of children's literature for young Arabic speakers. By providing stories in a more familiar dialect, opening new avenues for educational and cultural engagement. In conclusion, this research represents a significant step forward in Arabic dialect translation. Its findings and resources contribute to further advancements in this crucial area of Arabic Language processing and cultural preservation.

## 6 Future Work

**Expansion to Other Dialects:** The methodology developed in this study can be extended to other Arabic dialects, such as Levantine and Gulf Arabic. Creating parallel corpora and fine-tuning models for these dialects would further bridge the linguistic gap and enhance accessibility across the Arab world.

**Genre Diversification:** Future work could involve expanding the corpus to include a wider range of genres beyond children's literature, such as educational materials, and popular fiction texts. This diversification would provide a broader application of the developed models and resources.

**Data Augmentation:** To address the limited corpus size, we plan to use data augmentation techniques such as back-translation and paraphrasing. Additionally, incorporating synthetic data generated by LLMs could enhance the diversity and quantity of training examples.

## References


Latifa Al-Sulaiti, Noorhan Abbas, Claire Brierley, Eric Atwell, and Abdulmohsen Alghamdi. 2016. Compilation of an Arabic children's corpus. In *Proceedings of the Tenth International Conference on Language Resources and Evaluation (LREC'16)*, pages 1808–1812, Portorož, Slovenia. European Language Resources Association (ELRA). https://aclanthology.org/L16-1285

Abdulrahman Al-Thubaity, Abdullah Al-Khateeb, Bassam Al-Salhi, and Mohammed Al-Ghamdi. 2023. Evaluating ChatGPT and Bard AI on Arabic sentiment analysis. *Computing Research Repository*, arXiv:2305.14745.


[3] https://github.com/alaabouomar/Optimizing-Arabic-Dialect-Translation-for-Children-s-Literature-Using-Neural-Models.git

https://www.semanticscholar.org/paper/d4c0ee9f7ea7451216845c851d069dff95545faa

Zaid Alyafeai, Anwar Al-Omari, Iman Al-Kindi, Samah Al-Riyami, and Alaeddin Al-Maqaleh. 2023. Taqyim: evaluating Arabic NLP tasks using ChatGPT models. *Computing Research Repository*, arXiv:2305.14849. https://www.semanticscholar.org/paper/d14aa448b17fdc8d4ea12b43ee1a2b1254c38703

Houda Bouamor, Nizar Habash, Mohammad Salameh, Wajdi Zaghouani, Owen Rambow, Dana Abdulrahim, Ossama Obeid, Salam Khalifa, Fadhl Eryani, Alexander Erdmann, and Kemal Oflazer. 2018. The MADAR Arabic dialect corpus and lexicon. In *Proceedings of the Eleventh International Conference on Language Resources and Evaluation (LREC 2018)*, Miyazaki, Japan. European Language Resources Association (ELRA). https://aclanthology.org/L18-1535

Tom B. Brown, Benjamin Mann, Nick Ryder, Melanie Subbiah, Jared Kaplan, Prafulla Dhariwal, Arvind Neelakantan, Pranav Shyam, Girish Sastry, Amanda Askell, and Sandhini Agarwal. 2020. Language models are few-shot learners. In *Advances in Neural Information Processing Systems 33 (NeurIPS 2020)*, pages 1877-1901. Curran Associates, Inc. https://proceedings.neurips.cc/paper/2020/file/1457c0d6bfcb4967418bfb8ac142f64a-Paper.pdf

Taoufik Kadaoui, Houda Bouamor, Fathi Badran, and Nizar Habash. 2023. TARJAMAT: evaluation of Bard and ChatGPT on machine translation of ten Arabic varieties. *Computing Research Repository*, arXiv:2305.14786. https://www.semanticscholar.org/paper/796b894c4e1a3cb46715cc0b45a39e91ee5910e6

Quentin Malartic, Hamza Alobeidli, Danilo Mazzotta, Gabriel Penedo, Giulia Campesan, Muhammad Farooq, Mansoor Alhammadi, Julien Launay, and Badr Noune. 2023. AlGhafa evaluation benchmark for Arabic language models. In *Proceedings of ArabicNLP 2023*. Association for Computational Linguistics. https://aclanthology.org/2023.arabicnlp-1.1

Ritu Mullappilly, Mohammed Al-Awlaqi, Saleh Al-Yami, and Faisal Al-Dossary. 2023. Arabic Mini-ClimateGPT: a climate change and sustainability tailored Arabic LLM. *Computing Research Repository*, arXiv:2305.14824. https://www.semanticscholar.org/paper/6da8e97de0981b867b1038e12e98608928ad4c0e

El Moatez Billah Nagoudi, AbdelRahim Elmadany, and Muhammad Abdul-Mageed. 2022. AraT5: text-to-text transformers for Arabic language generation. In *Proceedings of the 60th Annual Meeting of the Association for Computational Linguistics (Volume 1: Long Papers)*, pages 628-647, Dublin, Ireland. Association for Computational Linguistics. https://aclanthology.org/2022.acl-long.46/

Ossama Obeid, Nasser Zalmout, Dima Taji, Salam Khalifa, Bashar Alhafni, Koichi Inoue, Fadhl Eryani, and Nizar Habash. 2020. CAMeL tools: an open source Python toolkit for Arabic natural language processing. In *Proceedings of the 12th Language Resources and Evaluation Conference*, pages 7022–7032, Marseille, France. European Language Resources Association. https://www.semanticscholar.org/paper/995ec006ac98a697ea38bd4eea8c1f3170a8adb4

Chatrine Qwaider, Nizar Habash, Houda Bouamor, and Fathi Badran. 2018. Shami: a corpus of Levantine Arabic dialects. *Computing Research Repository*, arXiv:1805.05190. https://www.semanticscholar.org/paper/654af2f5747126447e5d8fce220c6a1915761143

Ashish Vaswani, Noam Shazeer, Niki Parmar, Jakob Uszkoreit, Llion Jones, Aidan N. Gomez, Łukasz Kaiser, and Illia Polosukhin. 2017. Attention is all you need. In *Advances in Neural Information Processing Systems 30 (NeurIPS 2017)*, pages 5998-6008. Curran Associates, Inc. https://papers.nips.cc/paper/7181-attention-is-all-you-need.pdf

Ahmed Waheed, Muhammad Abdul-Mageed, El Moatez Billah Nagoudi, Badr Noune, Amir Hamdi, AbdelRahim Elmadany, and Massimo Poesio. 2023. GPTAraEval: a comprehensive evaluation of ChatGPT on Arabic NLP. *Computing Research Repository*, arXiv:2305.14976. https://arxiv.org/abs/2305.14976

Ahmed Abdelali, Hamdy Mubarak, Shammur Chowdhury, Maram Hasanain, Bekhzod Mousi, Sofiane Boughorbel, Said Abdaljalil, Yasir El Kheir, Dema Izham, Fahim Dalvi, Mohamad Hawasly, Nada Nazar, Youssef Elshahawy, Ahmed Ali, Nadir Durrani, Natasa Milic-Frayling, and Firoj Alam. 2024. LAraBench: benchmarking Arabic AI with large language models. In *Proceedings of the 18th Conference of the European Chapter of the Association for Computational Linguistics (Volume 1: Long Papers)*, pages 487-520, St. Julian's, Malta. Association for Computational Linguistics. https://aclanthology.org/2024.eacl-long.30

## 7 Limitations

**Dialectal Focus**: The current study primarily focuses on the Egyptian (Cairo) dialect, which may not fully represent the linguistic diversity within Egypt or the broader Arab world.

**Corpus Size**: While the study utilized 130 children's stories, a larger corpus could provide

more comprehensive insights and potentially improve model performance.
**Lack of Standardized Benchmarks**: The absence of standardized benchmarks for MSA to Egyptian dialect translation makes it challenging to compare results directly with other studies.
**Contextual Coherence in Line-by-Line Translation:** While the line-by-line translation approach ensured consistency, it occasionally fragmented the narrative flow. To quantify this limitation, we conducted manual evaluations of story-level coherence. Future work could involve incorporating context windows to address this issue.

## 8 Ethical Considerations

**Cultural Appropriateness:** Children's literature often contains cultural elements, moral lessons, and linguistic nuances that require careful handling during translation. Relying solely on automated translation and evaluation risks misrepresenting or losing these crucial cultural elements. Human reviewers can ensure that the translations are not only linguistically accurate but also culturally appropriate and engaging for the target audience.
**Age Appropriateness:** Ensuring that the translated content is age-appropriate is critical, particularly when dealing with children's literature. The translations must maintain the original intent, tone, and level of complexity suitable for the target age group. This includes avoiding any content that could be deemed inappropriate or too complex for young readers.

# Navigating Dialectal Bias and Ethical Complexities in Levantine Arabic Hate Speech Detection

**Ahmed Haj Ahmed[1], Rui-Jie Yew[2], Xerxes Minocher[1], Suresh Venkatasubramanian[2],**
[1]Haverford College, [2]Brown University
**Correspondence:** ahajahmed@haverford.edu

## Abstract

Social media platforms have become central to global communication, yet they also facilitate the spread of hate speech. For underrepresented dialects like Levantine Arabic, detecting hate speech presents unique cultural, ethical, and linguistic challenges. This paper explores the complex sociopolitical and linguistic landscape of Levantine Arabic and critically examines the limitations of current datasets used in hate speech detection. We highlight the scarcity of publicly available, diverse datasets and analyze the consequences of dialectal bias within existing resources. By emphasizing the need for culturally and contextually informed natural language processing (NLP) tools, we advocate for a more nuanced and inclusive approach to hate speech detection in the Arab world.

**Warning:** The content of this paper may be upsetting or triggering to some readers.

## 1 Introduction

In the Levant, deep-rooted socio-political tensions have turned language into a weapon. The rise of digital platforms has amplified hate speech, necessitating robust detection and mitigation mechanisms (Castaño-Pulgarín et al., 2021; Awan, 2014). Automated tools leveraging NLP are essential for curbing online hate speech (Jahan and Oussalah, 2023). However, these tools are not equally effective across all languages and dialects. While significant progress has been made for languages like English, Levantine Arabic remains underserved (Bender, 2019).

Levantine Arabic, spoken across Syria, Jordan, Palestine, and Lebanon, is a dialect continuum with significant regional variations, making it challenging for current NLP technologies to capture (Haff et al., 2022). Existing hate speech detection models often overlook the rich cultural and sociolinguistic nuances of the dialect. This paper addresses the ethical, cultural, and linguistic challenges in detecting hate speech in Levantine Arabic and highlights the critical need for more representative datasets.

## 2 The Linguistic Complexity of Levantine Arabic

### 2.1 Dialectal Variation

Levantine Arabic is a continuum of dialects differing significantly across countries and regions. In Syria, the Damascus dialect contrasts with that of Idlib or rural areas; for instance, "clothes" is "awaei" in Damascus but "teyab" in Aleppo, and "girl" is "bint" in Damascus and "sabiye" elsewhere, with pronunciation variations like consonant softening altering meanings (Naïm, 2012). Jordanian Arabic varies between urban centers like Amman and rural areas that preserve traditional forms; "now" is "halla" in urban settings and "hassa" in rural regions, and the letter jim may be pronounced as a soft "j" or a hard "g" (Sakarna, 2005). Palestinian Arabic differs between Jerusalem, the West Bank, Gaza, and diaspora communities; "cup" is "kasseh" in Jerusalem but "kubayeh" in Gaza. In Lebanon, Beirut's Arabic incorporates French loanwords due to historical influences—unlike regions like Tripoli or the south; the pronunciation of the letter qaf also varies between a glottal stop, a hard "k," or the standard "q" sound (Obégi, 1971; Naïm, 2012).

These regional differences are deeply tied to cultural and socio-political identities. Variations in expressions, idioms, and pronunciation can carry different meanings depending on locality, posing significant challenges for NLP tools. Generic models, often trained on standardized Arabic, may not capture these subtleties

### 2.2 The Role of Sociolinguistic Context

Understanding hate speech in Levantine Arabic requires not only linguistic proficiency but also a deep understanding of the socio-political context



*Proceedings of The 4th Workshop on Arabic Corpus Linguistics (WACL-4)*, pages 103–108
January 20th, 2025. 

in which the language is used. The Levant is a region marked by ongoing conflicts, occupation, and political instability. Hate speech is often employed strategically to exacerbate sectarian divisions, mobilize political supporters, or criticize opposition groups.

In Syria, for instance, even subtle linguistic features like the pronunciation of the qaf have become sociopolitical markers. Historically a neutral phonetic variation, the qaf pronunciation shifted during the conflict to signal regime alignment (Omran, 2021). Security forces used it in propaganda to stoke sectarian fears, while opposition groups mocked it as a regime identifier, transforming a simple linguistic trait into a symbol of allegiance and deepening societal divides.

Similar dynamics can be observed in Lebanon, where political factions often use divisive rhetoric to maintain control. Hate speech is not merely offensive language but part of broader strategies to sustain political dominance and suppress dissent. Any attempt to detect and mitigate hate speech in this context must account for these complex and shifting dynamics, including the sociopolitical significance of linguistic nuances.

## 3 The Problem with Current Datasets

### 3.1 Lack of Publicly Available Datasets

One of the most significant barriers to improving hate speech detection in Levantine Arabic is the lack of publicly available datasets. While several datasets exist for Modern Standard Arabic (MSA), Egyptian Arabic, Gulf Arabic, and others (Alakrot et al., 2018; Mubarak et al., 2017; Albadi et al., 2020; Al-Ajlan and Ykhlef, 2018), there is a striking absence of resources dedicated to Levantine Arabic. This gap limits the ability of researchers and developers to create effective hate speech detection models for the region.

The few datasets that do exist for Levantine Arabic are often restricted in scope, limiting their utility for broader research. Moreover, these datasets are rarely representative of the full spectrum of dialectal variation found within the Levant. Without publicly available, diverse datasets, the development of inclusive and effective NLP tools remains out of reach (Barocas et al., 2023).

### 3.2 Dialectal Bias in Existing Datasets

Even the best available datasets for Levantine Arabic are biased toward specific regional dialects. A prominent case in point is the Levantine Hate Speech and Abusive Language (L-HSAB) Twitter dataset—the first and only publicly available dataset dedicated to hate speech and abusive language in Levantine Arabic (Mulki et al., 2019). While L-HSAB is invaluable due to its size and scope, it disproportionately focuses on Lebanese Arabic. This bias stems primarily from its data collection methodology, which involved extracting tweets using keywords related to Lebanese political figures and events (Barocas and Selbst, 2016).

The most frequently mentioned entities in L-HSAB are predominantly Lebanese. "Gebran Bassil," a Lebanese politician, is mentioned over 1,000 times. The term "Lebanon" appears around 250 times, and "Wiam Wahhab," another Lebanese politician and journalist, is mentioned approximately 200 times. This concentration on specific individuals and topics skews the dataset toward Lebanese political discourse, thereby overlooking the linguistic and sociopolitical nuances present in other Levantine regions.

This skew introduces significant bias, as the linguistic features, idiomatic expressions, and even manifestations of hate speech in Lebanese Arabic differ markedly from other Levantine dialects. For instance, certain derogatory terms or politically charged phrases common in Lebanese discourse may be absent or hold different connotations in Syrian or Jordanian contexts. A term like "za‘ran", meaning "thugs" in Lebanese Arabic, is a strong insult in Lebanon but does not carry the same weight in Syrian Arabic. Conversely, a Syrian expression such as "shabbiha", referring to pro-regime militias, is a loaded term in Syria but might not evoke the same response or understanding among Lebanese speakers (Ümit Üngör, 2020).

Moreover, the focus on specific events and actors further narrows the dataset's applicability. The political landscape and issues prevalent in Lebanon are unique and may not reflect the concerns or conflicts in Syria, Jordan, or Palestine. Hate speech related to Lebanese political parties like the Free Patriotic Movement or events like the Lebanese protests of 2019 would not encompass the types of hate speech prevalent in other regions.

As a result, models trained on datasets like L-HSAB are less likely to generalize effectively to other dialects. They may fail to detect hate speech in Syrian, Jordanian, or Palestinian Arabic due to differences in vocabulary, idioms, and sociopolitical references. This limitation reduces the overall effectiveness of hate speech detection tools across the Levantine region.

Furthermore, this bias can lead to misclassification, where non-hateful speech in one dialect is incorrectly flagged as abusive because the model does not accurately interpret the linguistic nuances of that dialect. Conversely, actual hate speech may go undetected in underrepresented dialects, allowing harmful content to proliferate.

In summary, while datasets like L-HSAB are crucial stepping stones in advancing hate speech detection for Levantine Arabic, their dialectal and topical biases highlight the need for more inclusive data collection strategies. Expanding the dataset to include a broader range of dialects and sociopolitical contexts is essential. By doing so, we can develop NLP tools that are both effective and equitable, ensuring that all communities within the Levantine region are adequately represented and protected in the digital space (Barocas et al., 2023).

### 3.3 Limitations of Pre-trained Embeddings and the Need for Domain-Specific Models

In addition to dataset biases, the choice of language models and embeddings plays a crucial role in the effectiveness of hate speech detection systems. Our analyses and experiments on the L-HSAB dataset underscore the limitations of relying on pre-trained embeddings that are not tailored to the specific linguistic characteristics of Levantine Arabic.

We evaluated several embedding techniques to assess their performance in detecting hate speech within the L-HSAB dataset. The methods included traditional approaches like Bag-of-Words (BoW) (using unigrams) and Term Frequency-Inverse Document Frequency (TF-IDF), as well as neural embeddings such as pre-trained Arabic fastText, custom-trained Word2Vec on Levantine Arabic data, pre-trained GoogleNews Word2Vec, and pre-trained GloVe embeddings (Harris, 1954; Sparck Jones, 1988; Bojanowski et al., 2016; Mikolov et al., 2013; Pennington et al., 2014).

To provide a more concrete evaluation of the methods discussed, we conducted experiments using two classifiers: Logistic Regression (max_iter=1000) and a Support Vector Classifier (SVC) with a linear kernel. The results in terms of F1 scores are summarized in Table 1.

Notably, the custom dataset-trained Word2Vec model produced relatively low accuracy scores (0.4429 and 0.3527), which we attribute to the very limited size of our training corpus (approximately 21,959 words). We anticipate that performance would improve substantially with a larger, more representative Levantine Arabic corpus.

| **Model** | **Logistic Regression** | **SVC** |
| --- | --- | --- |
| BoW (U) | 0.7177 | 0.7147 |
| TF-IDF | 0.6553 | 0.7217 |
| Custom W2V | 0.4429 | 0.3527 |
| Arabic fastText | 0.6823 | 0.6964 |
| GloVe | 0.0606 | 0.0603 |
| GNews W2V | 0.0 | 0.0 |

Table 1: F1 scores for various embeddings and classifiers on the L-HSAB dataset. BoW (U) stands for Bag-of-Words (unigrams). Custom W2V refers to a Word2Vec model trained on a small custom Levantine Arabic corpus. Arabic fastText, GloVe, and GNews W2V refer to pre-trained embeddings from Arabic fastText, GloVe, and GoogleNews Word2Vec models respectively.

Effective Techniques: Our experiments revealed that BoW, TF-IDF, pre-trained Arabic fastText, and custom-trained Word2Vec embeddings significantly outperformed the other methods. These techniques achieved higher F1 scores, indicating better precision and recall in identifying hate speech content. However, it is important to note that the BoW approach, relying solely on unigrams, does not capture contextual relationships between words. As a result, its performance can vary significantly depending on the type and structure of the dataset used. The success of these models can be attributed to their alignment with the linguistic properties of Levantine Arabic, either through their focus on Arabic text or customization to the specific dialect.

Ineffective Techniques: In stark contrast, pre-trained embeddings like GoogleNews Word2Vec and GloVe, which are primarily trained on English corpora, scored nearly 0% in F1 metrics. This drastic underperformance highlights a critical issue: models trained predominantly on English data fail to recognize or interpret Arabic text accurately. Consequently, they are ineffective for tasks involving Levantine Arabic hate speech detection.

These findings emphasize the importance of domain-specific adaptations in NLP models. Utilizing embeddings and language models that are trained or fine-tuned on Levantine Arabic data is essential for capturing the unique linguistic features and nuances of the dialect. Relying on generic, pre-trained models not only reduces accuracy but also risks missing or misclassifying hate speech, thereby undermining the effectiveness of detection systems.

By investing in domain-specific models, researchers and technologists can create more accurate and reliable hate speech detection tools. Such tools will be better equipped to handle the linguistic diversity of Levantine Arabic, ultimately contributing to a safer and more inclusive online environment for speakers of all regional dialects.

## 4 Ethical Considerations in Hate Speech Detection

The dialectical bias identified above privileges one regional dialect over others, and risk marginalizing communities whose voices are already underrepresented in the digital sphere. There are also ethical concerns beyond issues of data bias. False positives—where non-hate speech is misclassified—can result in the suppression of legitimate cultural expressions, especially in a region where language is tightly bound to identity. A prominent example is the misclassification of the Arabic word "shaheed", meaning "martyr", by social media platforms like Meta (The Oversight Board, 2024). The term holds significant cultural and religious importance, often used to honor individuals who have died for a sacred cause. However, automated moderation systems have frequently removed content containing "shaheed," interpreting it as a reference to terrorism or violent extremism due to its association with entities on terrorism watchlists.

Conversely, false negatives—where actual hate speech goes undetected—allow harmful narratives to spread unchecked, fueling further violence. For example, derogatory terms or slurs specific to a particular region or group may go unnoticed by moderation systems trained primarily on other dialects or on Modern Standard Arabic. In the context of the Syrian conflict, hate speech containing region-specific pejoratives aimed at certain ethnic or sectarian groups might not be recognized as such by models lacking comprehensive dialectal data. This oversight enables the propagation of inflammatory content that can exacerbate tensions and incite real-world violence.

Technologists and researchers have a responsibility to develop models that not only detect hate speech but do so in a way that respects the linguistic and cultural integrity of Levantine Arabic. Practically, ethical considerations are particularly relevant within a conflict-ridden region like the Levant where the failure to identify and address hate speech content undermines efforts to promote peace and stability. By incorporating diverse linguistic inputs and cultural insights, developers can create more nuanced models that differentiate between harmful content and legitimate expression, thereby protecting both free speech and community safety.

## 5 Towards More Culturally Aware Language Technologies

Addressing the challenges of hate speech detection in Levantine Arabic requires practical solutions that consider the language's unique properties. Bergman and Diab (2022) offer valuable guidelines for developing effective and ethically sound NLP tools for underrepresented dialects. By incorporating these recommendations, we can create language technologies that are culturally aware and inclusive, specifically tailored to Levantine Arabic.

### 5.1 Engaging Local Communities

Engaging local communities is essential for capturing the full spectrum of dialectal variations and cultural contexts within Levantine Arabic. The language's rich diversity necessitates collaboration with native speakers from various regions. Involving annotators and experts who possess both language proficiency and deep understanding of local contexts ensures that the linguistic nuances specific to each dialect are accurately represented (Radiya-Dixit and Bogen, 2024).

### 5.2 Rethinking Data Collection and Annotation

To overcome dialectal bias, new data collection and annotation strategies must account for Levantine Arabic's specific properties. Given the significant dialectal variations, stratified sampling techniques are crucial for comprehensively capturing the linguistic landscape (Bergman and Diab, 2022). Annotation processes should prioritize using annotators proficient in specific regional dialects and familiar with local sociopolitical contexts (Caliskan et al., 2017; Radiya-Dixit and Bogen, 2024). Researchers must be mindful of potential consequences when collecting data from conflict-affected regions, as certain linguistic features can carry sociopolitical implications. Providing transparent annotation guidelines and support systems for annotators is also critical.

### 5.3 Prioritizing Ethical Design

Developing NLP tools for Levantine Arabic must be grounded in ethical design principles that account for the language's unique properties. Practitioners should carefully consider the granularity of language divisions within Levantine Arabic and strive for inclusivity without compromising annotation quality (Bergman and Diab, 2022). Providing support systems for annotators is essential, especially given potential exposure to disturbing content in conflict-affected regions. By adopting these strategies, researchers can develop hate speech detection models that are equipped to handle Levantine Arabic's dialectal diversity and cultural contexts, promoting an inclusive digital environment.

## 6 Conclusion

Detecting hate speech in Levantine Arabic presents unique cultural, linguistic, and ethical challenges due to intricate dialectal variations and biased datasets. This highlights the urgent need for more inclusive NLP approaches. By engaging local communities, reimagining data collection, and embedding ethical considerations into technology design, we can develop tools that effectively identify hate speech while honoring the Levant's rich linguistic diversity. This paper advocates for renewed cultural sensitivity in NLP applications targeting Levantine Arabic. Addressing sociolinguistic complexities and ethical implications enables us to create tools that serve all speakers, enhance detection accuracy, and promote a more just digital environment throughout the Arab world.

## 7 Limitations

This paper offers a conceptual discussion on the challenges of detecting hate speech in Levantine Arabic. While we provide experimental results to assess the effectiveness of different embedding techniques, the practical impact of our recommendations is still limited by the size and representativeness of our training data. Specifically, the custom dataset-trained Word2Vec model produced relatively lower F1 scores than the pre-trained Arabic fastText model, primarily due to the very limited size of our training corpus (approximately 21,959 words). We anticipate that performance would improve substantially with a larger Levantine Arabic corpus. To this end, we have identified three promising morphologically annotated Levantine corpora—Baladi (Lebanese, ~9.6K tokens), Curras (Palestinian, ~56K tokens), and Nabra (Syrian, ~60K tokens)—which we plan to combine into a more comprehensive Levantine corpus of approximately 125.6K tokens (Al-Haff et al., 2022; Nayouf et al., 2023). We expect that training our Word2Vec model on this expanded corpus will significantly enhance its performance.

Additionally, while we discuss dialectal variations across Syria, Jordan, Palestine, and Lebanon, the linguistic analysis is not exhaustive, and some regional nuances may not be fully represented. Although we reference frameworks such as the playbook by Bergman and Diab (2022), we do not offer a detailed roadmap for creating inclusive and effective hate speech detection models. Future work should therefore focus on both enriching the training data resources and developing concrete tools to operationalize these recommendations, ensuring more accurate, contextually aware, and inclusive hate speech detection in Levantine Arabic.

## Acknowledgments

We would like to express our sincere gratitude to Dr. Nagham El Karhili at the Global Internet Forum to Counter Terrorism, Professor Stevie Bergman at Brown University, Professor Manar Darwish at Haverford College, and Anna Lacy, Digital Scholarship Librarian at Haverford College, for their insightful feedback and guidance throughout this research. Special thanks to the authors of the L-HSAB dataset—Hala Mulki, Hatem Haddad, Chedi Bechikh Ali, and Halima Alshabani—whose valuable work significantly contributed to this study. We also extend our appreciation to Professor Daniel Ritchie, the Computer Science Department at Brown University, and Google Research for offering and directing the exploreCSR program and for their funding support. We are grateful to the Digital Scholarship team at Haverford College for their assistance and support. Lastly, we thank the Marian E. Koshland Integrated Natural Sciences Center at Haverford College for their funding and support. We are also deeply appreciative of the three anonymous reviewers, whose constructive feedback and suggestions helped us strengthen our work.

## References

Monirah A. Al-Ajlan and Mourad Ykhlef. 2018. Optimized twitter cyberbullying detection based on deep learning. In *2018 21st Saudi Computer Society National Computer Conference (NCC)*, pages 1–5.

Karim Al-Haff, Mustafa Jarrar, Tymaa Hammouda, and Fadi Zaraket. 2022. Curras + baladi: Towards a Levantine corpus. In *Proceedings of the Thirteenth Language Resources and Evaluation Conference*, pages 769–778, Marseille, France. European Language Resources Association.

Azalden Alakrot, Liam Murray, and Nikola S. Nikolov. 2018. Dataset construction for the detection of antisocial behaviour in online communication in arabic. *Procedia Computer Science*, 142:174–181. Arabic Computational Linguistics.

Nuha Albadi, Maram Kurdi, and Shivakant Mishra. 2020. Are they our brothers? analysis and detection of religious hate speech in the arabic twittersphere. In *Proceedings of the 2018 IEEE/ACM International Conference on Advances in Social Networks Analysis and Mining*, ASONAM '18, page 69–76. IEEE Press.

Imran Awan. 2014. Islamophobia and twitter: A typology of online hate against muslims on social media. *Policy & Internet*, 6(2):133–150.

Solon Barocas, Moritz Hardt, and Arvind Narayanan. 2023. *Fairness and Machine Learning: Limitations and Opportunities*. MIT Press.

Solon Barocas and Andrew D. Selbst. 2016. Big data's disparate impact. *California Law Review*, 104(3):671–732.

Emily Bender. 2019. The benderrule: On naming the languages we study and why it matters. *The Gradient*.

A. Stevie Bergman and Mona T. Diab. 2022. Towards responsible natural language annotation for the varieties of arabic. *Preprint*, arXiv:2203.09597.

Piotr Bojanowski, Edouard Grave, Armand Joulin, and Tomas Mikolov. 2016. Enriching word vectors with subword information. *arXiv preprint arXiv:1607.04606*.

Aylin Caliskan, Joanna J. Bryson, and Arvind Narayanan. 2017. Semantics derived automatically from language corpora contain human-like biases. *Science*, 356(6334):183–186.

Sergio Andrés Castaño-Pulgarín, Natalia Suárez-Betancur, Luz Magnolia Tilano Vega, and Harvey Mauricio Herrera López. 2021. Internet, social media and online hate speech. systematic review. *Aggression and Violent Behavior*, 58:101608.

Karim El Haff, Mustafa Jarrar, Tymaa Hammouda, and Fadi Zaraket. 2022. Curras + baladi: Towards a levantine corpus. *Preprint*, arXiv:2205.09692.

Zellig S. Harris. 1954. Distributional structure.

Md Saroar Jahan and Mourad Oussalah. 2023. A systematic review of hate speech automatic detection using natural language processing. *Neurocomputing*, 546:126232.

Tomas Mikolov, Kai Chen, Greg Corrado, and Jeffrey Dean. 2013. Efficient estimation of word representations in vector space. *Preprint*, arXiv:1301.3781.

Hamdy Mubarak, Kareem Darwish, and Walid Magdy. 2017. Abusive language detection on Arabic social media. In *Proceedings of the First Workshop on Abusive Language Online*, pages 52–56, Vancouver, BC, Canada. Association for Computational Linguistics.

Hala Mulki, Hatem Haddad, Chedi Bechikh Ali, and Halima Alshabani. 2019. L-HSAB: A Levantine Twitter dataset for hate speech and abusive language. In *Proceedings of the Third Workshop on Abusive Language Online*, pages 111–118, Florence, Italy. Association for Computational Linguistics.

Amal Nayouf, Tymaa Hammouda, Mustafa Jarrar, Fadi Zaraket, and Mohamad-Bassam Kurdy. 2023. Nâbra: Syrian Arabic dialects with morphological annotations. In *Proceedings of ArabicNLP 2023*, pages 12–23, Singapore (Hybrid). Association for Computational Linguistics.

Samia Naïm. 2012. *53. Dialects of the Levant*, pages 920–935. De Gruyter Mouton, Berlin, Boston.

M. Obégi. 1971. *The Phonemic System of a Lebanese Arabic Dialect: (microfilm)*. Theses (Dept. of Modern Languages). National Library of Canada.

Rasha Omran. 2021. The letter qaf and conflicting grievances. https://www.syria.tv/%D8%AD%D8%B1%D9%81-%D8%A7%D9%84%D9%82%D8%A7%D9%81-%D9%88%D8%A7%D9%84%D9%85%D8%B8%D9%84%D9%88%D9%85%D9%8A%D8%A7%D8%AA-%D8%A7%D9%84%D9%85%D8%AA%D8%B9%D8%A7%D8%B1%D8%B6%D8%A9.

Jeffrey Pennington, Richard Socher, and Christopher Manning. 2014. GloVe: Global vectors for word representation. In *Proceedings of the 2014 Conference on Empirical Methods in Natural Language Processing (EMNLP)*, pages 1532–1543, Doha, Qatar. Association for Computational Linguistics.

Evani Radiya-Dixit and Miranda Bogen. 2024. Beyond english-centric ai: Lessons on community participation from non-english nlp groups.

Ahmad Khalaf Sakarna. 2005. The linguistic status of the modern jordanian dialects. *Arabica*, 52(4):522–543.

Karen Sparck Jones. 1988. *A statistical interpretation of term specificity and its application in retrieval*, page 132–142. Taylor Graham Publishing, GBR.

The Oversight Board. 2024. Referring to designated dangerous individuals as "shaheed".

Uğur Ümit Üngör. 2020. Shabbiha: Paramilitary groups, mass violence and social polarization in homs. *Violence: An International Journal*, 1(1):59–79.

# Author Index


Abbas, Noorhan, 93
Afli, Haithem, 44
Aftiss, Azzedine, 77
Al-Laith, Ali, 68
Alahmari, Salwa Saad, 38
Aldallal, Zeina, 12
AlModhayan, Safwan, 12

Batista-Navarro, Riza, 50
Benkhedda, Youcef, 50
Berrada, Ismail, 86
Bezançon, Julien JB, 25
Bouomar, Alaa Hassan, 93
Bouvry, Pascal, 1
Brust, Matthias, 1

chafik, salmane, 86
Chrouf, Sara, 12

El Alaoui, Said Ouatik, 77
El amrany, Samir, 1
El-Ghawi, Yousra A., 63
Ezzini, Saad, 86

Haj Ahmed, Ahmed, 103
Hamed, Mohamed Motasim, 12
Hennara, Khalil, 12
Hossain, Shehenaz, 44
Hreden, Muhammad, 12

Karam, Rimane, 25
KEBDANI, RACHIDA, 68
Khered, Abdullah Salem, 50

Lamsiyah, Salima, 77
lamsiyah, salima, 1
Lejeune, Gaël, 25

Maggini, Marco, 1
Minocher, Xerxes, 103

Schommer, Christoph, 1, 77
Shammary, Bahaulddin, 44
Shammary, Fouad, 44

Venkatasubramanian, Suresh, 103

Yew, Rui-Jie, 103

Zeinalipour, Kamyar, 1